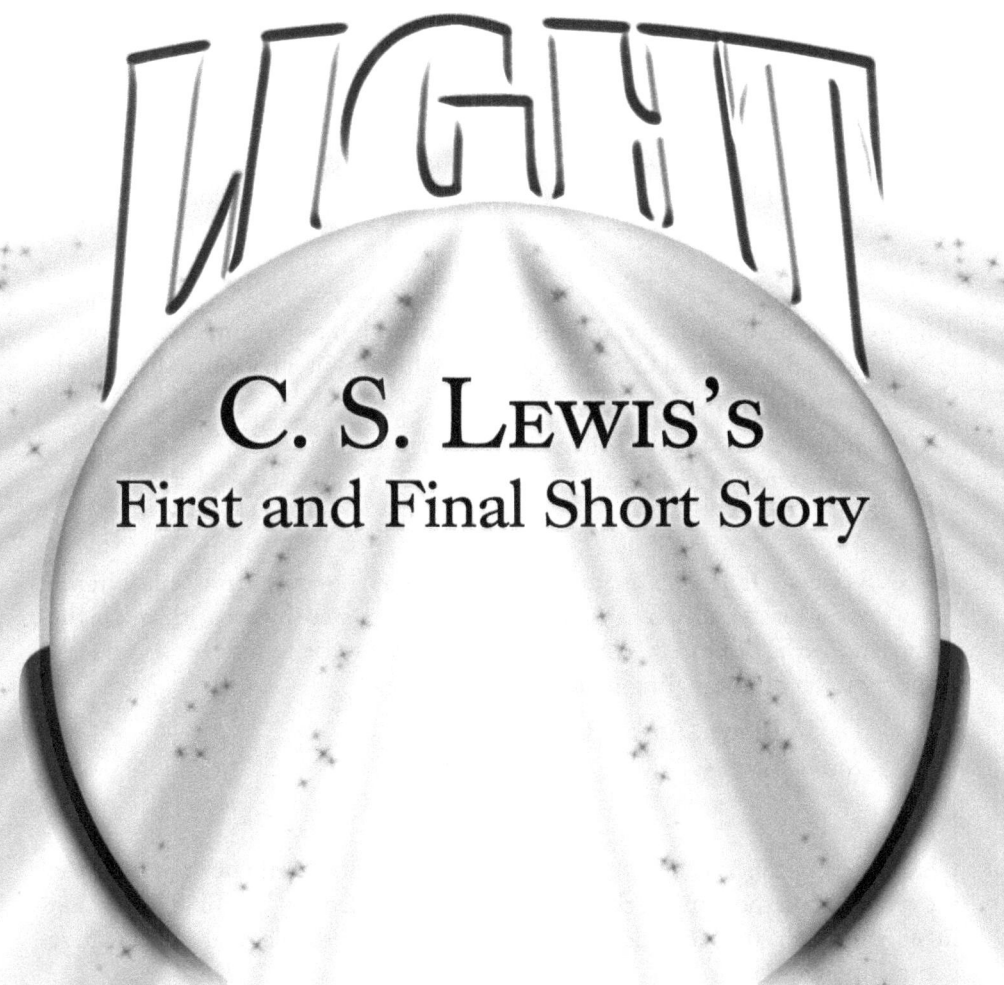

LIGHT

C. S. Lewis's
First and Final Short Story

Charlie W. Starr

Praise for *Light*

For someone who loves both C. S. Lewis and detective fiction this book will be a feast. Before I began reading, I feared it might be too much about too little. But once embarked, I was swept up into the most interesting who-done-it I've ever read.

>Walter Hooper, Trustee of the C. S. Lewis Estate, author of
>*C. S. Lewis Companion and Guide*

This book makes a necessary and serious contribution to our understanding of Lewis and to the world of C. S. Lewis scholarship. As literary journalism, both investigative and critical, it is top shelf.

>James Como, York College CUNY, author of
>*Remembering C. S. Lewis*

For C. S. Lewis fans, this is an amazing mystery not to be missed. Charlie Starr does a masterful job of not only guiding us, step-by-step, through the twists and turns of how this lost manuscript came to be found, he also does a wonderful job of untangling its possible meanings.

>Devin Brown, Asbury University, author of
>*Inside Narnia*

Charlie Starr's *Light* is an extraordinary volume that illuminates not only the provenance and meaning of this short story by C. S. Lewis, but all of his fiction in its thorough and engaging treatment of Lewis's theological and creative commitments.

>Bruce L. Edwards, Bowling Green State University, editor of
>*C. S. Lewis: Life, Work, Legacy*

If you, like me, rejoice whenever a previously unknown work by C. S. Lewis is discovered and published, then this is the book for you. Starr has done us all a great service not only by helping bring "Light" to a larger readership but also by trying, through careful argumentation, to make sense of this intriguing story. I can't recommend this book highly enough.

    Adam Barkman, Redeemer College University, author of
    C. S. Lewis and Philosophy as a Way of Life

Starr's book explores a hitherto virtually unexplored but vitally important theme in Lewis's work – light – a theme he explores in all Lewis's work, dare I say, brilliantly."

    Will Vaus, MDiv Princeton Seminary, author of
    Speaking of Jack: A C. S. Lewis Discussion Guide

Working from a newly discovered manuscript, Starr not only gives us the authentic text of a story by Lewis, previously known only in its transitional form, but also brings his considerable knowledge of Lewis's thought to bear on the interpretation of this puzzling work.

    Charles Huttar, Hope College, co-editor of
    Word and Story in C. S. Lewis

Starr shines a new and illuminating light on one of Lewis's most intriguing stories. He combines painstaking attention to detail with a refreshingly unstuffy tone, and the result is both informative and thoroughly thought-provoking.

    Michael Ward, St Peter's College, Oxford, author of
    Planet Narnia: The Seven Heavens in the Imagination of C. S. Lewis

LIGHT:
C. S. LEWIS'S FIRST AND FINAL SHORT STORY

Copyright © 2012 Charlie W. Starr

Winged Lion Press
Hamden, CT

All rights reserved. Except in the case of quotations embodied in critical articles or reviews, no part of this book may be reproduced or transmitted in any form or by any means, electronic or mechanical, including photocopying, recording, or by any information storage or retrieval system, without written permission of the publisher.
For information, contact Winged Lion Press www.WingedLionPress.com

Winged Lion Press titles may be purchased for business or promotional use or special sales.

10-9-8-7-6-5-4-3-2-1

WINGED LION PRESS
ISBN-13 978-1-936294-21-3

This book is dedicated with sincerest love to my in-laws,

Howard and Patricia Falgout,

for the unending mercy and grace
and the unconditional love
they have shown me over the last three decades.
I am grateful beyond words.

ACKNOWLEDGEMENTS

Very little ever gets done in committee, but a book is seldom the product of only one person. With this in mind, I first offer thanks to those who were with this project at its beginning. Thom Satterlee, who in the summer of 2010 was still on the faculty at Taylor University, was my initial contact, my initial encourager, and the person primarily responsible for starting the process of green lighting this book. Laura Constantine, assistant at the Center for the Study of Lewis and Friends at Taylor, got me access to the "Light" manuscript and copies when I needed them. She connected me with an invaluable appraisal document on the Brown collection, helped me with numerous questions and with analyzing the "Light" manuscript's surface features (how many folds?), and was also the first of many to check my transcription against the manuscript. Dan Bowell, Taylor University librarian, helped with the legalities and the question of "Quink." And of course, great thanks goes to Taylor University for giving me permission to write the first book on their prized Lewis short story and offering financial support for my research trip to Taylor and the Wade Center.

For advice, encouragement, and frequent responses to my desperate cries to find a quote source, my thanks to Devin Brown, David Lavery, Stan Mattson, Robert Trexler, Ted Sherman, Dave Neuhouser, Peter Schakel, Charles Huttar, Bruce Edwards, David Theroux, Charles Beach and Michael Ward.

Ed Brown gave his blessing to this project about a Lewis text on which he did the first serious work. Then he kindly responded to my request for an interview, and we spent a wonderful Sunday afternoon talking about the "Light" story and its origins, and Ed's continued love for Lewis's books, which ended in his giving me a priceless gift. His contribution to this project has been enormous.

Brian and Kelly Beesley housed a wandering soul on trips to Taylor and Wheaton. They fed, encouraged, and "churched" me, and even double checked a "reading" or two. Norm and Karin West also housed me on my trek to Wheaton, got me a cake on my birthday, and introduced me to a new friend.

Folks at the Wade Center at Wheaton College were invaluable in my research work during Spring Break of 2011. Laura Schmidt, Heidi Truty, (and Heidi's assistant Mariah) helped me access original Lewis manuscripts and resources I didn't even know I needed and wanted to see. Christopher Mitchell gave sage advice toward the project (and great directions for getting out of Chicagoland), and Marjorie Lamp Mead, who had already responded with help in the months leading up to my time in Wheaton, was gracious, kind, and a continued help.

In addition to a Chicago trip, this project yielded me a trip to Oxford as well. My sincerest thanks to folks at the Bodleian Library—especially Judith Priestman, Colin Harris, and Patricia Buckingham—for their help before and during my visit in the summer of 2011. Debbie Higgens, director of The Kilns, showed the greatest hospitality and helped me find my way in a country not my own. Thanks to Michael Ward for French food and fascinating conversation as well as his insights into the meaning of the "Light" story.

My thanks to Diana Glyer for her correspondence and work showing Lewis's history as a reviser, to Tony Fischier for his expertise and help with the "Quink" question, to Kentucky Christian University Head Librarian Naulayne Enders for answering the call every time I had a research question or need, and to my best buddy Bryan Rife for the book he gave me.

My Personal Assistant, Shawn Crawford, spent literally hours proofing the transcriptions of both "Light" and "The Man Born Blind" (including the marginal revisions). He caught several of my mistakes and was especially helpful in identifying illegible words and phrases. When he couldn't get a phrase (there were two or three which nearly did us in), my other Assistant, Logan Gray, offered his help, as did my son, Bryan Starr, who figured out in five minutes the phrase I'd come to call the "Shawn Killer," the one none of the rest of us could get: "it was nowhere to be found." My other, other Assistant Quinton McGlone offered assistance near the project's end. I'm also indebted to John Harvey who worked some Photoshop magic to help me examine some of the "hidden" words in the "Light" manuscript.

In addition to putting up with my obsessions and worries during this project, my wife Becky spent time examining the manuscripts with me, found a folder big enough to hold safe my photocopies of the manuscripts, and offered her artistic expertise during the process of designing the book's cover.

Dr. Perry Stepp, Vice President for Academic Affairs at Kentucky Christian University, helped me with my application for a reader's card at the Bodleian Library and found me some funding for the research trip to Oxford.

Other generous supporters of this project include Dr. Ronald and Doris Rife, Drs. Herschel and Dona Gower, my favorite in-laws Howard and Patricia

Falgout, my other favorite in-laws Tyrel and Molli Falgout, my parents Charlie and Cynthia Starr, Mark and Paula Berrier, Tom and Carol Scott, Kyle and Caitlin Martin, and Bobby and Dee Nusbaum. A special thanks to Dr. Robert C. Beesley and to Phil and Theresa Halff for their generosity as well.

Thanks to Kyle Martin for applying his excellent computer skills to the nightmare that was chapter nine.

My thanks to those who provided editorial advice after reading portions or all of the manuscript: Nathan Coleman, Ralph Hawkins, Dennis Durst, John M. Kirton II, Andrew Lazo, Devin Brown, James Como, Bruce Edwards, Charles Huttar, Dave Neuhouser, and Walter Hooper.

Douglas Gresham took time out of his busy schedule to answer every email I sent him with the most thoughtful detail.

The majestic feline Blessed Lucy of Narnia and her human Walter Hooper were an invaluable resource in my research for this book. In addition to offering answers to my questions, they opened their home to me, gave me tea and biscuits (Lewis's favorite kind), and told me the most wonderful stories.

A special thanks goes to Stan Archer for helping dreams come true.

Houghton Mifflin Harcourt graciously granted, *gratis*, permission for the publication of "The Man Born Blind."[1]

---

1   "The Man Born Blind" from THE DARK TOWER AND OTHER STORIES by C. S. Lewis. Copyright © 1977 by C. S. Lewis PTE Ltd. Used by permission of Houghton Mifflin Harcourt Publishing Company. All rights reserved.

TABLE OF CONTENTS

Foreword   ix

Introduction   1

PART ONE: LIGHT

Chapter 1   Light   6

PART TWO: THE ORIGINS OF LIGHT

Chapter 2   Rescued From the Fire   11
Chapter 3   Dr. Brown's Pursuit of C. S. Lewis   16
Chapter 4   Authenticating Light   20

PART THREE: THE MEANING OF LIGHT

CHAPTER 5	Contemplation, Enjoyment and War	46
CHAPTER 6	Toolsheds, Truth and Knowledge	57
CHAPTER 7	Beyond Reason and Imagination	70
CHAPTER 8	Earthly Longing, Heavenly Light	93

PART FOUR: LIGHT BY LETTERS AND LINES

CHAPTER 9	The Complete Parallel Light Stories	116
CHAPTER 10	Shedding Light on the Blind	139

APPENDIX	Describing the Manuscripts	148
BIBLIOGRAPHY		155
INDEX		167

FOREWORD

by
Walter Hooper

For someone who loves both C. S. Lewis *and* detective fiction this book will be a feast. Before I began reading it I feared it might be too much about too little. But once embarked, I was swept up into the most interesting who-done-it I've ever read.

If I have any contribution to make, it will not be to repeat what Charlie Starr has already done with great skill. I will, instead, try to add further illumination to C. S. Lewis's attitude towards writing and his manuscripts. Almost as soon as I met Lewis in June 1963 he realised I was interested not only in what he *said* in his books, but in his writing of them. During my first month in Oxford we met at least three times a week, on Mondays at the meetings of the Inklings, and always on Wednesdays and Sundays at his home, The Kilns, in Headington Quarry. When I arrived at The Kilns he was always at his desk, and sometimes he'd finish replying to a letter while I made the tea.

Watching him write took me back to my childhood, when children learned to write using dip pens dipped in an ink well. In my little hometown in North Carolina the post office and banks had dip pens and ink wells for writing. These old-fashioned nibs get splayed after a good deal of writing and have to be replaced from time to time. As I got older I went from using a dip pen to a fountain pen. But Lewis had gone from dip pens to a fountain pen, and then back to dip pens. The reason he gave me for continuing to write with a nib was that having to pause to dip the pen in the ink well after writing five or six words provided him with exactly the time needed to 'think of what's coming next.' He said that while writing he spoke every word aloud because 'it's as important to please the *ear* as it is the eye.' And there, in a nutshell, is perhaps the main reason his books sound so good when read aloud.

Lewis said the thing he most liked about writing was that it did two things at once. 'I don't know what I *mean*,' he said, 'until I see what I've *said*.' In other words, ink and thought come together in perfect symbiosis. What the chisel was to Michelangelo and the brush to Leonardo Da Vinci, the pen was to C. S. Lewis: when his imagination was assisted by the pen a breakthrough occurred.

He was so conscientious about his correspondence that he spent at least two hours a day answering letters. But his heart sang when he had time to compose. Sometimes this meant improving what he had already written, as when he edited 'The Man Born Blind,' revising it as 'Light.' At other times, he was not polishing existing works, but creating new literary gems in moments of special inspiration. One example that comes to mind is the last great passage in the Chronicles of Narnia:

> And as He spoke He no longer looked to them like a lion; but the things that began to happen after that were so great and beautiful that I cannot write them. And for us this is the end of all the stories, and we can most truly say that they all lived happily ever after. But for them it was only the beginning of the real story. All their life in this world and all their adventures in Narnia had only been the cover and the title page: now at last they were beginning Chapter One of the Great Story which no one on earth has read: which goes on forever: in which every chapter is better than the one before.[1]

I have a special reason for remembering our Wednesday meeting at The Kilns on Wednesday, 19 June. This was the first time Lewis made any reference to his manuscripts. We sat in his brother's study, where Lewis had been writing at a desk that had belonged to their father. As always, he was using a dip pen. Suddenly, he plucked out of the wastepaper basket a page of notes he had made. Handing it to me, he said: 'Would you like to have this?' 'Oh, yes!' I said. That was all he said about that page of scribbling – the first Lewis manuscript I ever owned. Delighted as I was by the gift I was somewhat mystified. I hadn't asked for a manuscript, but I had nonetheless been given one.

I didn't understand the gesture at the time. But looking back over the years I realise Lewis understood me far better than I thought, and I know now that this single page is related to the manuscript of *Letters to Malcolm*.

As I have explained elsewhere, Lewis asked me to become his secretary, and in July I moved into The Kilns. One day I asked what he did with his manuscripts. He told me that after writing a book, such as *The Lion, the Witch and the Wardrobe*, he turned the manuscript over and wrote another book on the other side. He then threw the manuscript away. 'I would not like the day to come,' he said, 'when someone says, "I have a First Edition of *That Hideous Strength*," and someone else says, 'But I have the unique manuscript!"' I realised then what I had always suspected, that Lewis was extremely modest.

---

1   *The Last Battle* (1956), Chap. 16.

C. S. Lewis's First and Final Short Story

And there the matter seemed to rest until Lewis handed me the manuscript of his latest book, *Letters to Malcolm*, which was then with the publisher. He asked if I'd like to read it, and of course this gave me immense pleasure. A few days later I offered to hand the manuscript back.

'Would you like to have it?' asked Lewis. I suspected that I was being tested. 'I remember what happened to Boromir,' I said, 'as a result of coveting the Ring.' 'I expect I know Tolkien's book better than you,' he replied. 'The question is – Would you like to have this manuscript?' 'Remember,' I countered, 'what you said about one person having a First Edition of *That Hideous Strength* to be outdone by someone else saying, 'Yes, but I have the unique manuscript!' 'I remember,' said Lewis, smiling, 'but that is not what I asked you – Would you like to have the manuscript of *Letters to Malcolm*?' 'Of course!' I said. 'But seeing how you feel about one-upmanship I promise to keep it very private.'

'That's an odd response for a scholar to make,' said Lewis. 'I'd have thought you would want to share it with others.' 'I would like that,' I said. And then I added, 'I'd like that *most* of all!' Lewis was beaming with pleasure and before sending me to make a celebratory pot of tea, he said 'I never knew a man who found it so hard to make up his mind!'

Lewis had come full circle. His humility had for years prevented him from preserving his manuscripts and sharing them with others. Now it was clear that no harm was likely to be done by giving me some of his manuscripts, to say nothing of the immense pleasure this afforded me. Almost immediately after this we talked about his great friend Roger Lancelyn Green, and I'm sure Lewis regretted not passing the manuscripts of the Narnian Chronicles to Roger, who read the stories as they were written and gave him much good advice. In any event, he evidently took pleasure in my enjoyment of his manuscripts. Not long afterwards he sent me to Cambridge to clear out his rooms in Magdalene College, with the instructions that if I came across manuscripts of things which had already been published I was to 'apply them to your own use.'

Following Lewis's death his brother, Warnie, seemed to derive as much pleasure as the younger brother in giving me many of C. S. Lewis's manuscripts. From this double generosity of the Lewis brothers many have benefited, one of whom is the author of this important book.

INTRODUCTION
A Most Mysterious Manuscript

It's astounding.

That an unknown manuscript by the twentieth century's most famous Christian author should suddenly appear out of seeming nowhere more than twenty years after his death is definitely astounding. That this manuscript is a piece of fiction by the author of such beloved works as *The Chronicles of Narnia* and *The Screwtape Letters* is remarkable. That this short story turns out to be a version of a previously published C. S. Lewis story which some have accused of being a forgery, transforms the remarkable into mystery.

Here are the facts.

C. S. Lewis's "Light" manuscript appeared as if out of nowhere in the mid 1980s. It came first to the hands of a London bookseller who never divulged his source. He quickly sold the manuscript to a second bookseller who then sold it to a third who then contacted the man most responsible for bringing the manuscript to the attention of Lewis scholars and fans: an American collector of Lewis books and manuscripts, Dr. Edwin W. Brown. Within a few months, the "Light" manuscript found a new and eventually permanent home in the American Midwest.

An earlier version of the story had been published in 1977 under the title, "The Man Born Blind." But in the late 80s, accusations were made that both the "Man Born Blind" and "Light" manuscripts were forgeries, sending ripples throughout the publishing world and causing a rift among Lewis scholars.

Both Lewis's stepson Douglas Gresham and his good friend Owen Barfield attested to the authenticity of the story, but Barfield dated its origin to the late 1920s—making it the earliest of any existing Lewis short stories—while Gresham dated it to the 1950s. Each claimed to be an eyewitness to the original. The manuscript which Gresham saw included the title "Light" in its heading. But that version then disappeared sometime in the 50s or early 60s. The version published from manuscript in 1977 is the one Barfield claimed to recognize, but the manuscript is untitled. Acting in his role as editor of Lewis's posthumous publications, Walter Hooper supplied as title, "The Man Born

Blind," because neither he nor Barfield saw the "Light" manuscript, as Lewis titled it, till it was shown to them almost a decade later by Edwin Brown.

Questions surrounding the "Light" manuscript abound.

Where did it disappear to for over two decades?

And could "Light" be the final version of the story, the missing polished text which should have been published all along (had it not been lost)?

What about the accusation of forgery? Professional appraisals authenticate both manuscripts as do handwriting analyses, but these same analyses shed doubt on any date ever proposed for the story's writing. Several facts seem not to fit previous testimony.

And is it truly possible, given its peculiarity, that this story could come from the mind of C. S. Lewis? No Lewis story ends so abruptly or shockingly as "Light," and it is this shocking ending which has contributed to so much doubt regarding the story's authenticity in addition to so much puzzling over its meaning.

And this may be the greater mystery: the question of what the "Light" story even means. Only a few Lewis specialists have tried to interpret it, and the generally accepted meaning may not stand up to the newest evidence and analysis of the story. The dating is critical. If the story was indeed written before Lewis's conversion, its meaning is likely very different from what the story written by a Christian Lewis would mean. But even beyond this, there may be no single meaning. The testimony, the textual evidence, and the totality of Lewis's writings suggest the possibility that this tiny little story called "Light" could be utterly thick with meanings.

The story may be a window into Lewis's pre-conversion thinking. It may be a key to understanding elements of a theory of knowledge which Lewis critics still wrestle to understand: enjoyment vs. contemplation, reason vs. imagination, thinking vs. experiencing, myth vs. fact, fact vs. truth—these key concepts in Lewis's thought find new explanation in this tale of a former blind man's search for Light. Besides these meanings, it may be that "Light" is Lewis's earliest image in fiction of that deep longing for Joy which was so central to his life. The insights into Lewis's thinking which his little four-page story may offer stretch across decades despite the manuscript's diminutive size. And of all the mysteries suggested and information so far offered, what may be the most astonishing fact of all is that this enigmatic story called "Light" has in all the years since its discovery never been published...until now. What may indeed be Lewis's earliest short story is here finally published in the form which Lewis intended.

In the pages that follow, you will be given the chance to first read the "Light" story in its revised form. Then we will delve together into a detective story: the story of a Lewis manuscript which appeared out of nowhere, demanded authentication, and defied previously held ideas about not only its meaning but even the decade in which it was written. Subsequent chapters consider the story's meaning—even multiple meanings—which may have changed in Lewis's mind over several decades of working with the story. Finally, we'll take advantage of an opportunity never before available in Lewis studies by looking at two versions of the same story side-by-side, including three partial revisions extending between them, to gain insight into Lewis's processes as a reviser and maker of literary meaning.

PART ONE

Light

Upon his death bed, Virgil asked that his *Aeneid* be burned because he didn't think it was good enough—he didn't want what he felt to be an imperfect text to be published.[1] Thankfully no one listened to his request. C. S. Lewis was himself in the habit of burning his manuscripts[2] (fortunately, at a very slow pace), many of which were preserved only by the intervention of Walter Hooper who writes of saving many of Lewis's notebooks and manuscripts from being burned in a bonfire by Lewis's gardener Fred Paxford under the orders of Lewis's brother Warnie.[3] Thanks to Hooper, we have had "The Man Born Blind" for decades. But this story is not the version which Lewis intended to publish. Imagine Virgil finishing *The Aeneid* to his liking before he died but never getting to publish this polished version, say, because it was lost, and only the imperfect version he wanted burned remained. A similar situation exists with the story known first as "The Man Born Blind" and now as "Light": the version in print was followed by another, more polished version. This book puts things in order by publishing what may be Lewis's first short story, and, in giving consideration to Lewis's intentions, the last of his short fiction to be released.[4] With this primary goal in mind, we begin with Lewis's "Light," presented with the slightest editorial corrections, Lewis's original punctuation, and without further comment or the distraction of notations.

---

1 Damen, ch. 11, part 2b, par. 5.
2 See Brown, *Pursuit*, 76 and Hooper, Preface to *Dark Tower*, 7.
3 Hooper, Preface to *Dark Tower*, 7.
4 As far as Walter Hooper knows, there are no more unpublished Lewis short stories (Hooper, Personal Interview, 18 July 2011).

Light

'Bless us!' said Anne, 'There's eleven o'clock. And you're nearly asleep, Robin.' She rose with a bustle of familiar noises, bundling her spools and her little cardboard boxes into the work basket. 'Come on, lazy-bones,' she added. 'You want to be nice and fresh for your first walk to-morrow.'

'That reminds me,' said Robin and then stopped. He had approached the subject three times already since his operation, once to the doctor, once to the nurse, and once before to Anne herself, and each time something seemed to have gone wrong. Now, he felt unreasonably nervous. 'I—I suppose,' he mumbled, 'there'll be lots of *light* out there—when we go for that walk?'

'You mean it will be lighter out of doors? Well, yes, of course. But I must say I always think this is a very light house. This room, now. We've had the sun on it all afternoon.'

'The sun makes it hot—?', said Robin tentatively.

'What *are* you talking about?' said Anne. That was what Robin couldn't understand; why they all sounded so angry or frightened whenever he got near the real question. It was as if they thought he was mad.

'I mean,' he said '—well, look here, dear. I've been wanting to ask you something ever since I got back from the nursing home. I expect it'll sound silly to you. But things must be different to a chap who's been blind all his life, mustn't they? It's all so new. As soon as I heard there was a chance of getting my sight—well, I looked forward. The last thing I thought of before the operation was *Light*. Wondering what it would be like. Then all those days afterwards before they took the bandages off; wondering, waiting—'

'But of course, darling. That was only natural.'

'Then—then' (his voice shook a little) 'why don't I—. I mean, where *is* the light?'

His three weeks of sight had not yet taught him to read the expression of her face, but he knew by her voice the warm wave of muddled, frightened affection that had swelled up in her as she said, 'Why not go to bed now, dearest? We can talk about all that in the morning. You know you're tired now.'

'No,' he said. 'I've got to have this out. You've got to tell me. Great Scot, don't you *want* me to know?'

'Know about what, Robin? Ask me anything you like. But there's nothing to worry about. Your sight is perfectly alright now. You're cured.'

'Very well, then. Is there light in this room at present?'

'Of course there is. Robin, do—'

'Then where is it?'

'Why, all round us.'

'Can you see it?'

'Yes. But really, Robin dear—'

'Then why can't I?'

'But, Robin, you can. You can see me, can't you?, and the mantelpiece, and the table, and—'

'That's what drives me mad. That's the sort of thing you all say. I want to see *light*. Are *you* light? Is the mantelpiece light? Is light only another name for all the other things?'

'Oh, I see what you mean. You're asking about *the* light. That's it there, hanging from the ceiling with the pink shade.'

'Then why did you tell me the light was all round us?'

'Darling, I mean that's what gives the light. The light comes from there.'

'Then where is the light itself? You see, you won't say. Nobody will say. You tell me there's light here and light there, and this is in the light and that is in the light, and people get in one another's light. But you won't point me out the light itself. If none of you know what light is, say so. If there's no such thing—if it was only a fairy tale all along—say so. If the operation was a failure and I still can't see what other people see, tell me. I can take *that*. It's this secrecy that I can't stand. You're all like conspirators. Why the devil—'

Anne began to cry and Robin apologised and comforted her. Then they went to bed.

This conversation made him more cautious. Clearly it was never going to be any use asking about light. Either there was no such thing or else he was all the time making some appalling mistake. If he was not careful he'd find himself in the hands of doctors again—psychotherapists, as likely as not. When Anne took him out for his walk next day he was on his guard. He kept on saying, 'It's lovely. All lovely. Just let me drink it in,' and that satisfied her. And he knew enough now to know that none of the things he saw could possibly be light. They were, as Anne volubly explained to him, only fields or cows or grass or the sun or trees or a quarry. Nothing could be attempted until he was able to go for walks on his own.

About six weeks went by before he first did so. During that time he had passed through every fluctuation of hope and despair but the steady trend of his feelings was towards an increasing, and presently a tormenting, desire. He no longer concealed from himself the fact that the visible world was a disappointment. He realised that he had never really wanted it except for the sake of light and that unless somewhere amongst them he could find that pure stream and bathe his eyes in it and drink it in, all the clouds and colours and animals and what Anne called the 'views' were of no account.

On the morning when he first went out alone there was a mist, but he had met mists before and this did not trouble him. He walked out over the railway bridge and up the steep hill and then along the field-path that skirted the lip of the quarry. Anne had taken him there a few days before to show him 'the view.' She had said, 'What a lovely light there is on the hills over there.' That clue he was now following, though with very faint hope. He was almost certain by now that she knew no more about light than he did. He was beginning to suspect that most of the un-blind were in the same position. What one heard among them was probably mere parrot-like repetition of a rumour—a rumour concerning something which the very few, the great poets and prophets, had really seen and known. Somewhere it must exist. Perhaps not in England—perhaps only rare deposits of it existed, far away to the East in deserts or high mountains. In that case, he would never see it. But if he did—ah yes, if—he would dive into its very heart, give all himself away to it, drink, drink, drink it till he died drinking.

The mist thinned rapidly. Trees brightened out of it, birds began singing. He found he was hot. His shadow lay before him, each moment blacker and more distinct. That violent yellow thing, the sun, which one could never see properly, stared at him on his left hand. He pulled the brim of his hat lower over his eyes, blinking. 'If only I could see any light!' he muttered.

At that moment he caught sight of a young man who was standing with his legs wide apart on the edge of the cliff, singing and making jabs with some slender instrument at a complicated two-legged object about the same height as himself. If Robin had had more experience he would have recognised this as a canvas on an easel. As it was, his eyes and those of the wild looking stranger met so unexpectedly that Robin blurted out, 'What are you doing?', before he had time to be self-conscious.

'Doing?' said the stranger with a certain light-hearted savagery. 'Doing? I'm trying to catch light, if you want to know. Damn it.'

'Good God! So am I,' said Robin.

'Oh—you know too, do you?', said the man. Then, almost vindictively, 'They're all fools. How many come out to paint on a day like this? How many will see it even if you show it 'em? And yet this is the only sort of day when you can *see* light—solid light—light you could drink in a cup or swim in! Look at it!' He pointed into the quarry. The fog was at death grips with the sun but not a stone on the quarry floor was yet visible. The bath of vapour shone like white metal and unfolded itself in ever widening spirals towards them. 'Do you see that?', shouted the violent stranger. 'There's light for you if you like it.'

A second later the expression on the painter's face changed. 'Here!', he cried, 'Are you mad?' The grab he made at Robin was too late. Already he was alone on the path. From a new-made and rapidly vanishing rift in the fog beneath him there came up no cry but only a sound so sharp and definite that you would hardly expect it to have been made by the fall of anything so soft as a human body: that, and the momentary rattling of a dislodged stone.

PART TWO
THE ORIGINS OF LIGHT

Chapter Two
Rescued from the Fire

An American from North Carolina named Walter Hooper started corresponding with C. S. Lewis in 1954.[1] His first letter expressed admiration for Lewis's books; he thanked Lewis for them and said that, though he was a Christian when he first read them, they had accomplished the valuable task of making the "faith clear."[2] Hooper wrote to Lewis in 1957 about going to England to see him, to which Lewis replied, "I shall be happy to meet you whenever you come to this country."[3] But it was not until 1962 that Hooper wrote with more serious intent about a trip to meet Lewis, explaining that he was visiting England with the hope of writing a book on Lewis for "an American series on English authors."[4] Lewis once again expressed an interest in meeting the young Hooper, though he did his best to dissuade him from writing a book about himself or "any living author."[5]

Walter Hooper finally met C. S. Lewis on the seventh of June, 1963 where they had tea at Lewis's home, The Kilns.[6] Hooper, who was on summer break from teaching at the University of Kentucky, and in England not only to meet Lewis but to participate in the International Summer School at Exeter College,[7] describes his visit as beginning with a nervous knock at the door after which Lewis welcomed him in a manner "so bright, loud and jovial that I

---

1 Hooper, *Companion & Guide*, 116.
2 Hooper's editorial note 383 in *Collected Letters 3*, 535.
3 2 December 1957; *Collected Letters 3*, 903.
4 Green and Hooper, 298. The series was the "Twayne's English Authors Series" (Hooper's editorial note 101 in *Collected Letters 3*, 1355).
5 2 July 1962; *Collected Letters 3*, 1355. Lewis was eventually successful in convincing Hooper to drop the project (Hooper's editorial note 101 in *Collected Letters 3*, 1355), but not before Hooper began work on a life long project: assembling a bibliography of the writings of C. S. Lewis (see Lewis's letter of 15 December 1962 in *Collected Letters 3*, 1393 in which Lewis says of Hooper, "You are now a very much better C.S.L. scholar than I am!").
6 Hooper, *Companion & Guide*, 116.
7 Hooper's editorial narrative in *Collected Letters 3*, 1446.

quickly forgot my fright."⁸ They talked for two hours. When Hooper thanked Lewis for taking so much time to meet with him, contrary to expressing any sense of burden, Lewis replied that he wanted to see Hooper again and so invited him to meet at a pub called the "Lamb and Flag" a few days later. This meeting was followed by others including Hooper's joining Lewis for church on Sundays, and meeting with Lewis's friends, the Inklings.⁹

Lewis's stepson Douglas Gresham writes of Hooper's visits to The Kilns that summer:

> I liked him at once. He was a handsome young man about fourteen years older than I, and he had a charming and gentle manner about him. He seemed at first to be almost in awe of Jack,¹⁰ and this I found slightly amusing, but, nonetheless, charming. He soon became popular with the whole household and his visits were looked forward to by all of us. Walter Hooper quickly took in the strange and difficult situation that existed at The Kilns and he tried to assist in every possible way.¹¹

The "strange and difficult situation" to which Gresham refers included the absence of Lewis's brother Warnie (who had "fled to the mists of Ireland and the fog of alcohol about the end of May"¹²), along with Lewis's increasingly poor health¹³ which took a turn for the worse in July. On the 14th, Hooper went to The Kilns to go with Lewis to church but found him too ill to do anything, even hold a cup of tea or a cigarette.¹⁴ Lewis explained that he was going to a nursing home the next day to be examined, and then, to Hooper's surprise, he asked him to stay in England to act as "a sort of secretary"¹⁵ for Lewis. Hooper accepted.

On July 15th Lewis went to the Acland Nursing Home as planned where he soon had a heart attack and fell into a coma from which the doctors did not expect him to wake.¹⁶ He surprised the doctors and delighted his friends when he woke at three p.m. the next day.¹⁷ The day after that, Walter Hooper took up

---

8   Green and Hooper, 299.
9   Hooper, *Companion & Guide*, 116.
10 The nickname Lewis preferred to be called (Sayer, 42).
11 Gresham, *Lenten Lands*, 153.
12 Ibid, 151.
13 Lewis faced multiple health problems in his last few years including kidney, prostate, and heart problems. See his letter of 6 December 1961 in *Collected Letters 3*, 1301-02 (and thanks to Walter Hooper for helping with this note). For additional details, see Sayer, chapter 22, pages 397-411.
14 Green and Hooper, 301.
15 Gresham, *Lenten Lands*, 154.
16 Green and Hooper, 301.
17 Hooper's editorial narrative in *Collected Letters 3*, 1446.

his duties (at the hospital) as Lewis's secretary.[18] One day later, Lewis's friend George Sayer visited him only to find that Lewis was somewhat delusional.[19] Thus, when Lewis asked Sayer if he'd met his new secretary, Sayer "was not quite sure that Walter Hooper was a real person." He learned otherwise the next day. Thereafter, Hooper was a regular part of Lewis's life for the next month and a half.

Hooper moved into The Kilns on July 26th where he was placed in Lewis's second floor bedroom, this because Lewis, before leaving the Acland, was forbidden to climb stairs (a bed was placed for him in a downstairs room). Lewis himself returned home on August 6th accompanied by a male nurse[20] wherein "he spent most of his time writing letters with Walter Hooper, who proved to be an admirable secretary."[21] Among the letters Lewis dictated to Hooper was his resignation from Cambridge[22] which was followed by the need for the undertaking of an enormous task: the fetching of Lewis's books from Cambridge to The Kilns. The task was taken up by Hooper and Douglas Gresham on August 14th. According to Gresham,[23] he and Hooper were sent to Cambridge with a list of instructions.[24] Hooper had voluntarily taken on the momentous work of sorting through and boxing up all the papers which Lewis had accumulated during his years at Cambridge. Gresham went with Hooper to help. They stayed for a week at the Blue Boar and spent their days organizing Lewis's books. Gresham writes, "I carried box after box of bound volumes to wherever Walter indicated. Walter, list in hand, labored on, checking, packing, sorting and generally organizing under a steadily increasing cloud of very learned dust."[25] Eventually, Lewis's Cambridge rooms were emptied and thousands of his books loaded on a truck and taken to Oxford[26] where they were "piled on the floor or pressed into the already crowded shelves at the Kilns."[27]

After offering Lewis some much-needed help in the summer of 1963, Hooper returned to America late in August[28] to teach for one more term at

---

18   Ibid, 1142-43.
19   Sayer, 405.
20   Hooper's editorial narrative in *Collected Letters 3*, 1446.
21   Sayer, 406.
22   Green and Hooper, 302.
23   See Gresham, *Lenten Lands*, 153-54.
24   Seven pages of instructions, according to Hooper's editorial narrative in *Collected Letters 3*, 1451.
25   Gresham, *Lenten Lands*, 154.
26   Hooper's editorial narrative in *Collected Letters 3*, 1451.
27   Sayer, 407.
28   Gresham, *Lenten Lands*, 154. Green and Hooper (304) and Sayer, (407) report Hooper leaving at the end of September, but a letter of 3 September 1963 (*Collected Letters 3*, 1454)

the University of Kentucky, this with the intention of returning to England to continue to help Lewis.[29] Over the next two months, Hooper corresponded with Lewis several times, mostly regarding Hooper's desire to return to his duties in January. Lewis tried to talk Hooper out of this plan, citing the poor pay and inadequately heated lodgings Lewis had to offer,[30] but Hooper persisted and Lewis acquiesced, writing, "Prudence having had her say, honor is now satisfied and I can settle down to enjoy the result which was the one I always hoped for. We look forward to seeing you on Jan 3rd or 4th."[31]

Unfortunately, the hoped-for reunion never happened. C. S. Lewis died on November 22, 1963. This did not deter Walter Hooper[32] from returning to England in January[33] to visit Lewis's brother Warnie and see what help or comfort he might offer. Hooper was there for Warnie "when Warnie was at his very worst."[34] He tried to help Warnie out of his drinking problem but to no avail.

It is here that the story of "Light," or rather its predecessor, "The Man Born Blind," enters the picture. While Hooper stayed with friends at Keble College in Oxford, Warnie Lewis began the process of "clearing out The Kilns" in preparation of moving to a smaller home where Hooper would later join him.[35] According to Hooper,

> The Lewis brothers felt little of that veneration for manuscripts so typical of many of us, and Major Lewis, after setting aside those papers which had a special significance for him, began disposing of the others. Thus it was that a great many things which I was never able to identify found their way on to a bonfire which burned steadily for three days.

Fortunately, Fred Paxford, Lewis's gardener, knew of Hooper's love for Lewis's work and so urged Lewis's brother Warnie to stop the burning process till Hooper could look through it. Hooper providentially appeared at The Kilns that same day and learned that, if he didn't carry the papers away immediately, they would be burned. He writes, "There were so many that it took all my strength and energy to carry them back to Keble College."[36]

---

from Lewis to Hooper indicates that Gresham's report is the accurate one here.
29 Sayer, 407.
30 20 September 1963; *Collected Letters 3*, 1457-58 and 11 October 1963; *Collected Letters 3*, 1461-62.
31 23 October 1963; *Collected Letters 3*, 1469-70 and Hooper's footnote 152 on 1470.
32 Who learned of Lewis's death via phone call from Douglas Gresham (Gresham, *Lenten Lands*, 157).
33 Hooper, *Dark Tower*, 7.
34 Gresham, *Lenten Lands*, 192.
35 Hooper, *Dark Tower*, 7.
36 Ibid. This story was somewhat confirmed by Dr. Edwin Brown. In his book, *In Pursuit*

C. S. Lewis's First and Final Short Story

Hooper has since acted as collector, preservationist, and editor in the publication of many Lewis documents which might have been lost to us without his painstaking work. Among the notebooks which Hooper saved from the fire was one containing the story which he first published (as editor) in *Church Times*[37] and *The Dark Tower and Other Stories* in 1977 under the title, "The Man Born Blind." Anyone wanting to read the story in this form can find the book easily enough. Anyone who would like to see the original notebook in which the story was found (which includes three revision paragraphs indicating that Lewis was still working on the story), will have to visit Oxford University where the notebook is preserved at the Bodleian Library.[38] The existence of the notebook, the story, and the three attempted revisions is critical to our investigation of "Light."

---

of C. S. Lewis, Brown writes of a former Blackwell's employee who knew Walter Hooper well, having met him while Lewis was still alive. "One day early in 1964 Walter came into Blackwell's in a mild state of panic to ask his friend if he might use their copier, one of the first xerographic copiers in Oxford. He explained that he had just retrieved a large quantity of Lewis papers that were about to be burned by Lewis's brother, Warnie, and he needed to make copies of those that had not yet been destroyed" (Brown, *Pursuit*, 92-93). The folks at Blackwell's helped Hooper out. I said above the story was "somewhat confirmed" by Brown's anecdote because Hooper read an earlier version of this footnote and returned a correction on the story: "Warnie gave me the notebooks I saved from the fire, so there was no need to copy them. What I took to Blackwell's to be copied were the eleven bound volumes of the 'Lewis Papers.' Warnie, having used them to write his first 'biography' of C. S. Lewis—which eventually became *Letters of C. S. Lewis* (1966), I feared he would destroy the Lewis Papers to provide more space on his shelves, so I got my friends at Blackwell's to photocopy them. In the end, he didn't destroy them, and the eleven volumes are now in the Wade" (Hooper, 31 August 2011; Email to Starr).

37 *Church Times*, No 5947 (4 February 1977) according to Hooper, *Companion & Guide*, 816.
38 Bodleian, Dep. d. 809, also called "Lewis ms no. 31."

Chapter Three
Dr. Brown's Pursuit of C. S. Lewis

Edwin W. Brown, M.D. is the man most responsible for bringing "Light" to…well…light. Though Brown is a Harvard trained medical doctor who has traveled to more than a hundred countries in the course of his career, he is also, to put it mildly, an admirer and collector of all things C. S. Lewis. The stories of Brown's experiences in collecting Lewis artifacts could fill a book. In fact they have: Brown recorded them in his book, *In Pursuit of C. S. Lewis: Adventures in Collecting His Works*.[1] There was a time when one could walk into Brown's Indianapolis basement library to find that he had converted it into a model of a proper English pub.[2] Brown was inspired by the "Eagle and Child," a favorite Oxford pub of Lewis and his friends, the Inklings. And on shelves along a wall in Brown's basement stood one of the finest private collections of C. S. Lewis first editions in well-preserved original dust jackets, part of a collection of Lewis rarities including hand-written Lewis manuscripts amassed by Brown during his travels over three decades. Brown's little *hobby* has allowed him to develop friendships with such Lewis family, friends, and associates as Walter Hooper,[3] George Sayer,[4] Pauline Baynes,[5] Owen Barfield,[6] and Douglas Gresham.[7]

Of interest to us is one very special manuscript which came into Ed Brown's possession and is now, thankfully, preserved for Lewis fans and scholars. The title Lewis gave to the document is "Light," and so we call it the

---
1   Written with Dan Hamilton.
2   Today the replica can be seen in the Brown Collection at Taylor University, Upland Indiana.
3   Brown, *Pursuit*, 43-45, 72.
4   Ibid, 47-48. George Sayer was a friend of Lewis's and wrote what many Lewis critics consider to be the best biography of C. S. Lewis to date: *Jack: A Life of C. S. Lewis*.
5   Ibid, 72-75. Pauline Baynes is the original illustrator of all the books in The Chronicles of Narnia.
6   Ibid, 83-87.
7   Ibid, 109-110. Douglas Gresham is the younger of Lewis's two stepsons; he is currently a producer on the Narnia movies.

"Light" manuscript.[8] Brown first learned about "Light" early in 1986[9] when he was contacted by a book seller, Peter Jolliffe, who specialized in Lewis and who had helped Brown acquire many first editions of Lewis's books.[10] Jolliffe was "a British bookseller who lived in Eynsham" outside Oxford in the 80s,[11] and he "may have had a shop in London with somebody else" at that time.[12] "Each time I went to England," says Brown, "I contacted him and visited" either at his house or shop. Brown recalls, "At that time he seemed to handle more C. S. Lewis material than any other bookseller because I bought more from him than" anyone else.[13]

Brown suspected that the appearance of the "Light" manuscript so many years after Lewis's death occurred because Lewis wrote the final version of his "Light" story and sent it off for publication to a magazine where it was neither published nor returned to Lewis and thus languished for some fifty years.[14] The story was secured "among some books and papers acquired from an unknown source by an obscure London book dealer" who sold it for a hundred pounds "to a more knowledgeable dealer, who immediately sold it" to Peter Jolliffe for 500 pounds, who then offered the manuscript to Brown for a price which "increased considerably."[15]

Jolliffe had contacted Brown in the States either by letter or phone and offered him an "interesting document."[16] I asked Brown when it was, exactly, that he realized this document was a version of the "Man Born Blind" story, and he replied that it was Jolliffe who identified the story and then told Brown what it was. Says Brown: "That's why I wanted it immediately." Jolliffe had obtained "Light" from a dealer named Julian Nangle. The manuscript appeared in 1985 when the "obscure London antiquarian bookseller" mentioned above "acquired the manuscript from a person well known to him [the dealer] who had owned it for many years."[17] This unknown bookseller (who was eventually identified as one Stanley Noble)[18] sold the manuscript to Nangle, who

---

8   Brown first uses the term on page 82 of his book.
9   Brown, Personal Interview, 13 March, 2011.
10 Brown, *Pursuit*, 82.
11 Brown, Interview.
12 Ibid. Jolliffe did have a shop in London later, with a partner, and still has a shop there today.
13 Brown, Interview.
14 See chapter four for newly discovered information regarding the manuscript's date and whereabouts.
15 Brown, *Pursuit*, 82.
16 Brown, Interview.
17 Ibid, Brown reading from an article he wrote about the "Light" manuscript.
18 In our interview, Brown confirmed that the "obscure" dealer had died by the time Brown learned of the "Light" manuscript. Shortly after the interview, Ed Brown contacted Julian

then sold it to Jolliffe, who then offered the manuscript to "his best Lewis customer," Ed Brown. The transaction of seller and collector occurred by mail between two continents. Brown says that he might have paid for "Light" with an "old Barclay's check." He remembers paying about twelve to thirteen hundred pounds for the manuscript which Jolliffe mailed to him folded up in an envelope![19] Having bought the "Light" manuscript, Brown spent the subsequent years studying and taking steps to authenticate it.

Brown's collection, which included materials related not just to Lewis, but to George MacDonald, Dorothy Sayers, Owen Barfield and Charles Williams as well, eventually came to the attention of Dr. David Neuhouser of Taylor University in Upland Indiana. Neuhouser learned of Brown's Lewis collection through a nephew of Brown's who had been a student of Neuhouser's at Taylor. The friendship struck up between these two men led to a tradition: a once-yearly field trip during which Neuhouser would bring fifteen students or so to view Brown's collection and listen to his wonderful stories. One day in February 1996, Neuhouser approached Brown to see if he was interested in donating his collection to "some institute"; however, because of its cost, Brown could not give the collection away outright. Still he responded by offering to sell Taylor the rare Lewis and Friends items he'd been collecting for more than two decades—including the "Light" manuscript—at a reasonable price.[20] Later that year an anonymous donor gave Taylor the money to make the purchase. Brown's collection arrived at Taylor on February 13, 1997. What Brown most fondly recalls about the whole process was how kind and "undemanding" Taylor was in pursuing the transaction.[21] "Light" now resides in the basement

---

Nangle by email, asking him for information about the "Light" manuscript and the unknown first bookseller (hoping that we might then track down the manuscript's previous owner). Nangle kindly replied, but Brown emailed me saying, "Unfortunately, he remembers nothing about it" (Brown, 23 March 2011; Email to Starr). Afterward (13 April 2011), while I was reviewing an appraisal of the "Light" manuscript conducted as part of a full appraisal of the Brown Collection for Taylor University, I ran across the name of the obscure first bookseller. Apparently Brown was still in possession of the seller's name in 1996 (which he later forgot) and was able to pass it on to the appraisers. According to the appraisal document, and here the appraisers are quoting Ed Brown, "An obscure (and recently deceased) London bookdealer, Stanley Noble, acquired it ["Light"] from an unknown source in 1986 [it was actually 1985] and sold it to another British dealer, Julian Nangle. Nangle promptly sold it to an Oxford dealer, Peter Jolliffe, who offered it to me" (Smith-Theobald, Part 115, par. 1). Brown thereafter contacted Julian Nangle one more time asking if he knew anything about Stanley Noble (Brown informed me of this in an email of 18 April 2011). Nangle never replied.

19   Brown, Interview.
20   Edwin W. Brown Collection Website.
21   Brown, Interview.

of Taylor's library as part of the Edwin W. Brown Collection.[22] But Ed Brown continues to collect Lewis bits and books today.[23]

For more than a decade, Lewis's short story, "Light," has been available to scholars and fans, but only to those who could make the trek to Taylor's campus to read the story in manuscript form. As Ed Brown made the story available to many by turning it over to Taylor, so Taylor University has now made it available to thousands more.

But the surfacing of a complete C. S. Lewis story more than twenty years after his death, calls for an examination of the manuscript's authenticity. "The Man Born Blind"[24] is the first piece of positive evidence in a trail we will take up in the next chapter. Thanks to Walter Hooper's work in preserving Lewis texts, the trail does not begin cold.

---

22 Additional history and information about the Brown Collection are available at Taylor University's website for the Edwin W. Brown Collection: http://www.taylor.edu/academics/supportservices/cslewis/collection/.

23 While half of our four hours together were spent on getting work done for the *Light* book, the other half was spent in Brown's basement, looking over and talking about Ed's amazing collection of rare Lewis books. A recent find at that time included a volume of Boswell's *Life of Dr. Johnson*, a favorite book of Lewis's, which Lewis bought as a teenager and in which he had written his name.

24 Hereafter the story will usually be referred to as MBB and the notebook in which it appears as the MBB notebook.

Chapter Four
Authenticating Light

That an entire C. S. Lewis short story should appear out of seeming nowhere in 1985 is amazing. Lewis's works are famous—they sell in the millions—and he is arguably the most important Christian writer of the twentieth century. How could one of his stories have been lost for decades? A partial answer is that Lewis was a prolific writer, another that he lived not very long ago. He wrote literally mounds of material, and he has only been gone from us for about 50 years. Given these facts we should not be surprised that new Lewis writings continue to surface, often in the form of private letters or forgotten short essays, on a still fairly regular basis.[1] But "Light" is a Lewis *story* and his fiction the most popular of his writings. It is strange to have a Lewis story surface so late and under somewhat mysterious circumstances. These circumstances raise questions which need answering: is the manuscript authentic, where did it disappear to, and when was it written?

Texts and Testimonials

In January of 2011, my search began, calmly and academically enough, among books by and about C. S. Lewis. I started with "The Man Born Blind" version of the story. Though some question has been raised as to the authenticity of MBB[2] what we have in it is a direct link to "Light." I accepted Ed Brown's theory that "Light" is the final draft of MBB[3] after reviewing both handwritten manuscripts, including the revisions Lewis attempted on the left facing pages of the MBB notebook. Otherwise, viewing the hand writing of the two texts side-by-side[4] shows not only their kinship in content but in authorship—both

---

1 See, for example, the recently published fragment, "Language and Human Nature" in volume 27 of *Seven*.
2 By Kathryn Lindskoog whose arguments have been thoroughly refuted.
3 Brown, *Pursuit*, 90.
4 Which I was able to do using photocopies; however, I visited both Taylor and the Bodleian to view each document directly to confirm all conclusions related to the manuscripts.

documents are written in Lewis's hand.[5] Furthermore, MBB appears in a notebook which contains additional content belonging to Lewis.

The next evidence I turned to was testimonial. According to Walter Hooper, the story was, to the best of his knowledge, "not seen by anyone during the author's lifetime with the exception of Owen Barfield and possibly J. R. R. Tolkien."[6] Hooper never asked Tolkien about the story but he discovered Tolkien's knowledge of it in a 1976 book by Clyde Kilby called *Tolkien and the Silmarillion*. Writes Kilby,

> Tolkien told me of C. S. Lewis's story about the man born with a cataract on each eye. He kept hearing people talk of light but could not understand what they meant. After an operation he had some sight but had not yet come to understand *light*. Then one day he saw a haze rising from a pond (actually, said Tolkien, the pond at the front of Lewis's home) and thought that at last he was seeing light. In his eagerness to experience real light, he rushed joyfully into it and was drowned.[7]

Hooper records that the differences between the published story and Tolkien's recollection of it suggest that, rather than reading the story, Tolkien was told the story—or at least this altered version of the story—by Lewis.[8] However, when I suggested this theory to him (forgetting to remind him that it was his own), Hooper answered that it's more likely that Lewis would have read the story to Tolkien.[9]

Barfield told Hooper that MBB "was written during the late 1920s when he and Lewis were deep in that 'Great War' debate over Appearance and Reality which Lewis refers to in his autobiography, *Surprised by Joy*."[10] Barfield records this testimony himself in his introduction to the 1965 book, *Light on C. S. Lewis*. In discussing the "Great War," he writes,

> it was about the same time, or a little later, that he [Lewis] further expressed his own position in the form of a short story about a man born blind, who recovered his sight by an operation. The result was disastrous for the protagonist, because he insisted on trying to *see* the mysterious thing he had heard people calling "light"; whereas you do not see light itself, but only the object which it illumines.[11]

---

5   Ed Brown made this same observation (Brown, *Pursuit*, 90-91).
6   Hooper, *Dark Tower*, 9.
7   Kilby, 27-28 (Hooper quotes the passage directly in *Dark Tower*, 9-10).
8   Hooper, *Dark Tower*, 10. Another possibility is that Tolkien simply misremembered the story and filled in his own details upon telling it to Kilby.
9   Hooper, Interview. Hooper even suggested that there might have been multiple versions of the story.
10 Ibid, 10. See also Brown's record of Barfield's testimony (*Pursuit*, 85).
11 Barfield, *Light on Lewis*, xviii.

Barfield claims that Lewis had not yet become a Christian when he wrote the story. If that is so, then Lewis must have written the story before his conversion late in 1931.[12] Early in my investigation, I had no reason to doubt this conclusion.[13]

Ed Brown visited Barfield soon after acquiring the "Light" manuscript[14] and left him a copy of "Light" to read. He had flown to England to show Walter Hooper a copy of the manuscript—this was the first time Hooper ever saw this version of the story. Barfield wrote a letter to Brown shortly thereafter. Brown rediscovered the letter Barfield sent him about "Light" a month or less before I visited him in Indianapolis.[15] In it, Barfield writes,

> I am afraid all I can tell you about Light / The Man Born Blind is that the printed version (latter title) is the only one I ever saw or heard of. It was sent to me by Lewis (and returned to him) shortly after it was written. I can't say just when: probably in the late '20s, certainly a long time ago. I never heard of the later revision.
>
> I suppose the later version is on the whole an improvement, but I am sorry Lewis cut out the touching episode of Robin going back to Braille, and his other habits when blind, for the comfort of them.[16]

Barfield here confirms his having read MBB, Lewis's authorship of the story, and a rough date (the late 20s) for the story's writing. Notice that Barfield leaves some room for doubting his date with the qualification, "certainly a long time ago." Nevertheless, Barfield attested to the story's date (the late 20s) as well as its authenticity throughout his lifetime.[17]

Another piece of evidence regarding the date of "Light" lies in the manuscript itself. Its heading reads, "From C. S. Lewis, Magdalen College,

---

12   It was 28 September 1931. See Hooper's editorial note in *Collected Letters 1*, 972, and Lewis's subsequent letters to Arthur Greeves of 1 October 1931 and 18 October 1931, 972-977.

13   See also Barfield's 1983 testimony to his dating and interpretation of MBB in "Owen Barfield's Response to John Fitzpatrick's essay on 'The Man Born Blind'" in *CSL* 14.8 (June 1983): 5.

14   In his book, Brown writes that it was 1988 (82); however, during our interview he realized that the year was 1986.

15   Brown, 6 February 2011; Email to Starr. Brown allowed the original to be photographed for this book. See figure 4.1 for the paragraphs pertaining to "Light."

16   Lewis's removal of MBB paragraph 30,* the "Braille" paragraph, constitutes the greatest difference between MBB and "Light." Lewis attempted to revise the paragraph three times in the MBB notebook before writing the "Light" manuscript.

*Paragraph references to MBB follow the original manuscript; the published version of MBB splits the opening paragraph into two.

17   Hooper, Interview.

C. S. Lewis's First and Final Short Story

Oxford." Lewis became a fellow of Magdalen in June of 1925[18] where he worked until the end of 1954.[19] This allowed me to narrow the date of the manuscript down to a mere three decades of Lewis's life—rather a weak start.

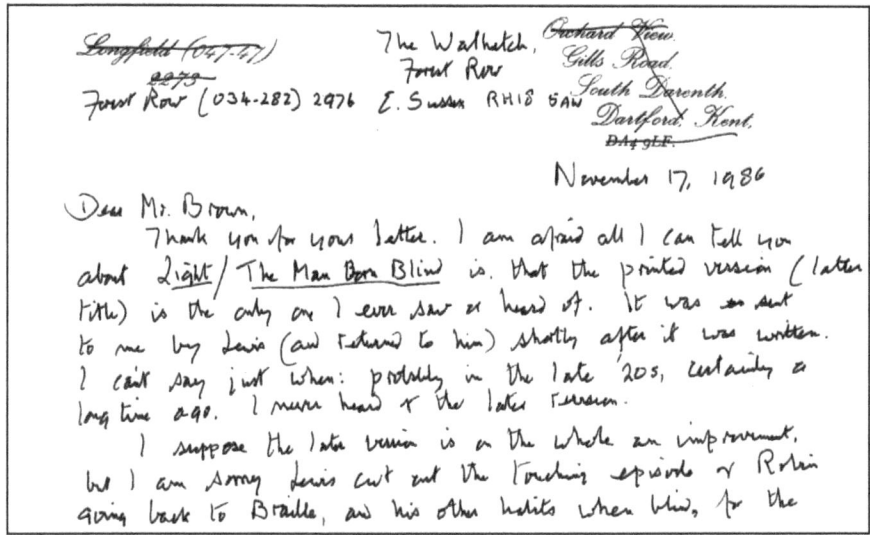

FIGURE 4.1, LETTER FROM OWEN BARFIELD TO ED BROWN, 17 NOVEMBER 1986

THE LOCATION OF THE "LIGHT" MANUSCRIPT

From Barfield's testimony and the manuscript's title, Ed Brown began drawing conclusions about the composition date and whereabouts of the "Light" manuscript. Brown writes that "Light" "was never published, but had apparently been sent to an unknown magazine for publication, as suggested by the entry [the heading] in the upper right-hand corner of the first page."[20] The manuscript "was neither published nor returned, turning up some 50 years later among some books and papers acquired from an unknown source by an obscure London book dealer." But did Lewis in fact send the manuscript off for publication as Brown suggests?

A potential argument against the idea is that Lewis sent his books off to be typed before sending them to a publisher.[21] Would he have sent a handwritten story to a magazine for publication? The answer is probably yes. A handwritten manuscript of Lewis's "Myth Became Fact" essay is preserved

---

18   Sayer, 183.
19   Sayer, 358.
20   Brown, *Pursuit*, 82.
21   A typed manuscript of *The Screwtape Letters* at the Wade Center (Wade Ms. CSL/MS-107) attests to this practice.

at the Wade Center under its original title, "—And Became Fact."²² At the top of the manuscript Lewis wrote a note clearly intended for a publication editor: "Will this do? If so, be sure and send me a proof."²³ Obviously Lewis was asking for proof sheets of this essay before it went to publication, and he was relying on the journal's publisher to type it up. In addition to this example of a handwritten short piece for publication, Walter Hooper told me that Lewis even sent handwritten book-length manuscripts to publishers.²⁴ This proof, along with the heading on the "Light" manuscript, provide evidence that Lewis might have sent "Light" off for publication and that it was neither published nor returned.²⁵ However, one clear piece of evidence raises problems for this theory.

Recall that Walter Hooper wrote in his Preface to *The Dark Tower* that, as far as he knew, no one besides Lewis, Barfield, and possibly Tolkien had seen the MBB story. Ed Brown made a similar claim about the "Light" manuscript, writing that, as of 1988, only Hooper, Barfield, the three dealers who had owned it, and Brown himself had ever read it.²⁶ My first adventure away from the books of my own library took me to Ed Brown's home in Indianapolis in March of 2011. Sitting in his formal living room, a legal pad of questions in my lap, a laptop on the coffee table before me and folders scattered about the couches, I asked Ed if he ever showed a copy of the manuscript to Douglas Gresham, Lewis's stepson, and he said he had not. It turns out he didn't have to. Gresham had seen the original while Lewis was still alive. I learned this fact in January of 1997 when emailing Gresham about the authenticity of MBB. At that time, I had not yet heard of "Light," so I only asked about MBB. Gresham replied, "Jack read me the story now entitled 'A [*sic*] Man

---

22   Wade Ms. CSL/MS-4.
23   The essay was originally published in *World Dominion*, Vol. XXII (September-October 1944), as noted by Lesley Walmsley (138). See also Bodleian collection Ms. Dep. d. 415 which contains Lewis's hand written essay "On Forgiveness" with a letter of 28 August 1947 in which he tells a "Mr. Irwin" that he may do what he likes with the article but that, if he publishes it, he should let Lewis see proofs first.
24   This occurred later in Lewis's life. Hooper said Lewis sent manuscripts such as *An Experiment in Criticism* and *The Discarded Image* to publishers because he found that they would make fewer mistakes when typing up the manuscript for publication because they had to slow down and type from something more difficult to read. Lewis had to do less correcting of proof sheets this way (Hooper, Interview).
25   I suppose there is a less likely possibility as to the manuscript's location for us to consider as well: that Lewis sent "Light" to a typist who never returned the original. But I have no reason to think so, and it raises the question of what happened to the supposed typescript which would have resulted (or, even less likely, did the typist keep "Light" and Lewis just forget about it?).
26   Brown, *Pursuit*, 91. I suppose we should also add as a likely reader the person who sold "Light" to the first dealer.

C. S. Lewis's First and Final Short Story

Born Blind' (which he called 'Light' at that time) sometime in the fifties, from its original hand written manuscript."[27] Gresham saw the manuscript in the 50s, more than two decades after Brown's conjecture that it disappeared in the late 20s.

I had emailed Gresham in February of 2011 to ask his permission to use the above quote, and his reply[28] confirmed his previous statement. Additionally, he wrote that he never saw the title Hooper gave the story until it was published,[29] and added that, not only did he know of the "Light" story in the 50s, but "my Mother [Lewis's wife, Joy] knew of it…and also Roger Lancelyn Green[30] almost certainly knew the story."[31] He later added, "I know about Mother because she was there when Jack [Lewis] read it to me, but I cannot remember why I am convinced that Roger also knew of it, it's just something that my mind has always accepted for some reason that I can no longer recall."[32]

I believe I succeeded in shocking Ed Brown when I shared these emails with him in our interview. He had not known that Douglas Gresham heard the story and saw the manuscript. But Ed said that Gresham's word was good enough for him.

Gresham's testimony still leaves questions unanswered and raises new ones. First of all, if Gresham saw "Light" in the 50s, was it indeed written in the 20s as Barfield had said? Or is it possible that MBB was written in the 20s and "Light" several decades later? The other important question is what happened to the "Light" manuscript *after* Gresham saw it in the 50s? I find it hard to believe that, given his fame, Lewis would've sent the manuscript off for publication and had it rejected and never returned. That theory worked

---

27 Gresham, 7 January 1997; Email to Starr.
28 Ibid, 22 February 2011; Email to Starr.
29 Ibid, 23 February 2011; Email to Starr. Gresham said that he preferred Lewis's title "Light" as well. I don't mean to sound conspiratorial regarding Hooper's titling of "The Man Born Blind." He did not have a titled "Light" manuscript, and he didn't know that it had existed and Gresham had seen it, just as Gresham doubtless didn't know that Hooper had found a notebook version of the story which he intended to publish as Lewis's literary executor and which story needed a title. Hooper not knowing about "Light" and Gresham not knowing about the notebook and Hooper's project, the two would've had no reason to communicate on the issue. In our interview, Hooper confirmed that he had chosen the title, "The Man Born Blind." He said that, whenever he was presented with an untitled Lewis text which he intended to publish, he created a title based on something Lewis said within the text itself (the one exception being "After Ten Years" which needed a sufficiently obscure title in order to keep the mystery of the opening chapter intact) (Hooper, Interview).
30 Green was a friend of Lewis's and an accomplished writer in his own rite (see Hooper, *Companion & Guide*, 661-663). He co-wrote with Walter Hooper the book *C. S. Lewis: A Biography*.
31 Gresham, 24 February 2011; Email to Starr.
32 Ibid, 25 February 2011; Email to Starr.

easily enough for a little known Lewis of the 20s, but not so much for this one. Given the morbidly stunning nature of its ending, the story might have been rejected and kept in a file cabinet or a stack of papers at a publishing house, but this doesn't seem likely.

There remains little to go on. "Light" was removed or sent from the Lewis household sometime after it was read to Gresham and his mother, either in Lewis's lifetime or after he died. Perhaps someone took it from the house in the late 50s or early 60s. Perhaps it was discovered in the house later by someone other than Hooper or Lewis's brother Warnie and taken for its value or as a keepsake. Lewis may have given or sent the story to a friend to read, and it was never returned. I found at least one instance where something similar happened: Lewis sent the typescript and handwritten preface of *The Screwtape Letters* to his friend Mr. Neylan. In an attached note, Lewis asked Neylan to hold onto the manuscript for safe keeping after he'd sent proofs to the publisher.[33] Another option is that Lewis folded the story up and stuck it in a book on a shelf where it was forgotten. Then the book was loaned out or given away before Lewis died or sold off after his death.[34] All we may ever know is that someone who wasn't Warnie Lewis or Walter Hooper somehow came into possession of the "Light" manuscript and kept it until 1985—for twenty-five to thirty years. This person then sold the manuscript to Stanley Noble, the now deceased first bookseller referenced in Brown's study. Beyond this conclusion, my search for the previous whereabouts of the "Light" manuscript came to a dead end in the spring of 2011. But there was still the mystery of dating the manuscript and some surprising answers.

The Question of Quink

When was the story written, both in MBB notebook and "Light" manuscript versions? Part of the difficulty in dating the story lies in a claim made by Nicolas Barker in a book review written in 1990. While Owen Barfield says the story was written in the late 20s or at least "a long time ago," Barker claims that the primary kind of ink used in writing MBB did not exist until around 1950.

According to Barker, the story in the MBB notebook is written in "Parker's Royal Blue 'Quink.'"[35] Barker claims that the "royal blue shade" of "Quink" was "introduced *c.* 1950, and briefly used by Lewis about then."[36] The Parker

---

33 Wade Ms. CSL/MS-107.
34 It may even be possible that Lewis wrote multiple versions of the story which scattered to the winds in various ways and the manuscript Douglas Gresham saw is not even the same one we now have. I have relegated this option to this footnote because I think it unlikely.
35 Barker, 364.
36 Barker, 363.

Pen Company was founded in 1888[37] in Janesville Wisconsin.[38] In 1928, the company began work on an ink that would "eliminate the need for blotting."[39] The result was an ink which dried by absorption rather than evaporation.[40] This new ink, called "Quink," was released in 1931 in four colors, one of which was "Tunis Blue,"[41] but this should not be confused with "Royal Blue" which was released later.[42] A little bit of internet digging found advertisements for "Quink" ink in period magazines. I eventually discovered a *Boy's Life* from March 1935 which contained one such advertisement including a complete list of "Quink" colors among which was the color "Royal Blue."[43] I suppose it might be argued that "Royal Blue Quink" was not available in England in 1935 (*Boy's Life* being an American magazine), but I find a fifteen year stretch rather doubtful.

Then comes the question of how Barker knew the ink he was looking at was "Quink." Granted his expertise with books and publishing,[44] did he nevertheless do any chemical testing or analysis? There's no indication in his essay that he did so. Referring to the MBB notebook marginal revisions, Barker mentions that Lewis "reverted to blue-black ink."[45] In an email to Douglas Gresham, I asked the question, "Did you ever take a look at the kinds of ink Lewis used for writing—the brand name? the colors of ink?" to which

---

37 "Parker Pen History."
38 "Parker Pen Company."
39 "Quink," par. 2.
40 Ibid, par. 3.
41 Ibid, par. 5.
42 In 1947 there was a new ink released by Parker called "Super Chrome" which dried almost instantly and came in a wider range of colors ("Quink," par. 7—there is no listing of the colors available). According to Tony Fischier, author of the website, "Parkercollector.com," "Superchrome and Quink are two different brands and two different mixtures," and they were advertised and sold quite distinctly (Fischier, 16 April 2011; Email to Starr). Thus Barker can only be talking about "Royal Blue Quink."
43 "Quink Advertisement," 35.
44 Barker has worked for such publishers as "Rupert Hart-Davis, Macmillan, and Oxford University Press. He became involved with *The Book Collector*, the journal for book-collectors, booksellers and librarians founded by Ian Fleming and edited by John Hayward, and in 1965" became the journal's editor.

"In 1976 Nicolas Barker was invited to become the first head of conservation at the newly founded British Library, and worked there in various other capacities, among them compiling *Treasures of the British Library*, until he retired in 1992. Since then, he has been libraries adviser to the National Trust, chairman of the London Library and the Royal Horticultural Society's Lindley Library, and consultant to many other libraries. He has also been furnishing the shelves of the old King's Library at The British Museum with appropriate books from the Library of the House of Commons" ("Nicolas Barker," par. 2-3).
45 Barker, 364.

he replied, "Yes. I sometimes got a fill of his ink for my fountain pens. In all the time I knew him, Jack always used 'Parker Quink' Blue-black ink."[46]

Upon first review, then, the "Quink" issue helps the dating of MBB and "Light" very little. Most of MBB is indeed written in a color which looks like "Royal Blue Quink," and a similar blue color exists in the heading and some corrections in the "Light" manuscript. "Blue-black Quink" was released in 1931, not far from Barfield's suggested date. "Royal Blue Quink" was available by 1935 (if not earlier). But without chemical analysis, we can't be certain of the ink used in MBB. What we can be certain of is that Barker's date for Royal Blue Quink is wrong. Even if it were released later than 1935 in the U.K., there are numerous examples of this shade of ink appearing in Lewis's handwriting in the years before 1950.

Let us suppose, though, that MBB *was* written in Royal Blue Quink. If so, then the notebook version of the story which Hooper dubbed "The Man Born Blind" was written after Lewis's conversion, not before. Lewis became a Christian in 1931. Quink was released in only four colors in 1931. If Royal Blue was released before 1935, I found no record of it. If Lewis wrote the story after his conversion to Christianity, traditional interpretations of the story, including Owen Barfield's, might be in need of revision.

Gresham's Testimony Redux

Early on, I had no definitive reason to doubt Barfield's date for the story, but as one discovery led to another, reasons to doubt began to rise. For example, Barfield claims the story "was sent to me by Lewis (and returned to him) shortly after it was written."[47] I wondered, if Lewis would have been more likely to send Barfield a notebook filled with other material besides the story Lewis wanted Barfield to read in it (several writings precede the story in the MBB notebook), or whether he would send him loose pages instead? I took my doubts one more time to Douglas Gresham.

I asked Gresham if he had any memory of the pages of the "Light" manuscript seeming old and stained, or crisp and new, or held together by a rusted paper clip. He replied, "Not really, I have the feeling that they were not old looking at all but I didn't think of them as being sparklingly new either. However, I had the distinct impression that this was a new story that he had recently written and that he was reading it to us to ask whether it "worked" or

---

46 Gresham, 16 April 2011; Email to Starr. Later Gresham added, "in all the years that I knew Jack he only ever used Quink Blue-black Permanent ink. And as a result it has become my favourite too" (Gresham, 26 April 2011, 4:47 a.m. [EDT—the email was sent from Malta]; Email to Starr).

47 Barfield, 17 November 1986; Letter to Brown.

not—it did."⁴⁸ Then I asked Gresham if he had any reason to doubt Barfield's argument that Lewis wrote the story in the late 20s? He answered, "Only that I was given the strong impression that when Jack read it to me in the 1950s, it was something he had just finished." In a follow-up, I sent Gresham an electronic photocopy of Barfield's letter to Brown. After reading it he replied, "This is very interesting but Owen was already in his late 80s when he wrote it and I wonder what he meant by 'a very long time ago'? However it does seem that the tale may have been around for a long time when I heard Jack read it. I wonder why he gave the impression that he had only just written it?"⁴⁹ In one more follow-up, I sent Gresham Barfield's statement from *Light on Lewis* that Lewis was not a Christian when he wrote the story. To this Gresham replied, "That, if correct, would date the story before 31 anyway, but the nature of the story and its troubles with Light might indicate that Jack was already leaning towards Christ at the time that he wrote it. It certainly is a mystery."⁵⁰ And the mystery continued.

Lewis's Handwriting

For a time, I entertained the notion that "Light" was a revision of MBB written decades after the original. But the evidence of Lewis's handwriting quickly turned me against this theory. Ed Brown argues that "Light" is the later draft, written from the MBB notebook,⁵¹ and I concur.⁵² Brown also argues that the two texts were written in the same time period. Though I didn't at first, I now agree with him. Having photocopies of both MBB and "Light" available to him (and he was the only person to have them for many years), Brown made copies of his copies and began clipping individual parallel lines and pasting them one above the other.⁵³ I have seen Brown's cutting-and-taping experiment and the visual parallels are indeed striking. But just holding copies of both manuscripts side-by-side is enough to see that Lewis's handwriting in each is from the same time period.

After visiting Ed Brown on my spring break in March of 2011, I went on to Taylor University to study the original "Light" manuscript⁵⁴ and then to Wheaton College for four days to study the vast Lewis collection at the

---

48   Gresham, 16 April 2011; Email to Starr.
49   Gresham, 26 April 2011, 4:47 a.m.; Email to Starr.
50   Gresham, 26 April 2011, 10:50 a.m.; Email to Starr.
51   Brown, *Pursuit*, 90.
52   See chapters nine and ten for proof.
53   Brown, *Pursuit*, 90-91.
54   Though I had seen the original the year before, for this book I had been working with the manuscript in photocopy form, and I wanted to double check my transcription and observations.

Marion E. Wade Center. That's where I made a surprising discovery.

There is a Lewis manuscript at the Wade Center called *The Moral Good: It's Place Among the Values*[55] which contains handwriting so unusual that it caused the folks at the Wade Center to wonder if it was truly written by C. S. Lewis.[56] They asked Walter Hooper whose reply rests as a note inside the manuscript folder:

> These notes are in C. S. Lewis's hand. I know that will sound odd to you, but he was experimenting a bit at this time with something of a "new" handwriting. If you could see the handwriting that preceded the notes, and see the changes that it went through to become the handwriting of the 1930s and onward, it would be clear to you.

Hooper's note continues, saying that the notebook in question contains Lewis's notes for lectures which he gave in 1924 when he was standing in for his old tutor at University College[57] and that Lewis describes the notes he was making for the lectures in a letter to his father of 28 August 1924.[58] The broader implication of Hooper's note struck me like a hammer. I realized that looking at Lewis's handwriting might help date his manuscripts not just in the 20s but perhaps throughout his entire life.

I soon discovered that *The Moral Good* contains a similar handwriting style to another 20s document called *Notes on Henry More*.[59] The notebook in which these notes appear is also one in which Lewis wrote his narrative poem, *Dymer*, a project he began in 1922 and published in 1926. Lewis was clearly making a concerted effort to change his handwriting style in the early to mid 20s. Among the peculiarities of his writing at the time is that, where Lewis's words had heretofore always slanted to the right, in these documents he slants them to the left. But this change is temporary.[60] Before 1926 ends, his writing is slanting to the right again.

To cover the complete range of changes in Lewis's handwriting throughout his lifetime is beyond the purview of this book.[61] But a few indicators made

---

55   Wade Ms. CSL/MS-76X.
56   This story was brought to my attention by Heidi Truty who is the Wade Center's Head of Public Services and Archivist.
57   Lewis was substituting for E. F. Carritt while he was away lecturing for a year at the University of Michigan. See Lewis's letter to his father of 11 May 1924; *Collected Letters 1*, 627-28.
58   See *Collected Letters 1*, 633-4.
59   Wade Ms. CSL/MS-170.
60   The first indication I found of this left slanting style (there are other marked differences as well) is a letter to Arthur Greeves of 25 July 1922 (Wade Manuscript Letters to Greeves, vol. 5). The last instance is a letter of 6 March 1926 (Bodleian Ms. Facs b 50).
61   However, what I found is that Lewis's handwriting can be divided into several periods, and this helped me date MBB and "Light." In rough, and certainly subject to change, these

me question a pre-conversion date for Lewis's writing of MBB. First, his lower case "t's" change over the years (though inconsistently), and the style of his "t's" in MBB and "Light" reflects later years more than earlier.[62] The same is true for Lewis's "s's," and, especially, his "f's." For the period in question, however,[63] a single indicator stands out (though there are others) and that is Lewis's letter "g." Within the period in which the "Great War" correspondence was written, the way Lewis writes his "g's," both small and large, is very distinct from any other time. The "g's" Lewis writes from 1926 to late in 1931 are sometimes little more than a barely curved line or a figure eight with the top loop unfinished (as in figure 4.2).[64] At the end of 1931, Lewis's "g's" change

---

periods are as follows:
    Juvenile
    Early 19-teens-May 1918
    May 1918-1922
    1922-1926
    1926- November 1931
    December 1931-1939/40
    1939/40-1947/8
    1947/8-early 1950s
    Mid and later 1950s (-60s)
    (1960s)

There are overlaps among years and, as one would expect with a writer who was not always purposely changing his handwriting style, there are inconsistencies. The starkest changes occur in the 20s and early 30s. After that the changes become more subtle. It might be possible to identify sub-periods within the 30s and 40s. Conversely, much of the writing in the late 40s through 60s is often difficult to date apart from this broad designation.

62   The way Lewis crosses his minuscule "t's" alters over the years. I don't think he ever crosses a "t" completely. He draws horizontal lines out from the right side of vertical lines. Early on, Lewis tends to make a long horizontal line (about a quarter of an inch or even a third) from the very top of the "t's" vertical line (see Wade Manuscript Letters to Greeves, vol. 2; the letter of 26 June 1927 in Wade Letters to Greeves vol. 5; and a letter of 10 June 1930 [Wade Ms. CSL/MS 140]). With the passage of years, however, Lewis starts to shorten the line and move it toward the middle of the *post* (see a letter with the poem "Caught" of 5 April 1935 [Wade Ms. CSL/MS-135], a letter of 29 October 1941 to Mr. Neylan [Wade Ms. CSL/MS-107], and a letter to Owen Barfield of 19 December 1945 [Wade Ms. CSL/MS-8]). Though there is not enough consistency in Lewis's doing this to carefully date any manuscripts, he *tends* to cross his "t's" with lines that are high and wide in his earlier writings (in the teens and 20s) and then to cross them with lines that are low and narrow in his later writings (in the 30s and on). But it is an inconsistent tendency (both kinds of "t's" are visible throughout Lewis's writings). Nevertheless, my impression from this tendency was to place MBB and "Light" in the "later" category.

63   The late 20s to the end of 1931.

64   See, for example, Lewis's "Great War" letters to Barfield (Bodleian Ms. Facs. c. 54), the *Summa* at Taylor University, and a letter to Arthur Greeves of 24 December 1930 (Bodleian Ms. Facs. b. 51). The first instance I found of this kind of "g" is in a letter to Cecil Harwood postmarked 28 October 1926 (Bodleian Ms. Eng. lett. c. 861). Lewis's "g's" before and after

Light

radically (see figure 4.3).⁶⁵ In the late 20s version, he never bothers to close the upper circle but simply "s-curves" into the down-line. Beginning in November 1931, he deliberately strokes in an upward semicircle to complete the upper circle of the "g" and then proceeds to draw the lower loop. This new "g" is the kind which appears in MBB and "Light," and Lewis does not start using it till after his conversion.

power of evoking spiritual experience

FIGURE 4.2, LEWIS'S LETTER "G" AS IT APPEARS IN THE *SUMMA*, CIRCA 1928

herself, and each time something

FIGURE 4.3, LEWIS'S LETTER "G" AS IT APPEARS IN THE "LIGHT" MANUSCRIPT

There are other subtle differences in Lewis's handwriting over the years which, by the end of my time at the Wade Center, gave me the impression that MBB and "Light" were not only written after Lewis's conversion but *many* years after. While Barfield's claims allow for the *possibility* of a post-conversion writing of the story, they do not allow for the date which I was considering given changes in Lewis's handwriting. Nevertheless, all I had was this *impression*, a subjective sense of how Lewis's handwriting changed over the years based on mostly inconsistent markers. The new "g's," after all, did appear in the early 30s. And I found no other clear cut markers at the time to indicate what I was thinking. Still, the *sense* that I had was that the manuscripts were written in the 40s. I left Wheaton absolutely second guessing myself. I was, at least, more confident that the writing did not occur in the 50s. Lewis's handwriting is messier in his later years—he writes in what I have come to call a "staccato" style: sharp lines and thin circles. But I had before me a number of incompatible elements including Barfield's claim that the story was written in the late 20s or shortly thereafter, Gresham's impression that the story seemed brand new in the 50s, Barker's claim about Royal Blue Quink which, with some adjustment, could have placed the manuscripts from the mid-30s to the 50s, and my impression based on only a week spent reading Lewis manuscripts that MBB and "Light" were written in the 40s.

---

this period are very different.
65 The first time Lewis abandons the "Great War" style "g" for the new version which he will use the rest of his life is in a letter to Arthur Greeves of 8 November 1931. Only three weeks earlier, in a letter to Greeves of 18 October 1931, he was still writing his "g's" in the "Great War" style (see Bodleian Ms. Facs. b. 51 for both these letters).

C. S. Lewis's First and Final Short Story

Surely Not...

By the beginning of summer, 2011, an idea was creeping into my head which I did my best to keep from taking seriously. One of the ideas that I personally consider "crack pot" coming out of the biblical higher criticism of the last hundred years or so is the existence of what certain biblical scholars have dubbed "Q." The "Q" manuscript was supposed to be a now non-existent gospel of Jesus Christ which the canonical gospels used as source material. This would explain why the gospels could be so similar to each other (when the idea that they're similar because they're written by or based on eye witness accounts was being rejected for no real reason other than the higher critics said so). The attitudes behind such criticism were born of the same 19th century intellectual arrogance that claimed Homer was written in committee, Shakespeare was written by Anonymous, and men in earlier ages didn't know anything about their times, but we do. I'm not a biblical scholar, but among the Bible scholars I know, the existence of the non-existent "Q" brings skeptical smiles or scoffing laughter. Nevertheless, a "Q" version of MBB and "Light" was exactly the idea creeping into my head, an idea which I didn't even want to entertain.

But in June I further confirmed the need to doubt Barfield's date, at least in terms of the existing manuscripts, when something that had been staring me in the face finally got my attention. I had obtained a photocopy of the manuscript of Lewis's *Summa*[66] from Taylor University so I could better understand the "Great War" and its connections to "Light." What I hadn't yet thought of, however, was that, since the *Summa* was written during the "Great War" years (Lewis dates the *Summa* November 1928), and if MBB and "Light" were written at the same time or even close to it, then I should find similar handwriting between the texts when comparing them. I grabbed my photocopies of the manuscripts and stared at them for half an hour. I saw every marker for the 1926-31 period of Lewis's handwriting in the *Summa*, and its handwriting was very different from that of MBB or "Light." At that point I became more convinced that these manuscripts were *not* written shortly after the *Summa*, nor even a few years later. And I said to myself, "Charlie, you may have to consider the existence of Q."

Documented Authentication

Dating the "Light" manuscript continued to be a struggle, but determining its authenticity was not. Lewis scholars who have seen it agree

---

[66] A lengthy, unpublished essay by Lewis on issues involving his "Great War" with Owen Barfield. Lewis gave it the title, *Clivi Hamiltonis Summae Metaphysices Contra Anthroposophos Libri II*. Scholars refer to it as the *Summa*.

that it is authentic.⁶⁷ This authenticity has, additionally, been documented in professional appraisal.

The MBB notebook was authenticated in 1989.⁶⁸ Dr. J. Stanley Mattson, the president of the C.S. Lewis Foundation in Redlands, California, sent a request to Oxford University "to provide a professional judgment on whether or not the manuscript in the Bodleian Library purporting to be by C.S. Lewis called The Dark Tower"⁶⁹ was indeed authentic. Mattson received the answer to his request on 6 February 1989⁷⁰ in a report from Francis Warner, the "Pro-Proctor elect of the University of Oxford and Vice-Master of St. Peter's College, Oxford, in the Vice-Master's capacity as sir Gordon White Fellow in English Literature."⁷¹ Because of his experience with Lewis's letters, Warner had been asked to render the requested judgment.

Warner added to his appraisal the expertise of "R. E. Alton, Fellow Emeritus of St. Edmund Hall, Oxford, and an acknowledged expert on handwriting."⁷² Together they examined several Lewis manuscripts "in the presence of Dr. Judith Priestman, curator of twentieth century literary manuscripts at the Bodleian Library, and Mr. Dennis Porter, formerly Senior Assistant Librarian, now retired, at the Bodleian Library." The manuscripts examined by Warner and Alton included separate leaves of the *Dark Tower* manuscript,⁷³ a notebook containing the *Encyclopedia Boxoniana*,⁷⁴ and the notebook containing several documents including "The Man Born Blind."⁷⁵ They concluded that "The Bodleian manuscript of The Dark Tower, shelf-mark Dep. c. 762, and the manuscript books referred to as Encyclopedia Boxoniana, and The Man Born Blind,…are in our opinion unquestionably in the hand of C.S. Lewis and are not forgeries."⁷⁶ The document is signed by Warner and Alton and dated 24 July 1989, Oxford.

The "Light" manuscript has also been authenticated by appraisal. When the Brown Collection was sold to Taylor University, Taylor requested an appraisal be made of the various books and documents in the collection by an outside source. Appraisal Associates International of West Lafayette, Indiana

---

67   Including Owen Barfield, Walter Hooper, Chris Mitchell, Marjorie Lamp Mead, David Neuhouser, and Michael Ward to name only a few.
68   The information which follows is taken from a document entitled, "C.S. Lewis Manuscripts: A Report." The photocopy was given to me by Ed Brown.
69   Warner, par. 1.
70   As noted by a stamp on the cover letter and first page of the report.
71   Warner, par. 1.
72   Ibid, par. 2.
73   Ibid, par. 3.
74   Ibid, par. 4.
75   Ibid, par. 5.
76   Ibid, par. 13.

C. S. Lewis's First and Final Short Story

sent their completed appraisal to Taylor University Provost/Executive Vice-President Daryl R. Yost on 10 December 1996.

The document was prepared by one of the two appraisers who reviewed the Brown Collection, Sharon Smith-Theobald, who "served on the faculty of the State University of New York and Wilfrid Laurier University, Waterloo, Ontario, Canada," as the "1996 Indiana State Director for the American Society of Appraisers." She also "served on the faculty of the Smithsonian Institution's summer course of studies held at George Washington University," and as the "Editor of the Quarterly Journal of the American Society of Appraisers."[77] The second appraiser was "Professor Emeritus Edwin Posey of the Purdue University Libraries, Book Consultant and Private Dealer"[78] who "served on the faculty of the Princeton University Library"[79] as well, "bringing over 40 years of experience to this assignment."[80] These appraisers do not doubt the authenticity of "Light." On the contrary, they conclude that the handwriting in "Light" possesses "remarkable uniformity"[81] with the handwriting of MBB, and so it "does establish the authenticity of the earlier manuscript in the Bodleian."[82]

The two manuscripts are written in the same hand, and I would add that the progressive differences between the two manuscripts as they stretch across the revisions attempted in the MBB notebook are too subtle, the thought processes too detailed and developed, for a consideration of forgery to be credible. If MBB were a forgery then the entire MBB notebook would have to be a forgery as well, for the handwriting in it appears to be Lewis's on either side of the MBB story (which does not appear until 22 pages into the notebook). And the material on either side of the story is so random, covering so many different projects and years, that it can only be explained as a notebook in which Lewis himself gradually wrote when he needed to find some clean paper to write on.

Oxford and Answers

In July of 2011, I was blessed with the opportunity to go to Oxford and see the MBB notebook myself at the Bodleian Library. But before seeing the notebook (which was unavailable during my first week in Oxford), I looked at

---

77   "AAI Appraisal," par. 4.
78   Ibid, par. 2.
79   Ibid, par. 3.
80   Additionally, "In 1995, AAI appraised the Riley Book Collection in Indianapolis, worked with James Canary of the Lilly Library at Indiana University and completed the appraisal of an Indiana rare book collection."
81   "AAI Appraisal," Part 115, par. 6.
82   Ibid, Part 115, par. 13.

a variety of other Lewis manuscripts which took me back to some old evidence. The Quink question reared its Royal Blue head in the form of numerous examples of what appeared to be the same kind of ink as what is used in MBB (and briefly in "Light"). The ink appeared several times in Lewis texts written in the 40s and 50s.[83] Lewis's use of this particular kind of light blue ink (possibly Quink Royal Blue) in the 1940s was bolstering my theory about the dating of MBB and "Light." In the end, however, Walter Hooper pointed out a limitation on any conclusions students of Lewis might draw regarding the dating of his manuscripts by the color of their ink:

> Lewis dipped his pens not only into *bottles* of ink but into *ink wells*. He did what most people with ink wells do—he poured into them inks of various shades, so that it would be impossible to say what shade he used when writing a certain document and what manufacturer made it. I have a bottle I use for this purpose. If I can't find blue-black ink I mix blue and black. I know Lewis did this for I saw him do it.[84]

Ink color aside, I continued to work on a system for dating Lewis's manuscripts by his handwriting. I began to map out a more elaborate system, and I worked on consciously identifying cues, whether significant or subtle, so that my subjective sense of Lewis's handwriting could be raised to a more objective analysis. In relation to the dating of "Light" and MBB, however, what I discovered that mattered most was an alteration in Lewis's "f's."

In 1934 Lewis starts looping the lower part of his "f's" backwards (to the left rather than the right) and in the shape of a triangle (if the "f" is the first letter of a word).[85] But it is not until the 1940s that some of Lewis's "f's," when appearing at the end of a word, begin to look like scarcely more than a curved line—like what I began to call an "end parenthesis."[86] Such "f's" exist in MBB and "Light" (see figure 4.4), placing these manuscripts in the 40s.

---

83 This included a poem called "The Birth of Language" (Bodleian Ms. Eng. lett. c. 220/3) which was first published in January of 1946 (Hooper, *Companion & Guide*, 846), some chapters from *The Great Divorce* (Bodleian , Ms. Dep. d. 241) which Lewis wrote in 1944, (Hooper, *Companion & Guide*, 281-82—Lewis's handwriting in these pages is very similar to that of MBB and "Light"), a letter to Cecil Harwood dated "Boxing Day 1945" (Bodleian Ms. Eng. lett. c. 861) in which the postscript is written in this same blue ink, and a letter of 11 May 1942 (Bodleian Ms. Eng. lett. c. 220/1). The MBB notebook itself contains examples of this ink besides the MBB story. I also found two letters in the Brown Collection at Taylor University which appear to be written in the same color ink: a letter to Jill Flewett (Freud) of 7 January 1948 and one to Mary Neylan of 17 April 1942.
84 Hooper, 30 January 2012; Email to Trexler.
85 See Lewis's letter to Arthur Greeves of 1 October 1934 (Bodleian Ms. Facs. b. 51).
86 See Lewis's letter to Greeves of 23 December 1941. (Bodleian Ms. Facs. b. 51).

C. S. Lewis's First and Final Short Story

His three weeks of sight had

Figure 4.4, Lewis's letter "f" from "Light" (compare with "f" in Figure 4.2, page 32)

But with Barfield's date for the story still a major issue in my mind, I felt I needed the expertise of someone who had spent far more time with Lewis's original handwriting than I ever will. I had arrived in Oxford on a Wednesday and spent the better part of the next two days at the Bodleian. On the following Monday, I still had not seen the MBB notebook, but I had no problem putting it off for one more day so I could accept Walter Hooper's gracious invitation to have tea with him and "Blessed Lucy of Narnia," his cat.

I arrived at Walter's address twenty minutes early and so sat on a bench outside his flat going over the questions I wanted to ask him. Expectations arise in one's head when going to meet the premiere C. S. Lewis scholar in the world. He would be serious and serene, scholarly in his speech and decorum—after all, he never seemed to smile in his pictures so he would doubtless be a man of gravity and deep thought. His rooms would be filled with books on dusty bookshelves and cluttered with paper, and the furniture would be a shabby collection of flotsam and jetsam because scholars just don't care about such things. In addition, this giant in Lewis studies would be a giant in stature—at least my average height or a full head taller. I was wrong on all counts.

The man who met me at his door was a head shorter than I. His first word was an enthusiastic "Hello!" followed by a conversation with his cat about not being allowed to go out of doors because they were entertaining a guest. It was the kind of conversation (and in the very kind of animated tone) that a mother has with a toddler, or a pet owner with a tail wagging dog.[87] Walter was friendly, smiling, engaging and, I would say, joyful. He told stories about Lewis as if he were doing so for the first time and I was the first person to ever hear them. He had a wonderful sense of humor, commenting, for example, on Owen Barfield's death as something which would have been a relief to the 99-year-old Barfield by saying that Barfield "had no interest in ever becoming a hundred." After I chuckled, Walter then explained that Barfield would've hated the fuss people would have made over his hundredth birthday. And far from being shabby, messy or dusty (though his tiny office did a wonderful job of fitting the bill), Walter's home was gorgeous, immaculately kept, and furnished and decorated as if by a professional in interior design.

After preparing my tea and offering me a plate of Lewis's favorite biscuits,[88]

---

87 There may be pet owners in the world who talk to their cats that way, but I was meeting the only one *I've* ever known for the first time, and he was Walter Hooper!
88 For Americans: "biscuits" in England are "cookies" to us.

Walter immediately asked about my question of dating the manuscripts. He began with Barfield who had been upset in the 90s by accusations that MBB was a forgery and that Barfield, at his age, could not be trusted to know the date of its writing.[89] Barfield had a very strong sense of certainty as to when the story was written, and from this he never wavered. In fact, Barfield even started writing, with Walter's help, a response to the attacks in the form of a mock story about losing his mind.

At that point in the conversation I told Walter that, while I had no question about the authenticity of the story, I did have doubts about the date. I had reasons to believe that the story in the notebook was written after Lewis's conversion, and I thought it might even be much later than any of Barfield's statements would explain. I asked Walter if he'd look at photocopies of the two manuscripts and consider when they were written based on Lewis's handwriting. If anyone would be able to tell, it was Walter. I assumed that he'd need several minutes to examine the texts carefully (while I sat in silent rapture, gazing at the master). Instead, his response was almost immediate: "Yes these look later than the 20s."[90] I felt a huge weight lift and a strong sense of vindication. But what then about Owen Barfield's date for the story?

Walter's answer was, "I don't think these are originals." And then he began to talk about Lewis the writer and re-writer: Lewis, he said, loved the very act of writing. For him it was a total experience. Lewis said, "I don't know what I mean till I see what I've said." Lewis wrote some things many times. He wrote some poems fifty times, and just as with, for example, *That Hideous Strength*, he often started a project in a notebook. Thus when Ed Brown showed Walter the "Light" manuscript in 1986, he "was delighted. I knew whatever was in the notebook couldn't be the final version" of the story. And here was proof.

Again, regarding the act of writing, Walter noted that Lewis "used a fountain pen in the 20s but then went back to his dip pen." This was because Lewis preferred the pause which dipping his pen in an inkwell afforded. That pause allowed him time to think. And Lewis whispered the words he penned aloud whether writing stories or letters. He said the words needed to appeal to the ear as well as the eye.[91] It was no wonder to Walter, then, that there might be many iterations of the same story. Rewriting was no drudgery to Lewis;

---

89   These accusations, again, made by Kathryn Lindskoog.
90   Later Walter reiterated that neither MBB nor "Light" in the manuscript versions we have "go back" to the 20s.
91   See also Hooper's Preface to *Collected Letters 1*: "When Lewis dictated letters to me, he always had me read them aloud afterwards. He told me that in writing letters, as well as books, he always 'whispered the words aloud'. Pausing to dip the pen in an inkwell provided exactly the rhythm needed. 'It's as important to please the *ear*,' he said, 'as it is the eye'" (x).

it was a pleasure. And besides poems, he may have even revised longer texts. Walter said Chad Walsh had claimed that Lewis sent him a copy of an early version of *The Lion, the Witch and the Wardrobe*, a very different version of the story, which Walsh subsequently threw away!

That there might have been many versions of "Light" is possible. Like me, Walter questioned whether Lewis would have sent an entire notebook to Barfield for the reading of one small story. He theorized that the version recorded in the MBB notebook could have easily been written from an earlier version of the story, one sent to Barfield during the time he had always said it was written, or perhaps even a version born of that version. Since Lewis often began a writing project in a notebook, he may have taken the earlier version of the story and transcribed it into the MBB notebook with the intention of rewriting it (which the revisions in the notebook and the "Light" manuscript show he did). And so Walter Hooper was suggesting the very theory of a "Q" manuscript which I had been reluctantly coming to!

"There's just so much we don't have," Walter said, and he repeated the statement several times in our conversation. He was speaking of the bonfire in which so many of Lewis's papers had been burned over a three day period in 1964. I was very familiar with this story, but Walter described it with a powerful image I had never before read: "I saw these stacks of ashes"—that's how he put it. If you've ever burned documents, newspapers, any kind of papers in stacks, you know that they can often retain their shape while being completely charred. I hadn't imagined it that way before: so many of Lewis's papers burned that, even on the fire, they sat in stacks—charred echoes of their former selves.

Walter's openness to the idea of multiple versions of the story even led me to wonder if the version Lewis read to Douglas Gresham and his mother in the 50s might be different from the one we have today, thus explaining Gresham's sense that the story was new.[92] Walter responded to this idea saying that Lewis wouldn't have said to Douglas, "Here's a story I wrote two decades ago." He would have said, "What do you think of this story?" and Douglas would have naturally gotten the impression that it was new.

As for the location of the "Light" manuscript for so many years between the 50s and 1985, Walter suggested, as I had theorized, that Lewis might have given the story to someone, or he might have folded it up and slipped it into a book which he either gave to a friend or misplaced and then forgot about.

I left Walter Hooper's home believing that my literary detective's journey was almost over, and I felt grateful for the chance to have met such a remarkable man. My questions were answered and the answers seemed satisfactory. There was one thing left to do: look at the MBB notebook itself. In the end, however,

---

92 As I mentioned in a previous note, I think this option possible, but I also think it unlikely.

I did come to the conclusion that Walter Hooper was wrong about one thing. When he first invited me to his home in the winter of 2011, he said to come have tea "with me and Blessed Lucy of Narnia (my cat)."[93] After I left Walter I came to the conclusion that he was wrong: Walter Hooper is Blessed Lucy's human.

The next day I finally had the MBB notebook before me.[94] Though I found several points of interest, a single discovery was the final stroke in identifying the date of MBB and, therefore, "Light." One of Lewis's peculiarities in working in notebooks is a tendency to write from both ends toward the middle.[95] He starts at one end, uses it for a while, and then flips the book over and begins writing from the other end. Nevertheless, I quickly learned that Lewis does not write a-chronologically on random pages. Whether he starts at the front end or the back end of a notebook, he writes on one page after another (each end moving toward the middle) and clearly in chronological order. The significance of this point is that MBB can be dated based on what Lewis wrote on either side of the story.

The earliest pages in the notebook, written from the front end, include material which may have been written in the 30s, but the handwriting suggests to me only the very late 30s or the 40s. Some of the content, however, keeps me from claiming so absolutely. For example, folio (or page) two begins the poem "Launcelot" which has since been published in *Narrative Poems*.[96] In the Preface to that book, Hooper says the poem was written in the early 30s "judging by the handwriting."[97] The notebook nevertheless quickly advances through time, if you will, so that on page nine there is a reference to John Foxe which Lewis wrote no earlier than 1940. The text begins, "The good fame of John Foxe (1517-1587), attacked by the Roman side in his own day and by many others in the century, has been ably defended in our time." A slightly altered version of this text appears in Lewis's *English Literature in the Sixteenth Century*: "In 1940, however, Mr. J. F. Mozley re-opened the whole question and defended Foxe's integrity, as it seems to me, with complete success."[98] This proves that by page nine of the MBB notebook, Lewis was writing in the 40s. MBB is on page 22.

---

93   Hooper, 31 January 2011; Email to Starr.
94   The manuscript number for the notebook in the Bodleian is Dep. d. 809.
95   Besides the MBB notebook, Lewis does this in a notebook at the Bodleian designated MS Dep. d. 811. This notebook is most famous for containing the "Lefay Fragment," an early attempt at the writing of *The Magician's Nephew*.
96   *Narrative Poems*, 93-103.
97   Hooper, Introduction to *Narrative Poems*, xii.
98   *English Literature*, 299.

C. S. Lewis's First and Final Short Story

Pages 14-18 of the notebook contain a neatly written essay about Milton and *Paradise Lost*. Comparison with Lewis's *A Preface to Paradise Lost* shows differences but enough similarities to indicate that the text in the notebook is a first draft of part of Lewis's introduction to the *Preface*, a book which he wrote in 1941.[99] Far more important is the reverse side of page 20 (the *verso* or left hand page across from page 21) and the top of page 21. What appears on these pages is an outline, not a complete essay, thus making it a bit more difficult to identify. The pages include the following:

> A limited number of visceral and cardiac sensations symbolise a much larger number of psychological states: just as a limited number of piano notes symbolise a much larger number of orchestral noises. Similar relations can be seen between toys and things, black & white pictures and paintings, 2-dimensional shapes (in art) and 3 dimensional shapes (in the real world), letters and sounds, algebra & arithmetic....[100]

> When the higher (e.g. intelligence) is explained by the lower (e.g. matter) it is the higher which does the explaining.

> To say that God is incarnate in J.C. is to say (perhaps) that the Divine Score is in one instance perfectly transposed to a human key board.[101]

What I've excerpted is not the entirety of the outline in the notebook; however, there are enough clues here (and more in the complete outline) to identify its final incarnation: almost every element of the outline can be found in Lewis's sermon "Transposition." And, since "Transposition" was preached in May of 1944, it was probably written shortly before.[102]

MBB itself is written on pages 22-28 of the notebook. Pages 29-37 are part outline, part essay, under the title, "Paper on Reason for the Socratic." The Socratic Club was established in Oxford in 1941 as a vehicle for philosophical interchange between Christians and unbelievers.[103] Lewis was its first president, and he participated in the Club's debates until the 50s when he moved to Cambridge. It is for this Socratic Club that Lewis wrote the essay begun in the notebook, and fortunately evidence exists for dating the essay to a specific meeting. The essay itself has been lost, but not the Club secretary's minutes for the meeting of 15 October 1945.[104] In part they read,

---

99 Hooper, *Companion & Guide*, 461-62.
100 MBB notebook, folio 20 rev.
101 From the top of folio 21 in the notebook.
102 If not, it was at least written after 1941, and it's difficult to imagine Lewis writing the outline in 1941 for a sermon he wouldn't preach for three years.
103 See Hooper, *Companion & Guide*, 786.
104 Hooper, "Oxford's Bonny Fighter," 152.

Light

> The President, Mr. C. S. Lewis, presented a paper on "The Nature of Reason" to a very large audience.
>
> We were said to be reasoning when the terms *must* and *must not* were used rather than *is* and *is not*, the language of observation.

On page 29 of the notebook we find this parallel sentence: "We are <u>reasoning</u> when our thought, if spoken, takes the form of <u>must be</u> or <u>cannot be</u>."[105]

And Then I Saw the Light

Here, at last, I had my answer to the question of dating the manuscripts. The solution is partial but here's what we now know and what is most likely:

1. Whether or not Owen Barfield was right about the date and context of the story and whether or not there was a "Q" predecessor to MBB and "Light" or even intermediary versions between them, the story published in 1977 as "The Man Born Blind" was written in the first half of the 1940s.
2. MBB was probably written in 1944, after "Transposition," but certainly after 1941. The later date for Transposition makes more sense because Lewis would have likely outlined it within a month or two before preaching it in May 1944. If "Transposition" was written in '44, MBB was written no earlier.
3. MBB may have been written in 1945, but before October of that year. However, the resonances between "Transposition" and MBB[106] suggest closer proximity in the time of composition.
4. As I will argue completely in Part Four, "Light" is a revision which follows MBB.[107] It too, therefore, was written after 1941 and most likely in 1944 or '45 soon after MBB.
5. Part of what convinces me that "Light" was written shortly after MBB is, first, the similarity of Lewis's handwriting between the two texts, and, second, my method of dating Lewis's handwriting. After completing my study of the MBB notebook, I spent the rest of the week at the Bodleian Library focusing on refining a system of dating Lewis's manuscripts by his handwriting. It's not perfect and by its nature shouldn't be—Lewis didn't *systematically* change his handwriting. It needs more work, and some of my tendencies in dating Lewis documents continue to lean toward subjective impressions. But I did identify more markers, more changes in Lewis's handwriting even to the point of allowing me to see differences between Lewis's

---

105 And there are other parallels between the notebook and the minutes as well.
106 Which I discuss in chapter seven.
107 Whether immediately, which I think is the case, or by a generation or two.

handwriting in 1944 and 1947. To this end, Walter Hooper was again helpful. He mentioned to me that he had developed the ability to date some of Lewis's letters by the nib he used.[108] Nibs used with dipping pens begin to wear out with use. They lose their sharpness, the lines they write become fatter, and their strokes show certain peculiarities.[109] This information helped me realize that there was a certain "look" to Lewis's letters beyond his handwriting, a thickness in the writing which seemed similar among some compositions and not among others. I saw several instances of one such "look," noticing it because I was familiar with it from the "Light" manuscript—my impression being, again, subjective—and the instances in which I saw it were often in texts dated 1944 or '45.[110] Now I think what I was seeing was Lewis's use of a single nib at that time. But about this point I am far less sure. That "Light" was written in the mid 40s, however, I am confident.

In summary, then, I have no proof that "Q" existed, but neither do I have a strong reason to think Owen Barfield could've been wrong by a decade or more. Though Barfield did not first record his statement that the story was written during the "Great War" of the late 20s till 1965, more than thirty years after the fact (thus giving us some reason to question his memory), he never wavered from his claim. Every time anyone asked him when the story was written (over the three decades which followed), his answer was the same. That said, I am certain that MBB was written in the 40s, probably in 1944 but

---

108 Hooper, Interview. See also Hooper's Introduction to *They Stand Together: The Letters of C. S. Lewis to Arthur Greeves (1914-1963)*. In discussing problems in dating Lewis's letters, Hooper says, "Often when there were no clues to be had from these kinds of sources, I was helped by something likely to strike those who rely on typewriters as trivial. Besides being very familiar with Lewis's handwriting, I happen, by preference, to write with the nearly obsolete nib pen which is dipped in an inkwell. Lewis nearly always wrote with one. Those of us who prefer this method of writing have at least one advantage over those who use fountain pens and the ballpoint sort. Nibs have to be changed every few weeks, and each nib being slightly different, and there being many kinds of them, it is fairly easy to tell which letters were written with the same one" (43-44).
109 Perhaps something like the way striations on a bullet from a gun's barrel can identify the particular gun which fired it—my image, not Hooper's.
110 The last time I encountered such a text was in the Bodleian while reading through some of Lewis's letters to A. C. Harwood (Bod. Ms. Eng. lett. c. 861). I had just finished reading a letter from 1937 when I turned the page of the folio and found myself staring at a letter which seemed to jump in years to the mid-40s. I didn't, at first, look at the date because I was trying to "practice" dating the text by Lewis's handwriting. The letter looked like one of these texts written with the same nib as "Light," and it certainly looked like Lewis's mid-40s handwriting. I found myself thinking, "this was written in 1944." I checked the date and found that I was close: 11 September 1945.

definitely before '45 was over. And I believe "Light" was written shortly after MBB. Any other versions of the story which may have existed before, between or after the two iterations we *do* have are apparently lost.

One mystery covered doesn't mean there are no mysteries left. What may be the greatest mystery of all is the meaning of "Light." We turn to that mystery next.

PART THREE
The Meaning of Light

CHAPTER FIVE
CONTEMPLATION, ENJOYMENT AND WAR

The immediate response of the astute critic after reading Lewis's "Light" story might be something like, "What?" And then he finds himself needing to read it again. Since the 1960s, critics have tended to accept one meaning (albeit with several variants)[1] based on the testimony of Lewis's friend Owen Barfield that Lewis wrote the story in the late 20s as part of their "Great War,"[2] over Barfield's belief in Anthroposophy and several philosophical implications related to it. Barfield's date is especially significant because it's near the time of Lewis's conversion to Christianity. The evidence presented in the last chapter regarding the dates of the manuscripts, however, opens up an opportunity for us to consider a variety of possible meanings in the story as revealed by both the text itself and the rest of Lewis's writings.

LEWIS AND BARFIELD

We will begin with the story's traditional interpretation and context. Owen Barfield was one of C. S. Lewis's closest friends. They met at Oxford, and remained friends for life. Barfield was, to Lewis, the epitome of what he called the "Second Friend."[3] A "First Friend" is one very much like the man who claims him as friend. Lewis called him a kind of *"alter ego"* and noted that his companion of teenage years, Arthur Greeves, was this first kind of friend. But a second friend, like Barfield, is one "who disagrees with you about everything." He is not an *"alter ego"* but an "antiself." He has the same interests as you do, or else he would never become your friend. But his approach to these interests is very different. "He has read all the right books but has got the wrong thing out of every one." This is the man whose "heresies" you intend to

---
1   See Barfield, *Light on Lewis*, xvii-xviii; Hooper, Preface to *The Dark Tower*, 10; Fitzpatrick, "The Short Stories"1-5; Thorson, "Knowing and Being," 1-9; Ward, *Planet Narnia*, 34.
2   As Lewis called it in his autobiography, *Surprised by Joy*, 207.
3   *Surprised*, 199.

C. S. Lewis's First and Final Short Story

correct only to find that he intends to straighten out yours.[4] Then, according to Lewis, "you go at it, hammer and tongs...each learning the weight of the other's punches, and often more like mutually respectful enemies than friends." And from this battle of wits emerges a "community of mind and a deep affection."

What most ignited the intellectual battle between Lewis and his friend was Barfield's conversion to the Anthroposophy[5] of Rudolf Steiner in 1923.[6] According to Lewis, this moment "marked the beginning of what I can only describe as the Great War between him and me."[7] It was never an angry fight, but it was a constant battle of minds, "sometimes by letter and sometimes face to face, which lasted for years. And this Great War was one of the turning points of my life."

The impact of the "Great War," according to Lewis, was first to rid him of "'chronological snobbery,' the uncritical acceptance of the intellectual climate common to our own age and the assumption that whatever has gone out of date is on that account discredited." More important to interpreting "Light," however, is Lewis's further claim that Barfield convinced him that any theory of knowledge based on a purely "realistic" view of the universe (where reality is defined only as the universe perceived by the senses) could not account for reasoned truth, valid moral judgments, or a philosophy of aesthetics.[8] The logical conclusion of such a "realistic" view would be to hold knowledge as invalid or accept or adopt some form of behaviorism. Lewis would accept neither option, so he had to admit that human "logic was participation in a cosmic *Logos*."[9] This was not the moment of Lewis's conversion, but it was a step down that road as Lewis shifted his thinking from "Realism" to "Idealism" (a belief in that "cosmic *Logos*" behind the universe).

"Great War" Interpretations of Light

But why does any of this matter to our exploration of the meaning of "Light"? Quite simply, because Barfield said it did. The generally accepted interpretation of this strange little story is born out of Barfield's testimony that the story was written at the time of and as a commentary on ideas he and Lewis were exchanging in the "Great War." Before we look at Barfield's interpretation of the story, however, we should consider two others because

---

4   Ibid, 200.
5   "Anthroposophy teaches a highly elaborated doctrine of the origin of the world, the original nobility of the human spirit, the various epochs of mankind, a doctrine of immortality, reincarnation, and 'Karma', but it places man in union with God in the centre" (Hooper, *Companion & Guide*, 748).
6   Bramlett, "The Great War," 188.
7   *Surprised*, 207.
8   Ibid, 208.
9   Ibid, 209.

they each focus on Lewis's transition from Realism to Idealism. Before Barfield ever *fully* explained his own interpretation of the story, John Fitzpatrick offered a reading in a 1983 article for *CSL*.[10]

Fitzpatrick argues that the story is about Lewis's battle over Realism and Idealism.[11] At first Fitzpatrick wonders if Lewis wrote the story as a Realist, warning Barfield about the dangers of his Idealism in the form of a character named Robin who would "accept nothing short of the Platonic ideal."[12] The story would exist, then, as a warning to Barfield against the pursuit of Idealism: Robin's diving into the light-filled fog results in an absolute encounter with the hard reality of the quarry floor.[13] However, Fitzpatrick doubts that this interpretation is the best one to take. He next explores the light imagery in the story and then Barfield's interpretation of it. In the end Fitzpatrick calls on Barfield and others to do more to explain the story's meaning. Two months later, Barfield did.

But first, there is another and more recent interpretation of the story, which again takes up the focus on Realism and Idealism. In his book *Planet Narnia*, Michael Ward offers a unique interpretation of "Light": "'The Man Born Blind' is a cautionary tale about pursuing to its end the logic of realism as represented by the 'stupidity' of Robin's wife and the 'savagery' of the painter."[14] Even though these characters have had their sight for decades, they cannot explain to Robin that light is something by which you see other things, not a thing you see. And so Robin's death is a sign of Lewis's "new-found agreement" with Barfield's contention that realism cannot offer a "satisfactory theory of knowledge." In Ward's interpretation, Robin fails at learning what Lewis the newly converted theist has come to understand: that thinking itself relies on the existence of a "cosmic *logos*" which is symbolized in MBB by invisible but omnipresent light.

---

10 "The Short Stories: A Critical Introduction."
11 Barfield first wrote about the story in 1965, but only in the most general of terms. Hooper published the story in the *Dark Tower* collection in 1977, and there he includes some similar thoughts from Barfield. Fitzpatrick's article is not the oldest critical analysis of the story either. He identifies a December 1977 article by Martha Sammons ("'The Man Born Blind': Light in C. S. Lewis") as the first "thorough treatment of any Lewis short story" (Fitzpatrick, 4). But while Sammons's reading of "The Man Born Blind" includes some thoughts on the story in the context of the "Great War," it also incorporates numerous other Lewis writings from throughout his lifetime in a study of MBB as it relates to Lewis's symbolic use of *light*. Though I came to Sammons's essay late in my study, I found that, in 1977, she had already covered many of the same issues which I explore in the next few chapters of this book, including the relationships between light and God, light and the Real, light and glory, and Lewis's use of light as an epistemological symbol.
12 Fitzpatrick, 3.
13 Ibid, 4.
14 Ward, *Planet Narnia*, 34.

C. S. Lewis's First and Final Short Story

Where both Fitzpatrick and Barfield (as we'll see in a moment) interpret "Light" as an expression of Lewis's *disagreement* with Barfield in the "Great War," Ward argues that the story is an expression of Lewis's *agreement* with Barfield: Lewis realized that any Realist-based philosophy undermined the efficacy of Reason, and, therefore, a new Idealist philosophy needed to be adopted. Lewis describes the stages of his conversion in this very way. He saw the complete Naturalism of the "popular scientific cosmology" of his own day as a boat which could not keep itself afloat: "Something like philosophical idealism or Theism must, at the very worst, be less untrue than that. And idealism turned out, when you took it seriously, to be disguised Theism. And once you accepted Theism, you could not ignore the claims of Christ."[15]

Now we turn to Barfield's interpretation of "Light"[16] which focuses on a different aspect of the "Great War"[17] though it still has to do with epistemology—the nature of human knowing. In 1965 Barfield explained for the first time in writing that Lewis tried to express his view about one area of their argument by writing a short story "about a man born blind" who has an operation and receives his sight.[18] The story ends badly for the newly sighted man because of his obsession with seeing the "mysterious thing he had heard people calling 'light'; whereas you do not see light itself, but only the objects it illumines." Barfield says Lewis was trying to emphasize that "Light is what you see *by*; it is not anything you see, or ever can or will see." At first this doesn't seem a very significant point. But that, then, is why exploring what may be the most complicated element[19] of the "Great War" is necessary—it's the only way to understand Barfield's interpretation of the "Light" story.

---

15 "Is Theology Poetry?" 91. Sammons's study of the story also sees Lewis as agreeing with Barfield, not on the issue of Realism vs. Idealism but rather on the issue of the existence of God (6) which the more philosophical debate represents; however, Sammons's argument shows some misunderstanding regarding the "Great War" debate, and she sees Robin's dive positively as a headlong plunge into Light "through faith" (7).
16 Unless referring specifically to the "Man Born Blind" manuscript or version of the story, I use Lewis's title for the story throughout this study.
17 Other than Realism vs. Idealism.
18 Barfield, *Light on Lewis*, xviii.
19 We haven't the space in this book to come to a complete understanding of the "Great War" concepts (if that were even possible). Readers interested in understanding this period in Lewis's intellectual history are directed to the works of the authors themselves (many of which are, unfortunately, unpublished) and to the following scholarly studies of the "Great War" (here listed in a roughly chronological order): Adey, "The Barfield-Lewis 'Great War'" and *C. S. Lewis' 'Great War' with Owen Barfield*; Thorson, "Knowing and Being in C. S. Lewis's 'Great War' with Owen Barfield"; Feinendegen, "Contemplating C. S. Lewis's Epistemology"; Thorson, "Enjoying the Spirit, Enjoying the Soul"; Feinendegen, "A Reply to Stephen Thorson"; Thorson, "Two Clarifying Points"; Starr, "Contemplating Norbert Feinendegen's Epistemological Contemplation"; Thorson and Feinendegen, "A Dialogue Concluded."

Enjoyment and Contemplation

In *Surprised by Joy*, Lewis writes of having read Samuel Alexander's *Space, Time, and Deity*. In it Alexander presents an epistemological distinction which Lewis claims had a significant influence on his own thinking: "I accepted this distinction at once and have ever since regarded it as an indispensable tool of thought."[20] Alexander's distinction was between "Enjoyment" and "Contemplation,"[21] but by these terms he means something very specific. As Lewis explains,

> When you see a table you "enjoy" the act of seeing and "contemplate" the table....We do not "think a thought" in the same sense in which we "think that Herodotus is unreliable." When we think a thought, "thought" is a cognate accusative (like "blow" in "strike a blow"). We enjoy the thought (that Herodotus is unreliable) and, in so doing, contemplate the unreliability of Herodotus.[22]

The easiest explanation for understanding this distinction is to consider it in terms of *experiencing* (enjoyment) and *thinking* (contemplation), though this explanation has its limitations. When I see a table, the act of seeing, the experience of seeing it, is *enjoyment* while my cognitive recognition of the table as a table is *contemplation*. When I think about something (like Herodotus), I am experiencing the act of thinking—that experience is enjoyment. In the midst of that experience is the thought which I am thinking: "Herodotus is unreliable." This thought is what I happen to be contemplating. In short, enjoyment is experience, and contemplation is thought.

However, keep in mind that this approach is somewhat misleading. If I say[23] we can laugh at a joke or analyze why it's funny but we can't do both at the same time, it becomes easier to see how well the experience=enjoyment/thought=contemplation dichotomy works. The laughing is experience, the analysis is thought. But Alexander's distinction is a bit more complex. When I go from laughing at a joke to analyzing it, I do not exactly go from experience to thought, I go from one kind of experience to another. Even my analysis and subsequent thoughts *about* the joke involve an experience: the act of thinking. It is by that experience—thinking—that I can produce resulting thoughts.[24] This discussion is further complicated by the fact that sometimes Lewis seems

---

20 *Surprised*, 218.
21 Ibid, 217.
22 Ibid, 217-218.
23 Borrowing an illustration from Lewis in "Myth Became Fact."
24 In "Meditation in a Toolshed," Lewis refers to these two kinds of experiences as looking at the beam (analyzing why the joke was funny in our example) and looking along the beam (experiencing the joke and laughing at it).

to write about enjoyment and contemplation as two completely separate activities while sometimes he writes of them as a single activity involving two very different qualities.[25]

One of the implications of Alexander's distinction for Lewis was a recognition about the nature of human knowing: that "the enjoyment and the contemplation of our inner activities are incompatible. You cannot hope and also think about hoping at the same moment; for in hope we look to hope's object and we interrupt this by (so to speak) turning round to look at the hope itself."[26] If we turn our attention from the object of our love to focus on our experience of loving, we, in a certain sense, stop loving. If we are afraid of something and begin to examine our fear, we stop being afraid of the thing feared because we're not paying attention to it anymore. Lewis explains how this new understanding helped him realize that the object of his Joy, the thing he had longed for all his life, was not, in fact, a thing to be found in his own mind but was instead a concrete reality outside himself which he ultimately realized was God.[27] But the real significance of the idea regarding "Light" and the "Great War" was in what Lewis, before finding God, claimed about Barfield's epistemological approach to the Transcendent.

Introspection and Abstraction

In distinguishing enjoyment from contemplation, Lewis sees a danger in the act of "introspection," where we look "inside ourselves" to try to see what's happening.[28] The moment we turn inside to look at what's occurring there, everything that's occurring stops by the act of looking inward! This doesn't mean "introspection finds nothing."[29] It unfortunately finds what is left behind when the mental activities we wanted to look at have been suspended, and what's left behind is "mainly images and physical sensations." We then run into the danger of mistaking these echoes for the real "activities themselves."

Barfield understood Lewis's mistrust for introspection as a central element of "The Great War" and as a main meaning in the "Light" story. Upon

---

25 Norbert Feinendegen emphasizes this unified experience of disparate activities as Alexander's meaning for the terms, and he points out where Lewis *does* explain enjoyment/contemplation in this fashion in his own writings (for example in the text quoted above from *Surprised by Joy*). See Feinendegen's "Contemplating C. S. Lewis's Epistemology," especially pages 31-32. I agree with Feinendegen's analysis; however, in applying the distinction, Lewis often seems to discuss enjoyment and contemplation as separate activities, and so I don't want to get caught up too much in philosophical minutiae. As we progress, we will let Lewis's texts determine for us how Lewis seems to be using the distinction in a given case.
26 *Surprised*, 218.
27 Ibid, 219-223.
28 Ibid, 218.
29 Ibid, 219.

first discussing the "Great War" in 1965, Barfield emphasizes that at a certain point in his life Lewis purposely stopped taking interest in himself "except as a kind of spiritual alumnus taking his moral finals."[30] For Lewis, self-knowledge came to mean recognizing one's own failures and limitations. To spend time examining oneself beyond this was for Lewis a potential "symptom of spiritual megalomania."

An example of Lewis sensing the danger of such spiritual self-centeredness in Barfield's beliefs appears in one of the letters Lewis wrote to Barfield regarding their "Great War" debate.[31] In the first letter of the series Lewis attacks a core tenet of Barfield's Anthroposophical system. According to Lionel Adey, who wrote the first serious study of "The Great War," what Steiner

> propounded was a development from supernatural inspiration in myth and prophecy to self-enlightenment by the modern self-conscious ego. During this evolution of consciousness, imagination had played a progressively larger part in the divine education of humanity. Now, moral action should be prompted rather by an 'inner lawgiver than divine fiat. For this reason, Steiner called his teaching Anthroposophy, 'human wisdom'....[32]

Adey says Lewis took issue with any belief that "the mind could profitably observe and direct its own operations." In the first "Great War" letter, Lewis writes that Barfield's belief that reason plus experience plus practiced habit could "produce a knowledge of the supersensible" is wrong.[33] Lewis maintains a distinction between the "real and the phenomenal." There is reality and there are the methods by which we seek to know reality, but all of these are reduced to phenomena in the mind. Whether targeting the reality of our senses or some higher reality beyond them, the mind remains Barfield's method, and all it can do is produce more phenomena.

If we apply the enjoyment/contemplation dichotomy here, we see Lewis saying that no true knowledge can result from introspection because the moment the mind turns inward to understand (via contemplation) its experience of the real, it stops experiencing the real and has only the residue of that experience to contemplate. Lewis even goes so far as to draw a set of pictures[34] which illustrate the dangers of Barfield's mystical, inward-turning approach to knowing. In the last of these pictures, the pursuer of

---

30 Barfield, *Light on Lewis*, xvi.
31 The ten extant "Great War" letters appear in *Collected Letters 3*, 1596-1646.
32 Adey, *C. S. Lewis' 'Great War'*, 6.
33 *Collected Letters 3*, 1600.
34 See *Collected Letters 3*, 1603-04.

such "occultism"[35] seems doomed to "ambulance, asylum, [and] cemetery"![36] In a later "Great War" document, the *Summa*,[37] Lewis continues to maintain that "we become more spiritual not by sinking into our own souls, that is by attending to what exists only in our souls, but by turning our eyes outward."[38]

But Barfield does not see the issue as a problem of introspection. He sees it as a problem in the very existence of the enjoyment/contemplation[39] dichotomy—not necessarily in Lewis's application of it, but in the fact of its existence. Barfield considers there to be something wrong with the very methods by which we are forced to think and know. In one of his "Great War" letters, Barfield writes,

> the idea of reality being a temporal continuum which we have to arrest and break up for the purposes of speech and logic is to me not merely an interesting fact, which I admit and then take no further note of.... It is a part of the whole meaning of the words 'logic,' 'term,' judgment' etc. to me, and is present in my consciousness every time I use them or hear them used. Now I *think* this corruption is more vivid and real to me than it is to you.[40]

For Barfield, the very nature of reasoning as a thing withdrawn from the totality of the real is a corruption of consciousness. He acknowledges that reason has to be used but sees using it as a problem in itself. The very fact that we have to separate contemplation from enjoyment—thought from experience—is the problem. In our minds we step away from space and time into abstraction

---

35 Ibid, 1600.

36 Ibid, 1604. This is the interpretation Stephen Thorson takes, responding to Fitzpatrick's initial approach to "Light" of focusing on Realism and Idealism. Thorson argues that Lewis was not attacking Barfield's Idealism but the danger of taking Idealism too far: "He was worried about Barfield's belief that one can (through Anthroposophical training) see Spirit.... Lewis wrote this story to show the grave danger of trying to *see* what is there to see *by*." Thorson references the pictures Lewis drew as proofs of this interpretation (Thorson, "Knowing," 7-8).

37 Lewis wrote a lengthy summary of his ideas as of the end of 1928 called *Clivi Hamiltonis Summae Metaphysices Contra Anthroposophos Libri II* (or *Summa*) which resulted in another round of exchanges between himself and Barfield before Lewis eventually abandoned their discussions on the "Great War" issues. The *Summa* is written in a single notebook, followed by a reply from Barfield with subsequent replies by Lewis.

38 The *Summa* is part of the Edwin W. Brown Collection at Taylor University (Upland Indiana). The transcription here was made for Taylor by Norbert Feinendegen. The quote is on page 44 of the Transcription, page 53 of the *Summa* Notebook, in section II.XV.

39 I should note here that Lewis and Barfield may have meant different things by these terms—see the essays by Thorson and Feinendegen referenced above for the subtle difficulties of this discussion.

40 Bodleian, Ms. Facs. c. 54, folio 17, par. 4.

to focus on some part or "term" within it. Barfield's ultimate belief was that any separation between reality and our knowledge of it could be eliminated through the spiritual disciplines of Anthroposophy.

Lewis may have actually come to agree with Barfield to some extent after his conversion. In chapter seven we'll return to the relationship between thinking and experiencing and the possible circumstances in which the separation between them might disappear, but a curious letter to Daphne Harwood suggests at least some kind of acquiescence on Lewis's part regarding humankind's ability to know the Transcendent. In the letter he says that the issue over which he was at odds with Anthroposophy at the time of the "Great War" was one on which Anthroposophy is "certainly right—i.e. the claim that it is possible for man, here and now, in the phenomenal world, to have commerce with the world beyond—which is what I was denying."[41]

Barfield on "Light"

So what does all this mean in relation to "Light"? Barfield's clearest explanation of his interpretation of the story appears in a June 1983 response in *CSL* to Fitzpatrick's article in the previous April issue.[42] Barfield claims the story is most associated in his mind with the "Great War." Next he says that one of Lewis's emphases in their philosophical battle was on the idea that contradictory things cannot be true at the same time.[43] As an example of this rule of logic, Lewis points to light and sight: "We can never see what we see *by*. For what would we be seeing by in *that bit* of seeing?"[44] What's true of seeing is true of "any kind of perception or thinking." Thus Lewis argues that Barfield is wrong in thinking that the immaterial world of the Transcendent, what they each called "Spirit" in the "Great War," is something which can be "*directly* perceive[d]." Barfield continues: "Later on he embodied this conviction in imagined and fictional form in 'The Man Born Blind.'"

Now it's hard at first to see how Barfield's wording here relates to the concepts of enjoyment and contemplation. Throughout the *Summa*, the pre-Christian Lewis makes a distinction between "Spirit" and "Soul" which Barfield accepts. The individual soul or self was born out of transcendent "Spirit."[45] The soul can enjoy Spirit, but it can only contemplate, not enjoy, the

---

41 28 March 1933; *Collected Letters 2*, 107. This letter lends force to Ward's contention that "Light" is a parable explicating Lewis's agreement with Barfield.
42 "Owen Barfield's Response to John Fitzpatrick's Essay on 'The Man Born Blind.'"
43 Lewis even produced, as part of the back-and-forth dialog written in the *Summa* a "Note on the Law of Contradiction" (pages 77-80 in the Feinendegen Transcription; pages 110-115 in the original *Summa* Notebook).
44 Barfield, "Response to Fitzpatrick," 5—this is Barfield's summary of Lewis's point.
45 Lewis, *Summa*, Transcription 7-11, Notebook 6-11, sections I.III-V.

phenomenal world outside itself (including other souls born of Spirit). Nor can the soul ever turn back and contemplate the source of its existence—Spirit. It would be like Hamlet looking back from the world of his play and perceiving Shakespeare.[46]

In Barfield's opinion, then, the "Light" story was written by Lewis to emphasize the "Law of Contradiction" and to reject the idea that transcendent Spirit could be contemplated as well as enjoyed. To attempt to do so might result in a mad leap into death. In the story, Robin fails to understand that light is the thing by which we see everything else. Light is the thing we enjoy which allows us to contemplate the many other things which it reveals to our eyes. But to then turn in toward light and try to see it directly will always result in failure.

Barfield's reply to Lewis, as he details it in his *CSL* article, is to return to the idea mentioned earlier regarding the problem of reasoning itself. Logical thought recognizes that contradictories can't be true, but humanity's job is to use imagination to overcome logical contradictories, including the "mutual exclusions of enjoyment and contemplation." He continues with what is certainly his best proof, though he says he never shared it with a not-yet-Christian Lewis during the "Great War." He argues that the marriage of enjoyment and contemplation is apparent in the opening of the Gospel of John. All things were made by Christ while at the same time He came into the world. By His mere existence we enjoy Him, but the gospel adds that when He came into the world, the world "knew Him not,"[47] which is to say, the world did not contemplate Him. "The Life in the Logos was always the light of men, i.e., the light they saw by, the light they 'enjoyed'. But it needed someone to 'bear witness' to it, before they could begin to learn—with the help of its temporary incarnation—to contemplate it."[48] Barfield concludes that he does not know how much Lewis came to agree with his position in later years.

Though Lewis rejected Barfield's idea of disciplined introspection toward enlightenment, he at least accepted some of the epistemological implications of the Incarnation. Where, in the *Summa*, Lewis had said Hamlet can't turn around and see Shakespeare, Lewis later argues, as an example of the Incarnation, that Shakespeare could put himself into Hamlet's world.[49] Perhaps this is what Lewis meant when he said in his letter to Daphne Harwood that, regarding man's ability to have commerce with the world beyond, the Anthroposophists were right.

---

46 Ibid, Transcription 12, Notebook 12-13, section I.VII.
47 John 1:10, *King James Version*.
48 Barfield, "Response to Fitzpatrick." 5. See also Barfield's poem, "C. S. L. Biographia Theologia" in Glyer, *Company*, 177.
49 *Surprised by Joy*, 227, text and Lewis's note.

Light

We have focused in this chapter on interpretations of "Light" which begin with Owen Barfield's testimony about the date and occasion of the story. But even here the interpretations are varied. If there's any one thing to take from these differing interpretations, a common thread which holds them all together apart from the "Great War" context, it is certainly an emphasis on epistemology. Each of these interpretations looks at "Light" as the imaginative telling of a philosophical position about the nature of knowing and truth. It is with such epistemological concerns that we will continue.

Chapter Six
Toolsheds, Truth and Knowledge

The reason we're not limited to Owen Barfield's interpretation of "Light" as a story about the "Great War" by a pre- (or even young) Christian Lewis is that neither "The Man Born Blind" nor the "Light" versions of the story which we have today were written in the late 20s or early 30s. I am not saying that Barfield was wrong and "Light" has to be completely reinterpreted. I am saying that the only versions of the story we have were written in the mid-40s. Furthermore, Douglas Gresham attests to Lewis's continued interest in the story in the 1950s, and so a more mature, Christian Lewis may have seen additional or new meanings in the story which made him return to and revise it decades after writing it during the "Great War." At any rate, Lewis was interested in this story several times throughout his life.

These revelations free us to consider other meanings in the story of un-blind Robin, meanings which have clear connections *to* "Light" *in* light of other Lewis writings from throughout his life. It is not my intention to argue a *definitive* interpretation of the "Light" story. But having discussed the interpretations based on Barfield's dating of the story in chapter five, I now want us to consider additional interpretations in this and subsequent chapters given these new dates for the manuscripts, and in relation to other Lewis texts which can be connected to "Light" in various ways.

Light and Knowing

Lewis often uses the word *light* as an epistemological symbol—one having to do with knowledge and truth. In *Miracles*, Lewis describes Reason itself as "like a beam of light which illuminates" the total self.[1] He furthermore describes "primary moral principles," the "self-evident" axioms upon which moral reasoning depends by saying, "Their intrinsic reasonableness shines by its own light."[2] He describes such principles as unchanging when he says that

---
1   *Miracles*, 45.
2   Ibid, 49. See also the quote Lewis takes from Aristotle for the beginning of chapter six: "For as bats' eyes are to daylight so is our intellectual eye to those truths which are, in their own

"The Light which has lightened every man from the beginning may shine more clearly but cannot change."[3] In *The Discarded Image*, Lewis writes of the sun's (or Sol's) effect in Medieval thinking: "Sol produces the noblest metal, gold, and is the eye and mind of the whole universe."[4] In the 1945 poem, "The Planets," Sol's arrow pierces the "mortal mind," parting "mists" and therein breathing "wisdom."[5] And both the epistemological and alchemic[6] qualities of Sol mentioned in *The Discarded Image* are reflected in the poem, "On a Theme from Nicolas of Cusa" where the soul partakes of the rays of goodness or truth which "By some far subtler chemistry"[7] transform the soul into something as "luminous as they."[8]

In addition to using light to talk about truth and knowledge, Lewis also uses metaphors of sight and light when discussing "enjoyment" and "contemplation." Barfield's references to "seeing" vs. "seeing by" have their counterparts in Lewis: "I believe in Christianity as I believe that the Sun has risen, not only because I see it, but because by it I see everything else."[9] Regarding the mystery of the Incarnation Lewis raises the sun to noonday but makes a similar claim: if the Incarnation is true, it will "illuminate" the "whole mass" of our knowledge.[10] It may be that the doctrine itself remains difficult to understand, but that is not important: "We believe that the sun is in the sky at midday in summer not because we can clearly see the sun (in fact, we cannot) but because we can see everything else."

A greater limitation than our understanding of certain doctrines is our knowledge of God. In trying to describe the God who is Love in *The Four Loves*, Lewis notes that any precision we apply in knowing God will be but a "model or a symbol"—that we can understand the "ultimate Being" only by "analogies."[11] And of this he concludes, "We cannot see light, though by light

---

nature, the most obvious of all" (*Miracles*, 55).

3   *Reflections on the Psalms*, 28. I.e. greater, clearer moral axioms may be revealed, but they will not be altered.
4   *Discarded Image*, 106 (see also Ward, *Planet Narnia* 100). Sol's sphere is also the "Heaven of theologians and philosophers" (*Discarded*, 106).
5   Lewis, "The Planets," lines 43-46, *Collected Poems*, 27.
6   I.e., gold making.
7   Lewis, "Cusa," line 11. See also Lewis's poems, "A Pageant Played in Vain" (*Collected Poems*, 110), and "Noon's Intensity" (*Collected Poems*, 128). Thanks to Michael Ward for pointing me (in discussion and in *Planet Narnia*, 103-04) to these solar connections to Lewis's light symbolism.
8   "Cusa," lines 9-16, *Collected Poems*, 84 (final quote from line 16).
9   "Is Theology Poetry?" 92.
10 *Miracles*, 145. See also Lewis's essay, "The Grand Miracle," where Lewis says, "What the story of the Incarnation seems to be doing is to flash a new light on a principle in nature" (85).
11 *Four Loves*, 174-75.

C. S. Lewis's First and Final Short Story

we can see things."[12] Lewis is doubtless echoing scripture: "The true light that gives light to every man was coming into the world,"[13] and "in your light we see light."[14] Lewis twice refers to God as "Father of Lights" and both times in the context of the reaches of human knowledge.[15]

Of Tools and Prepositions

One of the most immediate connections to be made between "Light" and the enjoyment/contemplation dichotomy is with Lewis's "Meditation in a Toolshed," an essay first published in 1945, which puts it very close to the time "Light" was written.[16] It is here, in fact, that the dilemma raised in the "Light" story is most clearly defined as an epistemological one.

Lewis writes of standing in a darkened toolshed with the sun shining from outside "through a crack at the top of the door."[17] Almost nothing else in the toolshed is visible, and so, says Lewis, "I was seeing the beam, not seeing things by it." Then he says he stepped into the beam and the view changed completely:

> I saw no toolshed, and (above all) no beam. Instead I saw, framed in the irregular cranny at the top of the door, green leaves moving on the branches of a tree outside and beyond that, 90 odd million miles away, the sun. Looking along the beam, and looking at the beam are very different experiences.

Several examples follow: A young man in love is looking "*along* the sexual impulse" while a scientist describing the man's behavior is "looking *at* it." A mathematician thinking "timeless and spaceless truths about Quantity" looks along while a neurologist examining the mathematician's thought processes is looking at.[18] The savage dancing before his god to bring rain and crops is looking along while the anthropologist observing this "fertility ritual" is looking at. A little girl crying over her "broken doll" is looking along while the psychologist taking notice of her "nascent maternal instinct" is looking at.

It is easy to see from these examples how the enjoyment/contemplation dichotomy can most easily be explained as one of experiencing vs. thinking. Those looking *along* are experiencing while those looking *at* are thinking about

---

12 Ibid, 175.
13 John 1:9, *New International Version*—echoed also in the quote from *Reflections on the Psalms* two paragraphs above.
14 Psalm 36:9, *New International Version*. Again, credit to Michael Ward for this connection.
15 *Reflections on the Psalms*, 69 and 93.
16 "Walter Hooper first wrote of the connection between "The Man Born Blind" and "Toolshed" in his 1977 Preface to *The Dark Tower and Other Stories* (10).
17 "Toolshed," 212.
18 Ibid, 213.

other people's experiences. But again, this is probably an oversimplification. While Lewis talks about experience as *opposed* to thinking in "Myth Became Fact,"[19] in "Toolshed" he clearly refers to looking along vs. looking at as two kinds of experiences: "You get one experience of a thing when you look along it and another when you look at it."[20] I'm not arguing that we should drop the simplified version of the distinction—only that we be aware of it, if for no other reason, because we will see it as Lewis's central conclusion at the end of "Toolshed."

Lewis continues with an important question: which of the two kinds of experiences is the more "true" or "valid"?[21] One answer, he says, has been accepted without a second thought for the whole of the twentieth century. In that time Western culture has believed that one doesn't go to a religious person to understand religion but to an anthropologist and one doesn't go to a person in love to understand romance but to a psychologist, and one doesn't go to believers of a social ideology to understand it but to sociologists. Looking *at* things from the outside is the dominant mode of knowing in Lewis's day while looking *along* them from the inside has been debunked. Lewis refers to this approach as the "whole basis of the specifically 'modern' types of thought." Now is this not the best course to take? We have been fooled by so many "inside" experiences that surely this more objective external approach is the most sensible, isn't it? Lewis's answer to this question is "no."[22]

The first reason a focus on looking *at* without looking *along* is a mistake is that the former, by itself, will produce inaccurate thinking and this because there is nothing to think *about*. The scientist who studies pain by looking at it will find that it equals "such and such neural events" in the mind, but the idea of pain would itself have no meaning for him beyond this unless he had at some point in his life looked along it by suffering himself.[23] If he only *looks* at pain he'll never really know what pain is. Pain, as a subject of inquiry for the scientist's thoughts, only so exists because he has at some point seen it from the inside.

Another reason it is a mistake to reject looking *along* in favor of looking *at* is that each subsequent experience can be rejected. If we reject what appears to us as we look along the beam of light—trees, sky, and sun—in favor of looking at the beam of light, we are still participating in an act of seeing. And this new act, then, "could also be looked at from the outside" as nothing more than "an agitation of my own optic nerves." So the image of the beam in the

---

19 See chapter seven.
20 "Toolshed," 213.
21 "Toolshed," 213.
22 Ibid, 213-14.
23 Ibid, 214.

toolshed is now no more accurate than the image of the trees outside it. But then this outside look could also be rejected since it too is an act of seeing—and this process of "debunking" can thus proceed (or rather recede) endlessly.

At this point Lewis makes his claim that "you can step outside one experience only by stepping inside another."[24] If all experiences of looking along—experiences which are from the inside—mislead us, we will always be misled. A neuroscientist may tell a mathematician that his thoughts are no more than "tiny physical movements of the grey matter," but then another neuroscientist may say the same thing to the first neuroscientist about his thought regarding the mathematician's thoughts. Where would it end? The answer is to never let it start. We should reject at the outset any idea which says looking *at* is better than looking *along*. The simple truth is we must "look both *along* and *at* everything."

In doing so we will find that looking from the inside is better in some situations, while in others it is better to look from the outside. In the case of reasoned thought, for example, the view from inside which accepts thinking as valid proves to be more accurate than the view from outside which reduces thought to the mere firing of neurons in the brain. To argue the reverse would be to say that thought has no truth value, and this is a contradiction: we cannot use reason to prove that reason cannot prove anything. On the other hand, the inside view of a native dancing to bring rain might be held suspect by the view from outside. What matters is that we hold no prejudice against one kind of view or the other but take each experience in turn and determine which is the most accurate way of seeing it. It's important to realize that looking *along* should not be dismissed automatically in favor of looking *at*, and this is the primary lesson of "Meditation in a Toolshed."

While there are differences, there are equally clear parallels between "Toolshed" and "Light." Robin wants to see Light itself, but light only allows us to see other things. In "Toolshed," however, Lewis is able to see light—a beam of it.[25] He is not using the beam to look at what's inside the toolshed; he is looking at the beam itself. Here we see something of the ambiguity of actual light which causes us to feel some sympathy for Robin. As readers, we are just as confused as Robin is as we follow his story—why can't he see light?

Our very language, as we find out in the stumbling conversation between Robin and Anne, makes us treat light as a seeable thing. Ubiquitous light illuminates everything, and thus Anne can, in one sense, say the light is "all round us."[26] There is indeed light in the room, but, strictly speaking, Robin is right in saying it can't be seen because they're seeing everything else by

---

24 Ibid, 215.
25 Again recall Psalm 36:9: "…in your light we see light."
26 "Light," par. 15.

its presence. The language betrays Anne's mis-thinking. She concludes Robin must be interested in the lamp, but that is only a source of light. Robin wants to see light *itself*. He too has been affected by language: the language of "poets and prophets"[27] who speak of light as if it's palpable—a visible thing unto itself.

Do we not sympathize with Robin? Even when Anne takes him out and notices, "What a lovely light there is on the hills over there," do we not think that the hill on which the sun is shining is more than just brighter than the hill in the shade—that light is not only pouring onto that hill but is also a thing we're seeing? When the clouds of a stormy day part and a beam of light breaks through, do we not think of it as seeing light itself? And from a scientific standpoint, isn't there some truth to the idea of light pouring onto a hill or beaming through a hole in the clouds? Robin wants light to be a *thing*, and to some extent he's right. Light is measurable with instruments, it has physical effects, it can burn human skin and blind human eyes. Over and over Lewis says light is not the thing we see but the thing we see by, but here in his dark "Toolshed," he is able (or at least uses the language of being able) to look *at* a beam of light. Unfortunately, it doesn't reveal very much.

To look at the beam of light shows very little. There is the beam itself, but the rest of the shed is almost completely dark. And so, though I might have sympathy for Robin, I cannot impose on his story (not yet anyway) any particular moment of redemption. Robin wants to see light itself, thinks he's found it, and dies for his epistemological misperceptions. In every interpretation discussed in chapter five,[28] Robin's end is a terrible one—his story a parable of mistaken philosophy. So even though Lewis can look *at* light in the toolshed, his every image in the essay seems to favor stepping into the beam and looking *along* it. Seeing by light seems far more important because doing so allows Lewis to experience the world outside: the trees and the sun, a world not of empty darkness but of light and wonder.

We might then suddenly be tempted to say that Robin's dive into the quarry is his attempt to step into the beam and see what's beyond (the world outside this earthly shed), and thus, though he dies, he's reborn.[29] But we might just as equally say that his dive is a fixation on the beam itself, not what it reveals either within or without, and thus he dies, end (literally) of story. We should, however, note that, while Lewis's imagery at the beginning

---

27 Ibid, par. 28.
28 Excepting the briefly noted reading by Sammons.
29 Consider the transcendent encounter of *looking along* as it's described in the coming of Venus to Earth in *That Hideous Strength*. As the planetary angels, the *Oyeresu*, come down to the terrestrial world, Venus holds the place of her descent "in her long beam," from which comes an ecstasy which is at once "fiery, sharp, bright and ruthless, ready to kill, ready to die, outspeeding light." To encounter Venus is to experience nothing less than the "translunary virtue" of "Charity" itself (*Hideous* 320).

of the "Toolshed" essay seems to favor the act of looking *along*,[30] he does say by the end of the essay that sometimes looking *at* will be superior to looking *along* (in the example of the native dancer, dancing for rain). What he rejects is any *predilection* to looking *at*. By extension, though, we should recognize that Lewis is not favoring looking *along* either. He argues the need to do both and then choose which is the more valuable mode of knowing in a particular instance.

Natural Blindness

There is clearly an underlying purpose in the "Toolshed" essay as evidenced in Lewis's emphasis on the fact that an *outside* approach to knowing is central to so called "modern" thought.[31] Besides being about knowledge (with a focus on enjoyment vs. contemplation) the essay is also a critique on the illusion of Objectivism as opposed to the "Poison of Subjectivism."[32] In that famous essay, Lewis laments moral relativism, the view that there's no one moral law, no absolute right & wrong. In "Toolshed," he's not contradicting himself. He's pointing out the problem of finite human knowledge. The *logical positivism* of his day argued that human beings are capable of knowing with perfect objectivity. The scientific method was touted as the means for mankind to step back and dispassionately observe the world so as to arrive at fact untainted by human error or personal point of view. What Lewis makes clear, however, is that to view an experience from the outside is simply to have stepped into another experience. The enjoyment/contemplation application may be something like this: Looking at the beam is perceived as an objective activity by the modernist scientist—he thinks he can contemplate it from the outside. What he fails to understand is that there is also an act of enjoyment which he cannot step out of: that of observer. Even observing is a subjective experience, not an objective one.

Lewis critiques the illusion of total human objectivity in other texts besides "Toolshed." The attack may be hinted at in "Light" in the form of Robin's fear of finding "himself in the hands of doctors again—psychotherapists, as likely as not."[33] Anyone looking at Robin's experience from the outside would doubtless think him delusional and in need of curing.[34]

---

30 Lewis's Narnia book, *The Voyage of the Dawn Treader*, contains an excellent example of this preeminence wherein the ship and crew are saved from the evils of the "Dark Island" by the coming of a "broad beam of light." When Lucy looks "along the beam" she sees an albatross which comes to lead the ship to safety.
31 "Toolshed," 213.
32 See *Christian Reflections*, 72-81.
33 "Light," par. 26.
34 See also Lewis's critique of contemporary philosophies of criminal rehabilitation in *That*

Lewis once wrote a paragraph about a community of people who were gradually going blind.[35] Words which imply anything to do with sight or color would linger in the language of these people for many years, even after the majority of them had gone completely blind. Critical thinkers among them would eventually start asking what the ancestors of their little community meant by such words and would conclude they meant nothing. During this time, if there were anyone who still retained his sight, he would find himself unable to prove to the blind thinkers of his community that the words having to do with sight had real meaning. Lewis suggests that this is a picture of Logical Positivism. Believers in this modern epistemology "make all ancient thought (e.g. Plato, Aquinas) look like a series of *sophismata per figuram dictionis*."[36] And if the Positivists were to talk about "The Form of Beauty," it is very likely that their words would have no meaning. Even so, Lewis asks if such words truly indicate the "experience of a kind of thought which most moderns have ceased to experience but wh.[37] was once commoner?"

Lewis answers this question in his poem "The Country of the Blind" which describes a country of men without eyes. The poem echoes the notebook paragraph perfectly.[38] The few men who can still see use the sight-language which belonged to their ancestors, but they cannot explain the reality of sight to the blind among whom are intellectuals who consider such men "Fools concocting a myth."[39] Near the end of the poem Lewis asks his reader if he thinks the picture painted in the poem is beyond belief. Then he replies that all anyone need do is go among the well known thinkers of his own day and attempt to talk to them about truths which once "stood plain to the inward

---

Hideous Strength (67-68) and "The Humanitarian Theory of Punishment" (287-300). In short, Lewis was concerned about any approach to criminal rehabilitation which treated criminals as diseased patients in need of psychological curing—the result would be that psychotherapists could submit their "patients" to any amount of torture for the sake of healing them.

35 This unpublished paragraph appears in Bodleian Ms. Dep. d. 811 on the sixth page from the back of the notebook.

36 Lewis used this phrase in his essay, "The Empty Universe" wherein he glossed the translation himself: "Sophism[s] disguised as language" (83). My thanks to Michael Ward for the reference.

37 Lewis's abbreviation for "which."

38 *Collected Poems*, 47-48. In fact the unpublished paragraph may be directly connected to "The Country of the Blind." Though different in several ways, the paragraph is similar to two paragraphs appearing near the end of Lewis's essay, "The Language of Religion" (140-41). The second of these paragraphs references a short story by H. G. Wells called "The Country of the Blind." Together the paragraphs cover material similar to that of the unpublished paragraph (see also Sammons, "Man," 4-5).

39 Ibid, 48, line 26.

eye."⁴⁰ Such obvious truths are obvious no more to the blind logical positivist, naturalist, materialists of the day.

Lewis connects an emphasis on looking *at* to naturalism and science in *The Four Loves* as well. One of the unusual qualities he notices about Eros—what we call being *in* love—is that it eliminates the separation between love which gives and love which receives.[41] Though Eros is the "king of pleasures," at its highest it regards "pleasure as a by-product."[42] The beloved object of our love gives us greatest pleasure, but Eros at its best focuses away from that pleasure and completely toward the one loved. To shift our attention to the pleasure we feel in the presence of the loved one would be to "plunge us back in ourselves, in our own nervous system. It would kill Eros, as you can 'kill' the finest mountain prospect by locating it all in your own retina and optic nerves."[43] Similarly, lovers of nature, whose focus is not on individual objects within nature but on the total experience[44]—a complete act of looking *along*—find themselves distracted by the man who looks *at* so many individual things. Says Lewis, "An enthusiastic botanist is for them a dreadful companion on a ramble," and the only companion worse than a botanist on such rambles would be a "landscape painter"[45] (perhaps such a painter as wants to "catch light"[46] and thus contributes to Robin's deadly leap).

In *Miracles*, Lewis reverses the sight image to favor looking *at*, doing so as part of an attack on naturalism. He argues that naturalism can't explain reason. It may be able to explain the gradual growth of and sophistication of the human brain's responses to its environment, but this is not the same as the power to reason one's way to truth. A brain's ability to respond to stimuli in increasingly sophisticated ways does not mean the brain would reach a point where it moves from such response to moments of real insight. "The relation between response and stimulus is utterly different from that between knowledge and the truth known."[47] To illustrate this point Lewis considers the possible evolution of the eye. Our eyesight is of much better use to us than in earlier life forms with only a "photo-sensitive spot." But having improved vision or having new improvements added to us would not bring us any closer to a "knowledge of light." Without eyes we would not know of light's existence, but *knowledge* about light isn't achieved by merely experiencing it with our senses. We learn knowledge about light by "experiments and inferences from

---

40 Ibid, line 32.
41 *Four Loves*, 137.
42 Ibid, 136.
43 Ibid, 136-37.
44 As described by Wordsworth.
45 *Four Loves*, 34.
46 "Light," par. 31.
47 *Miracles*, 29.

them, not by refinement of response. It is not men with specially good eyes who know about light, but men who have studied the relevant sciences."

Let's be sure we notice what Lewis has done here. He has argued against naturalism by pointing out that real knowledge is not the same thing as mental response—naturalism can't explain the existence of reason. He does this, however, by emphasizing looking *at* light rather than looking *along* it. In this illustration, thinking is given preeminence over experiencing, and looking *at* light is more important than looking *along* it. This is a clear instance in which Lewis's writings may suggest a positive interpretation of Robin's actions in "Light." Was it the inability of others to reason clearly, to move beyond mere response to their environments, which led to Robin's death? Perhaps he who had been blind was the only one who could clearly *see*. If so, the price he paid for it was (literally) steep.

Later in *Miracles*, Lewis does something which reminds us once again of the complexity of his enjoyment/contemplation epistemology. As I've said, it is too simple to merely say that enjoyment equals experience and contemplation thought. Where this description of the dichotomy seems accurate in passages in "Myth Became Fact"[48] or *Perelandra*,[49] here in *Miracles*, Lewis offers an instance in which thinking itself—or thinking by reason—is an act of both enjoyment *and* contemplation. In the case at hand, Lewis is considering a fair argument against the existence of the supernatural: if the supernatural is so central to life, so important to life, and so much a part of life, why do we need arguments to prove its existence at all? Shouldn't it be as "obvious as the sun in the sky?"[50]

To this Lewis responds with a series of illustrations: 1. When you're looking out of a second floor room at a garden you don't really notice that you're looking through a window. 2. When you read a book, you use your eyes to do it, but you don't really notice that you're using your eyes unless they start to hurt or you're reading a book on "optics." 3. We use grammar when we talk, but we don't pay attention to the fact unless we are speaking a foreign language.[51]

These examples show how the supernatural can be forgotten. Naturalists, having focused their thought on nature, have forgotten the "fact that they were *thinking*. The moment one attends to this it is obvious that one's own thinking cannot be merely a natural event, and that therefore something other than

---

48 See chapter seven.
49 *Perelandra*, 52. See the "Unconclusion" section of chapter eight for an explanation of this instance.
50 *Miracles*, 57.
51 Ibid, 57-58.

Nature exists."[52] Thinking itself is a supernatural activity, but because it's so common, we miss its supernatural quality. And not just because it's common, but also because we don't think about thinking. When we look at the garden, we don't care to think about the transparent quality of the glass which makes it possible to see through. Nor do we want to focus on our eyes when we're reading. When inquiring into objects, it is proper to focus on the objects and pay no attention to the act of inquiry itself—to the fact that we're thinking. To think about thinking is only necessary when we step back to try to develop a total philosophy. In thinking about nature, the naturalist forgets the fact that he's doing something unnatural: thinking. In forgetting this fact, he loses sight of the most universal proof of the supernatural: thinking itself.[53]

Now go back to the illustrations: the window allows us to see the garden, our eyes allow us to read, grammar allows us to communicate according to an accepted set of standards. In each of these instances, the thing we ignore is what allows us, metaphorically, to look *along*. The thing on which we're concentrating is what we're looking *at*. Applied to reason, we ignore the fact that we're thinking in order to think about an object. In other words, we are looking *along* reason in order to look *at* (to reason about) the object of our thinking. As applied to thought, these illustrations show that thinking is also a type of experience. When we use reason to look at things, that *use* of reason is an experience of looking along. Just as stepping into the beam of light and looking along the beam allows us to look at other things, so does stepping into the experience of thinking allow us to think about other things.

Once again, defining enjoyment as experience and contemplation as thought *is* an application Lewis makes. But it's only one application. Here in *Miracles* Lewis is saying that every act of knowing involves both enjoyment *and* contemplation. Thinking is not *just* contemplation; it's also the enjoyment which makes contemplation possible.

One of Lewis's arguments against naturalism comes from human nature, specifically our universal tendency to believe in moral standards despite our inability to live up to those standards.[54] This is important, says Lewis, because we cannot find out if there is anything behind the universe through science. All science can do is help us look at the universe. But if the thing behind the universe wanted to show itself to us, it might do so from "inside ourselves as an influence or a command trying to get us to behave a certain way."[55] Fortunately, there is one thing in the universe which we know more about than anything else, and that is us, mankind. We observe the universe, but we don't

---

52 Ibid, 58.
53 Ibid, 59.
54 See Lewis's *Mere Christianity*, 18-21.
55 Ibid, 21.

only observe people, we *are* people. "In this case we have, so to speak, inside information; we are in the know."[56] And what we know is that the *influence* to get us to behave a certain way is indeed in us. By looking, if you will, along *ourselves*, we find this proof of something beyond nature within ourselves. And that something beyond nature is speaking to us through light: "Nature is being lit up by a light from beyond Nature. Someone is speaking who knows more about her than can be known from the inside."[57] But what He reveals most is the person depicted in the gospels, a person as palpable and true as the Socrates described by Plato or the Johnson described by Boswell, and a person "also numinous, lit by a light from beyond the world, a god."[58] But if thought of as a god, then, since we are monotheists, not just a god but God Himself. In this moment in all of time and only here, the myth became fact, the Word became flesh, God became Man. The Incarnation is not religion or philosophy. It is the "summing up and actuality of them all."

In *Mere Christianity*, Lewis uses light to take one last jab, not specifically at naturalists or scientists, but at all atheists when he says that atheism is "too simple. If the whole universe has no meaning, we should never have found out that it has no meaning: just as, if there were no light in the universe and therefore no creatures with eyes, we should never know it was dark. *Dark* would be without meaning."[59] In contrast, *Mere Christianity* includes a version of the story about a blind community as an illustration of how Christians, as they become more Christlike, also become more individual—more uniquely themselves. Imagine that we found a group of people who had always lived in the dark and invited them into the light so they could become visible to each other for the first time. Before stepping into the light, these people might mistakenly think that, because they were all about to be lit up by the same kind of light, they would all look exactly the same. They would of course be wrong. The light would show how very different they are from one another in ways they could not have known while in the darkness. The body of Christ is like that.[60]

It's worth pointing out that the people in the darkness are at least in one instance capable of putting themselves there. They are not blind; they simply refuse to see. The unbelieving dwarfs in *The Last Battle*, are thrown with the story's heroes into a dark stable which turns out not to be dark at all but a doorway into the real Narnia—into heaven. When the friends of Narnia try to tell the dwarfs that they are not in a stable and there is light all about them, the

---

56   Ibid, 20.
57   Miracles, 159.
58   *Surprised by Joy*, 236.
59   *Mere*, 34.
60   Ibid, 189.

dwarfs refuse to believe them. Lucy begs them to look around and see the sky and trees and flowers and herself, but the dwarf leader, Diggle, merely replies, "How in the name of all Humbug can I see what ain't there? And how can I see you any more than you can see me in this pitch darkness?"[61] When Aslan appears, Lucy asks him to help the dwarfs, but, try as he might, he cannot. He concludes, "They will not let us help them. They have chosen cunning instead of belief. Their prison is only in their own minds, yet they are in that prison; and so afraid of being taken in that they cannot be taken out."[62]

Lewis's last use of a place set in darkness occurs in reflections he recorded after his wife died in a book called *A Grief Observed*. Only this time the person in the dark—and it too is a prison—is Lewis himself:

> One moment last night can be described in similes: otherwise it won't go into languages at all. Imagine a man in total darkness. He thinks he is in a cellar or dungeon. Then there comes a sound. He thinks it might be a sound from far off—waves or wind-blown trees or cattle half a mile away. And if so, it proves he's not in a cellar, but free, in the open air. Or it may be a much smaller sound close at hand—a chuckle of laughter. And if so, there is a friend just beside him in the dark. Either way, a good, good sound. I'm not mad enough to take such an experience as evidence for anything. It is simply the leaping into imaginative activity of an idea which I would always have theoretically admitted—the idea that I, or any mortal at any time, may be utterly mistaken as to the situation he is really in.[63]

Unlike the dwarfs in his last Narnia book, Lewis allows himself to be freed from his prison. Notice that in his uses of light metaphors he ends here where he often begins: epistemology—knowledge—what we can and cannot see.

Lewis's post-conversion writings, especially "Meditation in a Toolshed," add new possibilities to an interpretation of "Light." They clearly share the same interest in an epistemological problem: the qualities of and differences between looking at the beam and looking along it. An accurate epistemology will recognize the insight that all acts of knowing involve a dichotomy of enjoyment and contemplation. But as we move into the next chapter, we'll see that there are times to favor looking along over looking at and that it may be possible to eliminate the separation within the dichotomy and see instances in which enjoyment and contemplation become one and the same.

---

61 Lewis, *Last Battle*, 181.
62 Ibid, 185-86.
63 *Grief*, 75-76.

Chapter Seven
Beyond Reason and Imagination

Robin's constant problem in "Light" is a problem of perception. Upon first learning that he might receive his sight, he looks forward to a certain sort of experience: the chance to see *"Light"* itself.[1] When this doesn't happen, his experiential mishaps continue as just that—failures caused through lack of experience. In the story's first paragraph, Anne rises with a "bustle of familiar noises." Lewis emphasizes "noises" rather than activities because he is describing Robin's experiential viewpoint. It is the noises of Anne's actions which are familiar to Robin, not the sights, and experiences involving sight continue to be unfamiliar to him throughout the story. At the beginning of the story, Robin hasn't been outside for a walk with his working eyes yet, and in paragraph two he considers broaching the subject of "Light" with Anne but hesitates remembering that, in previous conversations with a doctor, a nurse, and Anne, "something seemed to have gone wrong." "Seemed" is the double-meaning symbol of Robin's problems with perception. He doesn't know what light is in the first place—not experientially—and so doesn't understand a point of perception taken for granted by the sighted. This in turn results in the next thing he fails to understand: why every conversation about light goes wrong. This idea of *seeming* (which is rooted in seeing[2]), then, becomes a metaphor for the entire story. It is a metaphor for failed understanding due to a lack of experience. In "Light," seeing is connected to the concept of knowing through experience, and this is the issue we take up in this chapter.

Consider how the conversation between Robin and Anne at the beginning of "Light" is one of utter language confusion because each person's initial premises—based on their experiences—are wrong. Robin wants to know where Light is; Anne says it's all around them. Robin wants her to point it out, then Anne thinks he means *"the* light" and points to a bulbed thing with an ugly shade. But Robin doesn't love lamp, he loves Light, and their conversation

---
1 "Light," par. 20.
2 Consider how we often use the synonym "appeared" for "seemed."

ends at a frustrated impasse for both.[3] Language has gotten in the way of meaning because experience has not allowed Robin and Anne to share the same perceptions. What seems like one clear truth to one of them appears as something very different to the other. Notice that everyone "sounded so angry" in paragraph five and Robin can't read Anne's facial expression in paragraph nine, only the "warm wave of muddled, frightened affection" in her voice. The emphasis here remains on Robin's perceptions and misperceptions. Later (in the MBB version of the story) Robin retreats into his old, comfortable experiences, walking and eating with his eyes closed and reading in Braille.[4]

As a story about epistemology, "Light" is an introduction to a theme in Lewis's thinking about knowledge and truth which has gone largely unnoticed, a theme which matters to us on the most practical levels and in our most spiritual insights. The Apostle John wrote, "Whoever does not love does not know God, because God is love."[5] He makes the point to which this chapter is ultimately heading: besides reason and imagination, knowledge also comes from experience; sometimes it's the most critical knowledge we can have.

Imaginative Truth?

There has been a conversation going on about Lewis's theory of knowledge which has focused on a dichotomy different from that of enjoyment vs. contemplation. This conversation has been a point of critical emphasis at least since Peter Schakel first wrote in 1983 about reason and imagination in C. S. Lewis.[6] Critics have been especially concerned, in this conversation, with the relationship between truth and imagination in Lewis's thinking.[7] I was first drawn to the "Great War" letters because they address this issue. In the letters, Lewis denies the existence of imaginative truth.[8] But did his thinking on the matter change when he converted to Christianity? Walter Hooper ends his own exploration (in which he describes Lewis as having struggled to "find a clear connection between imagination and truth"[9]) by turning to

---

3   "Light," pars. 10-25.
4   "The Man Born Blind," par. 30. See chapters nine and ten for reasons why Lewis may have cut this section from "Light."
5   I John 4:8, *New International Version*.
6   In "Seeing and Knowing: The Epistemology of C. S. Lewis's *Till We Have Faces*." See also Schakel's *Reason and Imagination in C. S. Lewis*, published in 1984.
7   See, for example, Schakel: *Reason and Imagination*, 123-24; 138-39; Carnell: "Imagination." 214-15; Neuhouser: "Higher Dimensions," 45-64; Sammons: *A Far Off Country*, 266; Honda: *The Imaginative World of C. S. Lewis*, 6; Camery-Hoggatt: "God in the Plot," 451-470; and, especially, Hooper: *Companion & Guide*, 568-574.
8   See "Series 1, Letter 2," 1606-13 in *Collected Letters 3*.
9   Hooper, *Companion & Guide*, 569.

two secondary sources:[10] Owen Barfield in his *Owen Barfield on C. S. Lewis*[11] eventually concludes a reluctance on Lewis's part to develop a complete theory of imagination (and by implication a conclusion on the connection between imagination and truth), while Peter Schakel's *Reason and Imagination* suggests at least the possibility of Lewis's coming to terms with the place of imagination in the expression of truth later in his life.

However, even Lewis's later writings[12] show a reluctance to say that imagination produces truth. This is especially the case in *An Experiment in Criticism*[13] where Lewis very specifically rejects any view that "literature is to be valued…for telling us truths about life."[14] He says, "To value [works of literature] chiefly for reflections which they may suggest to us or morals we may draw from them, is a flagrant instance of 'using' [texts for our own purposes] instead of 'receiving'" them for what they are.[15]

But now notice that this new dichotomy of using vs. receiving, which runs throughout *Experiment*,[16] echoes the enjoyment/contemplation dichotomy where *using* is something of an act of *contemplation* and *receiving* an act of *enjoyment*.[17] I think this dichotomy takes us in a direction which will help us understand both the "Light" story and Lewis's overall epistemological thinking[18] in ways better than a focus on reason and imagination alone can.

The enjoyment/contemplation distinction, especially where perceived in its most basic form as thinking vs. experiencing, moves us towards a tripartite approach to understanding Lewis's epistemology, one that emphasizes Lewis's views on *Fact* or *Reality* as well as on *Reason* and *Imagination*. If critical study on Lewis's theory of knowing has been focused too much on only the two

---

10   Ibid, 572-74.
11   See the essay entitled "Lewis, Truth, and Imagination."
12   For example, Lewis's 1951 essay, "The World's Last Night": "For a God who can be ignorant is less baffling than a God who falsely professes ignorance. The answer of theologians is that the God-Man was omniscient as God, and ignorant as Man. This, no doubt, is true, though it cannot be imagined. Nor indeed can the unconsciousness of Christ in sleep be imagined, nor the twilight of reason in his infancy; still less his merely organic life in his mother's womb. But the physical sciences, no less than theology, propose for our belief much that cannot be imagined" (99).
13   Which was published in 1961.
14   *Experiment*, 130.
15   Ibid, 82-83.
16   Beginning on page 19.
17   See Feinendegen, "Contemplating C. S. Lewis's Epistemology," 45.
18   I specifically use the term "epistemological thinking" in this instance as opposed to "epistemology" because of a recommendation from Peter Schakel who kindly served as one of my dissertation readers and who helped me see that a complete synthesis of Lewis's epistemology would be somewhat artificial since Lewis never synthesized it himself. I'm not trying to systematize Lewis's epistemology. I'm trying to understand it better.

terms—Reason and Imagination—it is not because of any blindness on the part of students of Lewis but because of Lewis himself. We can blame him for the approach in that he so often centered issues of knowing in these two modes of thought, starting especially with his poem on the subject, "Reason"[19] in which he seems to make knowledge an issue of the dichotomy between reason and imagination.[20] But the concept of *Enjoyment* in the enjoyment/contemplation dichotomy brings a third element into this mix: the kind of knowing which comes by experience.

My own study of Lewis's theory of knowledge began with a single sentence in *Perelandra* in which the protagonist, Ransom, realizes that the "triple distinction of truth from myth and of both from fact"[21] might not exist outside a fallen world. In trying to understand what Lewis meant by this enigmatic statement, I came to what eventually ballooned into a doctoral dissertation on Lewis's epistemological thinking. But rather than focusing on Reason and Imagination, I began with the concepts of Fact, Truth and Myth, turning eventually to the correspondences between Reason and Truth and Imagination and Myth. Among the conclusions which this approach yielded was the most surprising of all: that Lewis seemed less concerned about knowing *truth* than he was about knowing *reality*. If Lewis's epistemology has a center, it is in *fact*, not *truth*, because truth is always *about* reality—one step removed from the thing itself.

Truly Mythic Facts

And here we turn to the essay in which Lewis says as much. Lewis published "Myth Became Fact" in 1944,[22] very near the time the extant versions of MBB and "Light" were written. In the essay we find not only Lewis's epistemology of fact, truth and myth in its plainest form, but we also find the enjoyment/contemplation dichotomy considered specifically in terms of experience vs. thinking. Together these elements emphasize that the experience of reality is central to knowing. As we study this essay, we'll find three important ideas emerging. The first is that human beings approach reality epistemologically in two ways: as thinkers and as experiencers.[23] The second is that experiencing—stepping into and looking along the beam—will at times be the superior approach in knowing. The third is that it may be possible in some circumstances to break the divide and merge these kinds of knowing.

---

19 Lewis, *Poems*, 81.
20 See also *Surprised by Joy*—the Reason/Imagination dichotomy is ubiquitous there.
21 *Perelandra*, 122.
22 Hooper, *Companion & Guide*, 583.
23 And this problem takes us back to Barfield's concern about the very nature of reason as a mode of knowing stripped from time and abstracted out of reality.

Lewis begins the essay with a charge by his friend "Corineus" that modern Christianity is nothing like ancient Christianity, and all that remains of that primitive religion are the trappings of mythology. Lewis thinks this assertion false, but, if it were true, he wonders why Christians continue to hold onto the mythology. It would be much easier for them if they let it go. Lewis's answer is that, even if classical Christianity were purely mythical (which Lewis denies), it is *that* myth which vitalizes and nourishes the religion most of all and endures when philosophical heresies rise and fall. To explain how this is possible, Lewis determines to look more closely at myth. In doing so, he begins with the problem of knowing.[24]

"Human intellect is incurably abstract,"[25] Lewis says, and yet the "only realities we experience are concrete—this pain, this pleasure, this dog, this man." While we interact with the man, endure the pain, or delight in the pleasure, we are never able to think about the concepts of "Pleasure, Pain or Personality." These lofty universals,[26] significant as they are, remain in the abstract intellect. When we experience them in reality, those experiences are reduced to "mere instances or examples." And this is our epistemological dilemma:

> either to taste and not to know or to know and not to taste—or more strictly, to lack one kind of knowledge because we are in an experience or to lack another kind because we are outside it. As thinkers we are cut off from what we think about….The more lucidly we think, the more we are cut off: the more deeply we enter into reality, the less we can think. You cannot *study* Pleasure in the moment of nuptial embrace, nor repentance while repenting, nor analyse the nature of humour while roaring with laughter. But when else can you really know these things? 'If only my toothache would stop, I could write another chapter about Pain.' But once it stops, what do I know about pain?[27]

This is Lewis's clearest expression of the enjoyment/contemplation dichotomy at the most basic level of experiencing vs. thinking.[28] As used in this way, the

---

24 Lewis, "Myth Became Fact," 38-40.
25 Ibid, 40.
26 Take note of the capitalizations—we'll see how these universals matter as we work through the essay.
27 "Myth Became Fact," 40.
28 For another clear example, see *A Preface to Paradise Lost* where Lewis references Alexander specifically: In Milton, "The cosmic story—the ultimate *plot* in which all other stories are episodes—is set before us. We are invited, for the time being, to look at it from outside. And that is not, in itself, a religious exercise….In the religious life man faces God and God faces man. But in the epic it is feigned, for the moment, that we, as readers, can step aside and see the faces both of God and man in profile. We are not invited (as Alexander would have said)

concept is saying we can do one or the other but not both at the same time. And this is a huge epistemological dilemma, for neither kind of knowing is sufficient in itself. Lewis calls the problem a "tragic dilemma" but says that myth is, at least partially, a solution to it.

Here we begin to see Lewis acknowledging the importance of knowing reality through *experience*, but he goes even further. He says that in the "enjoyment"[29] of a myth we can come close to "experiencing as a concrete what can otherwise be understood only as an abstraction."[30] As an example of myth bridging the divide between thinking and experiencing, Lewis takes up the myth of Orpheus and Eurydice. In trying to understand the barest tasting of reality with our "discursive reason," a taste which vanishes as we apply reason to it, we are like Orpheus, able to hold his beloved Eurydice by the hand but not able to turn and look at her or else she'll disappear. The difficult concepts of this dilemma about knowing become "imaginable" when spoken of in mythic terms (notice here that the imagination apprehends myth like an experience of reality).

The reader may respond that the abstract idea which Lewis has just applied to the myth of Orpheus and Eurydice was not a meaning the reader had ever seen before. Lewis answers that this is exactly his point: the reader was not looking for any "abstract 'meaning' at all." To look for abstract meanings in myth is to receive it allegorically not mythically. In receiving the myth as an experience, the reader doesn't *know*, the reader *tastes*, but what he is tasting "turns out to be a universal principle." If we state the principle, we go back to abstracting, but if we receive the myth in the imaginative form of a story, we are able to experience concretely what is otherwise only abstract.

Interlude

Let's try to collect some of these ideas together before continuing with the "Myth Became Fact" essay. Imagine a situation in which there were no distinction between enjoyment and contemplation, where the intensity of experience met the cool-headed reflection of reason, where concrete realities were known with the precision of abstract thought, where our most carefully worked out thoughts were known with the palpable immediacy of experience. In such a situation, looking along the beam and looking at the beam would be one and the same. Lewis says that such a situation comes close to existing in our reception of myth but only if we look along the beam: to experience myth,

---

to *enjoy* the spiritual life, but to *contemplate* the whole pattern within which the spiritual life arises" (132).
29 I suspect Lewis uses this word both for its common meaning and the technical one given to it by Alexander.
30 "Myth Became Fact," 41.

rather than to analyze it, puts us into an epistemological situation wherein we can come close to being able to do both simultaneously—to do what Owen Barfield called "concrete thinking."[31]

Recall Barfield's concern about the very nature of knowing by reason: it's abstract, it's withdrawn from Space, it requires time withdrawn from actions *in* Time—it stands in contrast to experience. Barfield believed a more perfect mode of knowing could be possible, one in which experiencing and thinking were merged. This idea is a central tenet in his book *Poetic Diction*.[32] Through the study of ancient languages, Barfield concludes that myth was born of a time when "our distinction between subjective and objective cannot have existed."[33] The age of myth-making occurred in "pre-logical times." Reasoning, or "discursive thought operating in abstract ideas" depends upon a "subjective— or self—consciousness." Barfield claims that no such subjectivity—the separation of self from objective reality—existed till later in human history. It developed gradually—in an evolutionary fashion—and "was associated with the origin and development of language."[34] This is why humanity was a race of myth-makers before one of philosophers. Meaning permeated the world in the earlier age, apart from individual thinkers,[35] and relationships were perceived as realities in the world, not just thoughts in the mind.

Barfield is adamant: "the dualism, *objective:subjective*, is fundamental neither psychologically, historically, nor philosophically."[36] He argues that the "distinction of objective from subjective is a relatively late arrival in human consciousness" and that "the seemingly fundamental distinction between self and world" is not fundamental at all.[37] In relation to enjoyment/contemplation, what Barfield is saying is that the dilemma of thinking vs. experiencing did not exist in the past. Only when humanity began to distinguish between self and world did there begin to arise a distinction between "thinking and perceiving." Originally, thinking was "at the same time perceiving—a picture thinking, a figurative, or imaginative, consciousness."[38]

Much of Barfield's epistemology is born of ideas garnered from his belief in Anthroposophy, a quasi-religious philosophy which has its differences with orthodox Christian thinking, differences which may give us pause regarding Barfield's conclusions. But we need neither to critique Barfield's system nor accept it completely. What we must do, however, is realize that it had a

---

31 Barfield, *Poetic Diction*, 210.
32 Which Barfield dedicated to Lewis.
33 *Poetic Diction*, 204.
34 Barfield, *Saving the Appearances*, 169.
35 *Poetic Diction*, 86.
36 Ibid, 204.
37 Ibid, 206.
38 Ibid, 206-07.

significant influence on the thinking of C. S. Lewis. Earlier in this chapter, I quoted a passage from *Perelandra* in which Lewis suggests that the distinctions among truth, fact and myth might not exist outside of a fallen world. Indeed Lewis suggests that those distinctions might exist *because of* the fall,[39] and, echoing Barfield, he suggests that they gradually appeared as our thinking evolved (or perhaps devolved) while we moved through time further from paradise. In *That Hideous Strength*, Lewis writes of an age—the one in which Merlin lived—when "The Earth itself was more like an animal....And mental processes were much more like physical actions."[40] This is vintage Barfield.

Lewis even goes so far as to chronicle the increasing separation of subject from object (and thus thinking from experiencing) in the time from the late Middle Ages to the Romantic Period in his *English Literature in the Sixteenth Century*. He says that the achievement of the new scientists was to use mathematics to construct hypotheses which were tested not by mere observation but by observation—which was carefully controlled—of phenomena which could be measured precisely. The result for our activities is that nature was delivered into our hands. The results for our thinking and feeling were equally profound:

> By reducing Nature to her mathematical elements it substituted a mechanical for a genial or animistic conception of the universe. The world was emptied, first of her indwelling spirits, then of her occult sympathies and antipathies, finally of her colours, smells, and tastes....The result was dualism rather than materialism. The mind, on whose ideal constructions the whole method depended, stood over against its object in ever sharper dissimilarity....This process, slowly working, ensured during the next century the loss of the old mythical imagination: the conceit, and later the personified abstraction, takes its place. Later still, as a desperate attempt to bridge a gulf which begins to be found intolerable, we have the Nature poetry of the Romantics.[41]

Here an historical perspective, and then Lewis goes on in *Miracles* to predict an *end* to this increasing rift between knower and known, between our thinking and the reality we experience. He says the kind of thinking that combined imagination and reason, which we can see as late as Plato, must first give in to a "process of logical analysis"[42] which kills but remains necessary. In that process, distinctions between "nature and spirit, matter and mind, fact and myth, the literal and the metaphorical," must be sharpened more and more until finally a "purely mathematical universe and a purely subjective mind

---

39 *Perelandra*, 122.
40 *Hideous*, 235.
41 *English Literature*, 3-4.
42 *Miracles*, 211.

confront one another across an unbridgeable chasm." But if thought itself is going to survive this descent, there has to be a re-ascent, and the Christian vision allows for it. "Those who attain the glorious resurrection will see the dry bones clothed again with flesh, the fact and myth remarried, the literal and the metaphorical rushing together."[43]

Until that final, eschatological remarriage of knowing and known, Lewis argues that concrete thinking might be achieved by looking *along* a myth: by receiving it experientially. We should remember from the "Toolshed" essay that Lewis suggested there would be times when looking *at* was superior to looking *along* and times when the reverse was true. This is clearly an instance where looking along matters more, and notice, then, how looking along a myth is achieved: where we can define looking along as experiencing things in the concrete world, in looking along a myth we are experiencing things in a world perceived by our imaginations. Mythic thinking is achieved only through imaginative experience.

Is it possible that this is the source of Robin's fatal fall in "Light"? We've seen that Robin's attraction to Light was born of his love of the poets. Was Robin, in his sightless imagination, able to experience imageless mythic images which gave him tastes of a palpable thing called Light, a thing which does not exist in our common human experience but which exists in a higher, mythic one? If "God is light"[44] means anything, does it not mean that there is a place where Light is far more solid than any place we have imagined on earth? As we again take up "Myth Became Fact," it is to this place which we turn. I want us to notice that mythic encounter is not the only situation in which the enjoyment/contemplation distinction may break down into simultaneous knowing—more than a situation, in fact, there is a *reality* in which such concrete thinking may occur.

More Myth, More Fact

According to "Myth Became Fact," when we "translate" myth we get "abstractions"—lots of them.[45] But the myth itself is not abstraction. Myth "flows" into us, giving us "not truth but reality (truth is always *about* something, but reality is that *about which* truth is)." Here is Lewis's plainest explanation of truth, myth and fact: reality is what's real; myth gives us imaginative experiences (mimicking concrete experience) of reality; truth is abstract thinking about reality (which corresponds to it). But this plain description of myth needs qualifying. Because myth gives us reality, it can

---

43 Ibid, 212.
44 I John 1:5, *New International Version*.
45 "Myth Became Fact," 41.

foster numerous abstract truths. Lewis says, "Myth is the mountain[46] whence all the different streams arise which become truths down here in the valley, *in hac valle abstractionis*"[47]—the valley of abstraction. Several times now Lewis has suggested what he has not explicitly said: that in talking about reality he is considering several levels of it. His next metaphor for myth is not vertically hierarchical, but it certainly suggests levels of importance: myth in this image is an "isthmus" connecting the "peninsula" of thought to the "vast continent" to which we "really belong."

The use of the word "really," and the sentence which follows, where Lewis says myth is not abstract like truth nor "bound to the particular" like experience, are key to so much. "Myth Became Fact" is not, as it may first seem, an essay which argues that experience, or looking *along*, is better than thinking or looking *at*. Lewis finds that mere experience of the reality around us is just as limited as is thinking about reality. To experience Love here in our world is only to experience an example, an instance of it. What Lewis has been saying throughout this essay is that neither our thinking about such higher (dare I say Platonic) ideas as Pleasure, Personality, or Pain, nor our experiencing specific instances of them is a sufficient mode of knowing. What he *is* saying is that looking along myth (rather than at it) can get us closest to the Reality—the "vast continent we really belong to"—in which those higher ideas abide.

This hierarchical concept of reality continues throughout the remainder of the essay: "myth transcends thought" and "Incarnation transcends myth."[48] The ubiquitous pagan myth of the dying and reviving God becomes fact while remaining myth. It comes down to us from the "heaven of legend and imagination" to factual history here on earth. The hierarchical in Lewis's thinking about reality is clear. As Lewis goes on to talk about the story of Christ as myth become fact, which should be received by our imaginations with mythic wonder and our reason with factual certitude, he concludes that the "marriage of heaven and earth" is the coming together of "perfect myth and perfect fact."[49]

---

46 In the original manuscript of "Myth Became Fact" (Wade Ms. CSL/MS-4—originally titled by Lewis as "—And Became Fact"), the word "mountain" is written in over the word "fountain." I like "fountain" for its possible connection to the "pure ethereal stream whose fountain who can tell" in the "third revision" (as I call it) in the "Man Born Blind" Notebook (see chapter nine) for which Robin longs to search. "Mountain" is perhaps the better word because of the hierarchical nature of the *reality*—the concrete universals—which myth communicates to us.
47 Textual gloss on page 41: "In this valley of separation."
48 "Myth Became Fact," 41.
49 Ibid, 42.

Light

Higher Reality

The sources of myth include the heavenly. Myth is "a real though unfocused gleam of divine truth falling on human imagination."[50] It is "gleams of celestial strength and beauty falling on a jungle of filth and imbecility."[51]

---

[50] Lewis, *Miracles*, 176n.

[51] *Perelandra*, 173. Lewis argues that myth is a revelation of God to man. In a letter to Arthur Greeves he says, "the Pagan stories are God expressing Himself through the minds of poets using such images as He found there, while Christianity is God expressing Himself through what we call 'real things'" (18 October 1931; *They Stand Together*, 427). Three months later Lewis wrote that the sacrificial gods of all the "greater myths" (including Balder, Dionysus, and Adonis) were "the first shadowy approach of something whose reality came with Christ" (10 January 1932, Ibid, 437).

Perhaps these "shadowy" myths originate archetypally, which for Lewis would be to say God has woven them into the fabric of the human psyche. Lewis was intrigued by Carl Jung's archetypal theory: "For Jung, fairy tale liberates Archetypes which dwell in the collective unconscious, and when we read a good fairy tale we are obeying the old precept 'know thyself'" ("On Three Ways of Writing for Children," 27). Lewis did not absolutely embrace Jung, however: "Jung's theory of myth is as exciting as a good myth and in the same way....But I have an idea that the true analysis of a thing ought not to be so like the thing itself. I should not expect a true theory of the comic to be itself funny" ("De Audiendis Poetis," 16-17). Lewis treats Jung at length in his essay "Psycho-Analysis and Literary Criticism." He concludes that the origin of primordial images is more remote than Jung theorizes ("Psycho-Analysis," 300), but that, if Jung's theory "turns out to be bad science it is excellent poetry" (297).

Nevertheless, Lewis does agree that there is a subconscious quality to myth. In *Mere Christianity* he calls myth "good dreams" sent to the human race by God: "I mean those queer stories scattered all through the heathen religions about a god who dies and comes to life again and, by his death, has somehow given new life to men" (44). Also, in comparing myth to allegory, Lewis says, "Into an allegory a man can put only what he already knows: in a myth he puts what he does not yet know and cd not come to know in any other way" (22 September 1956; *Letters*, 458).

If any of us are uncomfortable with a metaphor from psychology, the metaphor of distance may be more acceptable. Near the end of *Perelandra* Ransom asks the *Oyeresu* of Venus and Mars how they came to be known on Earth: "It comes, they told him, a long way round and through many stages. There is an environment of minds as well as of space. The universe is one—a spider's web wherein each mind lives along every line, a vast whispering gallery where (save for the direct action of Maleldil [God]) though no news travels unchanged yet no secret can be rigorously kept. In the mind of the fallen Archon under whom our planet groans, the memory of Deep Heaven and the gods with whom he once consorted is still alive. Nay, in the very matter of our world, the traces of the celestial commonwealth are not quite lost. Memory passes through the womb and hovers in the air. The Muse is a real thing. A faint breath, as Virgil says, reaches even the late generations. Our mythology is based on a solider reality than we dream: but it is also at an almost infinite distance from that base" (*Perelandra*, 172-73).

The idea that "traces of the celestial commonwealth" are never quite lost in the fabric of our world resonates with a myth passage on death, resurrection, and atonement in *The Problem*

If myth can help us know in a way which takes us up into concrete essences because of its connection to the heavenly realm, then the heavenly realm itself must be a place of constant concrete knowing—a place where the separation of enjoyment from contemplation does not exist.

Lewis suggests this very possibility in *The Great Divorce*. The novel first paints a picture of heaven as a higher reality, a more *real* reality than earth. Everything is so much more solid than the souls first arriving there that even the grass will not bend beneath their nearly weightless feet.[52] Later in the novel we are told that on earth, hell is smaller than a pebble while in heaven hell is smaller than one heavenly atom.[53] The heavenly New Narnia is described in the same way in *The Last Battle*. Though old Narnia is very much like this new one, the new Narnia looks "More like the real thing."[54] The old Narnia "was not the real Narnia. That had a beginning and an end. It was only a shadow or a copy of the real Narnia which has always been here and always will be here."[55] The Platonic imagery of hierarchy is pretty clear in this instance, but, in case we doubt, we need only listen to Professor Digory's explanation of the phenomenon: that it is as different as a real thing is from a shadow or as waking is from a dream. And then he says, "It's all in Plato, all in Plato."[56] Lewis describes the new Narnia as "a deeper country: every rock and flower and blade of grass looked as if it meant more."[57]

And why wouldn't it if to enter heaven means to enter a place where abstract reason and mere instances of experience give way to concrete thought and experience of the absolute? This possibility is offered in *The Great Divorce* where a ghostly man who has a passion for inquiry, (though not for truth) is visiting the outskirts of heaven. There he meets an old friend who has moved beyond the ghostly stage to full presence, full being in heaven. The glorified man is there to invite the ghost to go further in. But the ghost refuses unless certain guarantees are met, especially "an atmosphere of free inquiry."[58] The glorified man tells his friend he will find no such thing; he will find final answers. The ghost responds that there is "something stifling about the idea of finality" to which the other replies, "You think that, because hitherto you

---

of Pain, wherein Lewis says that "Nature herself has written it large across the world in the repeated drama of the buried seed and the re-arising corn. From nature, perhaps, the oldest agriculture communities learned it and with animal, or human, sacrifices showed forth for centuries the truth that 'without shedding of blood is no remission'" (103).

52   *Divorce*, 20-21.
53   Ibid, 138.
54   *Last Battle*, 210.
55   Ibid, 211-12.
56   Ibid, 212.
57   Ibid, 212-213.
58   *Divorce*, 40.

have experienced truth only with the abstract intellect. I will bring you where you can taste it like honey and be embraced by it as by a bridegroom." Thus, in Lewis's vision, what can only be an abstract idea on earth is concrete reality in heaven. On earth, truth is an idea—it is abstract thought, reason removed from reality. In heaven, Truth is a person.[59] In such a world, experiencing and thinking simply become knowing. To look along *is* to look at. To contemplate the beam is to step in and enjoy it.

And here I return briefly to the question of imaginative truth. A full review of the many Lewis references necessary for a complete discussion on the issue is beyond the scope of our study of "Light." But here I think we can gather an inkling of an answer. In his essay "Bluspels and Flalansferes," Lewis calls imagination the "organ of meaning" on which our ability to reason to truth depends.[60] Neither truth nor falsehood can exist without meaning, and I think this a key point: for Lewis, imagination here in the "valley of abstraction" is, if you will, "truth neutral." It can be used to make true meanings and false ones.

More than once Lewis writes of what I call the *dangerous imagination*. In his poem "Relapse," for example, he speaks of how images born of hurt or temptation can grow within us like cancer and then shoot their venomous poison into our hearts when we least expect it.[61] In a letter written in 1958, Lewis refers to both the "physical (and still more the imaginative) sins" related to sexuality.[62] Several times he points out how the imagination or texts which appeal to it can be corrupted to produce false beliefs and desires about sexuality,[63] and he even goes so far as to say that, more than reason, "It is your senses and your imagination that are going to attack belief."[64] Imagination can be an enemy of faith!

More clearly than anywhere else, Lewis points out the limitations of imagination as a truth-bearing faculty in chapter ten of *Miracles*. There he says that accurate knowledge of the earth's distance from the sun is an example of clear thinking which would most likely be "accompanied by *imagining* which is ludicrously false to what we know that the reality must be."[65] Thinking is different from imagining and often quite distinct, and what, in our thinking, we know to be true can be accompanied by images which are "entirely false."

---

59 As, I think, must be Justice, Goodness, Beauty, Wisdom (Proverbs 8:22-31), Word (John 1:1), Love (I John 4:8) and even Light (I John 1:5). See also "The Poison of Subjectivism" where Lewis deals with the dilemma of which has preeminence, God or Good, by suggesting this very idea (79-80).
60 "Bluspels," 265.
61 "Relapse," lines 5-11, *Poems* 103.
62 13 February 1958; *Collected Letters 3*, 920.
63 See *Mere Christianity*, 84-85 and *The Screwtape Letters*, 106-07.
64 In "Religion: Reality or Substitute," 136.
65 *Miracles*, 95.

C. S. Lewis's First and Final Short Story

Furthermore we can know these images to be false while still thinking correctly, or we can think correctly while also having false images which we do *not* know are false.[66] Lewis tells a story of a little girl who thought poison was always red.[67] She knew rightly that poison was bad, but she had a false image accompanying her right thinking. Clearly, Lewis believes imagination can produce falsehood.

Nevertheless, Lewis does see connections between truth and imagination. In the *Miracles* passage above, he notes that the only way to talk about things beyond our senses (such as God or heaven) is to talk about them with that imaginative device called metaphor, and he denies that metaphors must automatically be taken as false.[68] Elsewhere he says, "I think that all things, in their way, reflect heavenly truth, the imagination not least,"[69] and these passages together provide a hint as to the real connection between truth and imagination, which is in that place where truth and reality merge—the heavenly world. In heaven, the distinction between fact, truth and myth disappears (and so the distinction between experience, reason and imagination). Until then, on earth, when imagination allows us to experience higher, mythic reality, it is allowing us to experience concrete (but not abstract) truth.

Imagination allows us to have experiences. Myth allows us to have experiences of the heavenly reality wherein truth is a concrete thing. Imagination allows us to experience truth in the form of concrete thought. But this, for Lewis, is not earthly, abstract truth. Were he to explain his vision any clearer, he might say that imagination does not allow us to see truth, but (in myth) to experience higher reality. If we try to articulate that reality into truth statements, we have moved beyond experience and imagination. So long as we continue to perceive through imaginative experience, we perceive mythic reality, and that reality so perceived, comes closest to concrete truth.

The Moral Imperative

But there might yet be one more place where concrete thought is possible. Besides heaven, and besides looking along myth, it might be possible to look along a direct, divine encounter in the earthly realm and there experience a knowledge even to the point of salvation. Lewis writes of this possibility in *The Voyage of the Dawn Treader*. Here we find one last instance where looking along the beam is the superior mode of knowing.

---

66   Ibid, 96.
67   See also Lewis's essay, "Horrid Red Things," which shares the same title with this chapter in *Miracles*.
68   *Miracles*, 96-98.
69   *Surprised*, 167.

In chapter twelve of the novel, the Dawn Treader and her heroes draw near to a "Darkness" so thick that it is described as a "smooth, solid blackness."[70] They enter this horizontal ocean abyss leaving the sun behind them with some reluctance.[71] Indeed, it is only the chastisement of the brave mouse Reepicheep which drives them forward. Not long into the Darkness, they hear a cry and come upon a man whom they rescue from the water. He tells them to turn the boat around and "Fly!" from that place as quickly as possible[72] because ahead of them is the "Island where Dreams come true."[73] At first the crew thinks this wonderful news till the man, who turns out to be one of the lost Lords of Narnia for whom they've been searching, explains that it is not a place where wishes or desires come true but one where *actual* dreams do. Upon realizing that the objects of their worst nightmares might come into existence in that place, the travelers scramble to turn the ship about and head out of that darkness back into daylight.

Only Reepicheep, never wavering in his courage, questions this course of action. Caspian replies, "You can say what you like, Reepicheep. There are some things no man can face."[74] To this, Reep replies, "It is, then, my good fortune not to be a man." Unfortunately, they begin to succumb to fear as they hear their worst dreams coming to life out in the darkness.[75] They fear they will never get out—that they'll be trapped in that darkness forever. At that point Lucy cries out to Aslan for help. Suddenly there is a "speck of light ahead, and while they watched a broad beam of light fell from it upon the ship."[76] Like Lewis in his toolshed, the ship has come into the beam, and, as similarly described in the "Toolshed" essay, Lucy looks "along the beam" where she sees what looks like a "cross" and then an "aeroplane" and then a "kite" until it draws near enough for her to recognize it as an "albatross,"[77] the magical bird symbolizing divine presence in Coleridge's *Rime of the Ancient Mariner*. The bird whisper's to Lucy in the voice of Aslan; he tells her to be brave. Then the albatross leads the Dawn Treader out of darkness and back into the light of day.

As applied to Alexander's dichotomy, this scene in Lewis's third Narnia book[78] is a parable showing the value of looking along and the danger of

---

70 *Dawn Treader*, 190.
71 Ibid, 192.
72 Ibid, 196.
73 Ibid, 197.
74 Ibid, 198.
75 Ibid, 199.
76 Ibid, 200.
77 Ibid, 200-01.
78 This is my subtle way of acknowledging that all the Lewis critics who argue that the original published order is the best way to read the Narnia books are right!

looking at. Encountering God (appearing here in the form of the albatross/Aslan) is best accomplished by looking *along* the beam—by experiencing Him. Despite his courage, Reepicheep is wrong in this instance. No one should ever look *at* one's nightmares, and to draw them out into the real world would make that very thing occur. Let horrible dreams sit safely tucked inside our subconscious minds to be encountered in our sleep. Some things are not meant to be faced in any other way.

Or it may be that Reepicheep is not so much wrong, here, but merely that he is not human. He thinks it an advantage that he is not, and this perhaps hints at the possibility that he is blind to the significance of the moment, not because he is fearless, but because mice don't have nightmares.[79] On the other hand, perhaps Reep's courage is born of the excessive desire, often found in adventurers, to complete some new quest or conquer some new object. But whether he simply lacks the same experiences as human beings or is driven to excess in a desire to own the object of his quest, he is a type of the character we know as Robin in Lewis's "Light" story. It may be that Robin leaps to his death for lacking the experience of light which others had. Or it may be that he dies out of a desire to own what no one can. Recall that the painter in the story tells Robin he is trying to "catch light"[80] to which Robin replies, "so am I." Such a desire to own light—to capture it—is indicative of an inability to enjoy (look along) something through experience. Instead the painter pursues capturing light and holding it frozen so that it can be contemplated—looked at. Robin is perhaps so obsessed with knowing light as an object (like an object of art), that he cannot enjoy it.

But the Divine is not something to be owned. He is not "a tame lion."[81] Scripture tells us that knowing God requires a surrender to experiences of Him—especially to actions which mimic His nature. According to Proverbs wisdom doesn't begin till one fears the Lord,[82] and the Apostle John tells us that love in action is necessary for anyone who wants to know God.[83] God plants truth and wisdom within us,[84] and the wicked are blind to what they do not know.[85] Only those who want to do God's will can know His

---

79 Of course, I cannot verify this interpretation without the testimony of any psychologists who are experts in the subconscious minds of talking (preferably Narnian) animals. Any reader who knows of such experts would help this study immensely by running down an answer to this query about the dreams of Narnian mice.
80 "Light," par. 31.
81 Lewis, *The Lion, the Witch and the Wardrobe*, 200.
82 Proverbs 1:7.
83 I John 4:8.
84 Psalm 51:6.
85 See Proverbs 4:19, 5:6, and 7:23 among others.

teaching,[86] and He reveals Himself only to those who love Him and keep His commandments.[87] In fact, the only way to be certain we know God *is* by keeping His commandments.[88]

Lewis echoes this idea using light as a metaphor for it. In a letter to a former student, he points out the limits of theoretical knowing by saying that "one can begin to try to be a disciple before one is a professed theologian. In fact they tell us, don't they, that in these matters to act on the light one has is almost the only way to more light."[89] Regarding self knowledge Lewis writes, "Virtue—even attempted virtue—brings light; indulgence brings fog,"[90] and of knowing God he says that, in matters of knowledge of God, the "initiative lies on His side."[91] Nothing we do can make Him reveal more of Himself to us, and He shows Himself more to some people than others based, not on favoritism, but on their spiritual conditions: "it is impossible for Him to show Himself to a man whose whole mind and character are in the wrong condition. Just as sunlight, though it has no favourites, cannot be reflected in a dusty mirror as clearly as in a clean one."[92] Lewis teaches us that the question of light and knowledge is not merely an epistemological one. It is a moral and spiritual one.

Transposition and Sacrament

A tripartite approach to Lewis's epistemology, one which focuses on reason, imagination *and* reality (including our experiences of it), carries us into one more important Lewis text which may be intimately connected to "Light." In May of 1944,[93] C. S. Lewis preached a sermon entitled "Transposition" at Mansfield College Chapel in Oxford.[94] I believe this sermon may have been the impetus for Lewis's renewed interest in the story he had written for Owen Barfield more than a decade before. As I argue in the last two chapters of this book, "Light" is a revision of its previously published predecessor, "The Man Born Blind." This version begins on page 22 of the MBB notebook.

---

86 John 7:17.
87 John 14:20-21.
88 I John 2:3. Additionally, anyone who says he knows God but does not keep God's commandments is a liar (I John 2:4). See also I John 2:29, 4:7, 5:20 and 2:11: "But the one who hates his brother is in the darkness and walks in the darkness, and does not know where he is going because the darkness has blinded his eyes" (New American Standard Bible).
89 4 January 1941; *The Letters of C. S. Lewis*, 357.
90 *Mere Christianity*, 87. See also page 127 where the people in heaven are described as being filled with goodness "as a mirror is filled with light."
91 Ibid, 140.
92 Ibid, 141.
93 See Bramlett, "Transposition," 408.
94 Lewis, *Transposition and Other Addresses*, 9.

C.S. Lewis's First and Final Short Story

Right before the story is an outline—brainstorming notes, if you will—for the sermon which Lewis called "Transposition," and though Lewis's story about a blind man given sight may not be the very next thing he wrote, it *is* the very next thing he wrote down in this notebook.

More than anything else, "Transposition" is about Lewis's view of hierarchical reality—of nature and supernature and the ways in which they interact. And as I said before, I think it might have been the inspiration for Lewis's return to his story about blindness and light. Like "Light," "Meditation in a Toolshed," and "Myth Became Fact" among other Lewis writings, "Transposition" is concerned with the problem of knowing. Since we've spent a great deal of time on the epistemological difficulty of enjoyment vs. contemplation, let's remember that, in the interpretations offered in chapter five, the question was not just that of Alexander's dichotomy but also of knowing the higher spiritual reality behind the visible world. "Transposition" begins in this same place. Starting with the specific question of whether or not the phenomenon of speaking in tongues is a truly spiritual experience (as opposed to some kind of "hysteria"), Lewis raises the broader question of how we can know any alleged spiritual activity is authentic. Because there is a continuity between the natural and supernatural worlds, it is difficult to know when a supernatural event is occurring in the world of nature.[95]

One of Lewis's answers in "Transposition" repeats almost exactly one of the interpretations of the meaning of "Light" discussed in chapter five. The interpretation that says "Light" is a parable of the dangers of spiritual introspection—of looking within oneself to encounter the divine beyond—finds wording in the last third of "Transposition": "I suspect that, save by God's direct miracle, spiritual experience can never abide introspection."[96] Lewis adds that trying to "discover by introspective analysis our own spiritual condition is to me a horrible thing" which will, at its best, show us only ourselves and not God in us or the true state of our spiritual condition, and, at its worst, "may be the quickest road to presumption or despair."[97]

If introspection can't show us when the higher reality of supernature encounters the lower reality of nature, what can? Lewis's answer is for us to become aware of the problem and look for instances of what he calls *Transposition*. The first instance of Transposition which Lewis offers as proof of spiritual phenomena is the relationship between our emotions and our physical sensations. Taking aesthetic pleasure as an example, he notes that the joy of experiencing beauty can have the same effect on the body's feelings as being

---

95 "Transposition," 268.
96 Ibid, 274.
97 See also pages 269-70 where Lewis points out the limitations of introspection on identifying moments of transposition.

sick or hearing bad news.[98] His point is that our "emotional life" is "higher" than the life of our physical sensations. Our emotions are more varied and subtle than our sensations, and so multiple emotions (say the feeling of being in love and the feeling of fear) will have the same effect on the body though we recognize them as very different feelings.

To look for anything spiritual in the natural world, then, means first of all *not* looking for one-to-one correspondences. In any relationship of higher to lower, the higher is deeper, fuller, richer than the lower. If it is to appear in the lower, it can only do so by having multiple meanings in the lower. The English language has only five vowels, but in order for the language to make use of those vowels, each vowel must represent multiple pronunciations.[99] If a song written for an orchestra were rewritten for piano only, then some of the piano notes which represented flutes in one part of the original score will also have to represent violins in a different part. Musicians talk of transposing songs from major to minor keys; thus Lewis uses the word *Transposition* to describe the relationship between the higher and the lower.

Lewis's primary metaphor for describing this relationship is art: drawing and painting. Here we have a strong connection between "Transposition" and "Light" via the illustrations in the former and the painter in the latter. If "Light" was rewritten just after "Transposition," this art connection suggests that Lewis was discovering a new meaning in (or perhaps even adding one to) his "Light" story.

In the sermon, Lewis notes that the very act of trying to capture a three-dimensional world on a two-dimensional canvas is an act of transposition. The clear example of transposition in drawing exists in the challenge of representing three dimensions of space on a flat piece of paper. The solution has to do with manipulating perspective, and this can only be done by giving more than a single value to two-dimensional shapes. For example, the shape an artist uses to draw a receding road is the same shape he would use to draw a spear's tip. Shading works in a similar fashion: "Your brightest light in the picture is, in literal fact, only plain white paper: and this must do for the sun, or a lake in evening light, or snow, or human flesh."

Lewis's point regarding the presence of higher reality in the lower is to say that, if it appears, it will do so using the forms of lower reality in a way which will not replace the meanings of those forms but only add to them. And as to how we can tell if higher reality is indeed appearing in the lower world, Lewis answers that we can't, not without already knowing something of the higher. Imagine a drawing of a man on a straight road. If the man were to come to life, he would not be able to see anything above the page since he is only a two-

---

98   "Transposition," 270.
99   Ibid, 271.

dimensional creature. The lines of the road would, to him, be nothing more than a triangle. If we were to talk to the man and try to explain to him that the various shapes in the picture represent our higher, three-dimensional reality, he would be doubtful about its existence because all of the shapes on the paper already have their two-dimensional meanings. He would wonder why we keep trying to prove the existence of our three-dimensional world only having as proof his two dimensional shapes,[100] and he would likely conclude, "Is it not obvious that your vaunted other world, so far from being the archetype, is a dream which borrows all its elements from this one?"[101]

In my thinking, light is an apt metaphor for this process[102] and another reason that "Transposition" might have sent Lewis back to his "Light" story though this time with a focus on both knowing *and* the hierarchical nature of reality.[103] Is it true that we never see light, that we only see what light illuminates? In his toolshed, Lewis looked both along *and* at the beam of light. If even that wasn't really light, however, only the lighting of a thread width portion of the toolshed, is there no higher place where light *itself* can be seen? No place on earth where light takes the world up into itself and shows us not only the world but the light itself?

Lewis hints at possibilities as "Transposition" continues, next considering the best term for identifying the transpositional relationship between higher and lower realities. He says that a word that won't work in describing the relationship of the higher being transposed into the lower is the word "*symbolism.*"[104] Though the word might work in some cases (as in the relationship between words spoken and words written), in others it won't. Here we come to a passage which above all others makes me think that Lewis might have renewed his interest in the "Light" story after writing this sermon:

> Pictures are part of the visible world themselves and represent it only by being part of it. Their visibility has the same source. The suns and lamps in pictures seem to shine only because real suns or lamps shine on them: that is, they seem to shine a great deal because they really shine a

---

100 Ibid, 271-72.
101 Ibid, 272.
102 Michael Ward points to light as a metaphor for Transposition in Lewis's poem, "Noon's Intensity," where the sun transforms "All baser virtues" (line 11, *Poems*, 114) not through alchemy—the *transformation* into gold of baser metals—but through *transmutation* (Ward, *Planet Narnia*, 104-105). "This," says Ward, "is that theme which Lewis elsewhere calls 'Transposition': the flooding of a lower medium and the raising of it to a new significance by incorporation into a higher medium" (*Planet Narnia*, 105).
103 And this idea of light as Platonic metaphor will be the final interpretation of "Light" to which we turn in chapter eight.
104 "Transposition," 272, Lewis's italics.

little in reflecting their archetypes. The sunlight in a picture is therefore not related to real sunlight simply as written words to spoken. It is a sign, but also something more than a sign: and only a sign because it is also more than a sign, because in it the thing signified is really in a certain mode present. If I had to name the relation I should call it not symbolical but sacramental.

Did this illustration take Lewis back to his story about a man born blind with its painter trying to capture light? We can only speculate. But what we *can* see in this passage is that possibility mentioned above of light as the thing both seen and by which we see and therefore the perfect metaphor for the concept of Transposition. Lewis says, "Transposition occurs whenever the higher reproduces itself in the lower." And so just as light in a painting is both reflecting and in a "certain mode" giving off light, so light in the world may allow us not only to see other things but to see something of itself, or, perhaps more fitting to the analogy, to see something of a larger light: that "light from beyond Nature" which is lighting nature up.[105] Maybe this is what it really means to both see by *and* see light: we see the higher light reproducing itself in the lower light, revealing something of itself through it.[106]

This idea of sacramentalism is reflected in Lewis's views of nature and mankind in *The Four Loves*. Of nature he says, "The created glory may be expected to give us hints of the uncreated; for the one is derived from the other and in some fashion reflects it."[107] And of humanity: "It is easy to acknowledge, but almost impossible to realise for long, that we are mirrors whose brightness, if we are bright, is wholly derived from the sun that shines upon us."[108] This is true of humanity with the exception of the man Jesus Christ who was God and who in the Incarnation achieved the greatest act of Transposition and of sacramentalism. While on earth He both *reflected* and *was* light. In the Incarnation God takes

> the whole environment of Nature, all the creaturely predicament, into His own being. So that "He came down from Heaven"[109] can almost be transposed into "Heaven drew earth up into it,"[110] and locality,

---

105 *Miracles*, 159.
106 Lewis suggests something similar using a metaphor of wind in *Letters to Malcolm*: "When the wind roars I don't just hear the roar: I 'hear the wind'" (89). And so, when the light shines, does he not see more than just what it's shining upon? In this sacramental way, does he not also see light?
107 *Four Loves*, 38.
108 Ibid, 180.
109 The title of a book by Lewis's friend and fellow Inkling Charles Williams, taken by both from the Nicene Creed.
110 An allusion to the Athanasian Creed. Thanks to Charles Huttar for this and the above

limitation, sleep, sweat, footsore weariness, frustration, pain, doubt, and death, are, from before all worlds, known by God from within. The pure light walks the earth; the darkness received into the heart of Deity, is there swallowed up. Where, except in uncreated light, can darkness be drowned?[111]

Lewis's use of drawing and painting metaphors continues in "Transposition" as he takes up the question of heavenly hope. The idea of Transposition, if believed, allows us to see that it's possible to get a glimpse of heaven.[112] Lewis shows us how through a fable:[113] a woman who has been thrown into a dungeon[114] gives birth to and raises a son there. The boy grows up never seeing the outside world save for a bit of sky in a high window. His mother, who is also an artist and just happens to have her drawing pencils and paper with her, teaches the boy about the outside world in the hope that they will one day be released. Her instructional method consists primarily of drawing pictures for the boy of all aspects, objects, and terrains of nature and human creation. The boy does his best to learn from and believe his mother about the outside world until one day he says something which makes her realize that he thinks the world outside the dungeon is filled with lines drawn with a pencil. She tells him it isn't so, and his whole conception of the outside world falls apart. He could only imagine it with lines, and now he's told there are none. He doesn't understand that the lines were only a transposition of something far more real: three-dimensional objects which do not need lines to demarcate their existence for they do so themselves. The result is that the boy "will get the idea that the real world is somehow less visible than his mother's pictures" when in actuality the real world has no lines "because it is incomparably more visible."[115]

Lewis says this is the situation we face in trying to imagine and therefore hope in heaven. We don't know what we'll be like there, but we'll certainly be more than what we are on earth, not less. Our experiences in this life are like lines drawn in pencil on flat paper. If those experiences disappear from our lives in heaven, they will do so only in the same way that penciled lines would disappear if a picture suddenly became an actual landscape or as the flame of a candle would disappear not because someone snuffed it out but because he raised the shades and "let in the blaze of the risen sun." Lewis then clarifies that pictures do not turn into real places, forming dirt and sprouting

---

reference.
111 *Malcolm*, 70-71. See also the "Transposition" sermon, 277. It is there, in the context of discussing the Incarnation, that Lewis first says the lower can be taken up into the higher.
112 "Transposition," 274.
113 Ibid, 275-76.
114 See *A Grief Observed*, 75-76 for a similar dungeon with a similar theme.
115 "Transposition," 276.

plant life. Instead "real landscapes" enter into pictures.[116] The higher draws the lower up into itself. Understanding this idea of Transposition may then help us recognize the spiritual when it appears in the natural world.

Lewis concludes "Transposition" with the pencil drawing and light. He reminds us that he had previously said that the drawing had only white paper to represent sunlight and clouds. In one sense this is "miserably inadequate!"[117] But in another sense it is perfect. "If the shadows are properly done, that patch of white paper will, in some curious way, be very like blazing sunshine; we shall almost feel cold while we look at the paper snow and almost warm our hands at the paper fire." Likewise, Lewis thinks that there will be no experience of spiritual, transcendent, supernatural things which is so far from our imaginations and feelings that there isn't some earthly counterpart which can be found to correspond appropriately. There may be all manner of earthly transpositions of many heavenly things.

What we have come to is that light reveals earthly things to us, but it may also reveal something of itself or of the light behind all light. By looking along the beam we sometimes encounter opportunities to look at the beam—to see the light of divine, higher reality by being awash in it. It is to light as a symbol of that higher reality that we now turn.

---

116 Ibid, 277.
117 Ibid, 278.

Chapter Eight

Earthly Longing, Heavenly Light

In this chapter my interpretation of "Light" envisions the story as a Christian parable of a man's extreme desire for transcendent *Light*, a desire so strong and a *Light* so great that it is worth dying for. To read Robin's death positively may be a stretch, and not one I commit to completely, but it's a stretch worth taking in order to consider every interpretation of this story which Lewis's pen makes possible.

Concrete Light

"Transposition" offers us a hint that there may be a "thingyness" to light. Yes, I know, "thingyness" is a terrible word, but apart from my penchant for whimsy, I like it better than "weight," "gravity," "thickness," "concreteness," or even my second favorite choice, "palpability." In physical terms light is a *thing*: whether as a particle or a wave, light can be measured. It strikes the earth and heats it up. It burns our skin if we stay out in it or blinds our eyes if we stare at it for too long. But there remains this dilemma—Robin's dilemma—of visibility and invisibility, of light being the thing by which we see but not visible in itself. We have seen hints in Lewis's works that he thought this invisibility might not always be a given, but Robin wants more than just to see Light. He wants to touch it. He wants to "bathe his eyes in it."[1] He wants to "drink it in." He wants solid light. Whether he wants to look at it or experience it or both, it is palpable Light (a light with "thingyness") that he is looking for. Over and over again, Lewis suggests that such light exists.

Let's begin with Robin's hope that it does. The last thing Robin thought of before his operation was what "*Light*" would be like.[2] The italics (underlined in the original) and capital "L" are Lewis's. For Robin, light is an object, one he very much wants to see. That the object is specific, or particular, is clear in Robin's use of an article in paragraph eight when he asks where "*the* light"[3] is.

---

1 "Light," par. 27.
2 Ibid, par. 6.
3 My italics.

Robin is not looking for a universal invisible presence but a specific, palpable thing. This causes Anne to think he must be interested in seeing the source of light in the room they're in, which is merely a lamp with a pink shade.[4] But as their mutual clarification failure continues and Robin learns that the lamp is just a source of light, he continues to demand, "Then where is the light itself?"[5] Not only does he wonder if his operation was a failure, he even begins to wonder if light "was only a fairy tale all along," a hoped for thing which yet turns out to be unreal.

As time passes, Robin can no longer hide from himself "the fact that the visible world was a disappointment."[6] Even more startling is Robin's recognition that he hadn't really wanted to see the visible world "except for the sake of light." This sentence in "Light" does not appear in the MBB version of the story. It's only in this later version that we see Robin's true desire. The description of this desire continues in the same paragraph: unless he could find somewhere among the visible objects of the world "that pure stream [of light] and bathe his eyes in it and drink it in, all the clouds and colours and animals and what Anne called the 'views' were of no account" to him. Robin wants the *thing*, light. He wants to bathe in it. He wants to drink it in.

Robin comes to realize that Light must be far less common than he had been led to believe. Most of the "un-blind"[7] did not know what light was. They only knew of rumors "concerning something which the very few, the great poets and prophets, had really seen and known." Light had to exist somewhere; if not in England, then in "rare deposits" in deserts or mountains in the far East. It's clear from this idea of "deposits" of light that Robin is looking for something concrete, substantial. If he could find it, he would "dive into its very heart, give all himself away to it, drink, drink, drink it till he died drinking."

The transcendent quality of this *Concrete Light* is hinted at both in the earlier reference to the visible world being a disappointment—perhaps because Robin is actually searching for a world beyond the visible—and in the reference to "great poets and prophets" just mentioned. In the left hand pages of the notebook in which MBB is written, Lewis attempted three revisions of this passage.[8] In two of these revisions he mentions some of these poets and prophets: Shelley and Ruskin in Lewis's second revision and Milton in both the second and third. The third revision is the one which most immediately precedes the final version of the passage in "Light." There Lewis writes of Robin doubting the existence of *Light*, but then "Great lines from Milton that

---

4   "Light," par. 21.
5   Ibid, par. 24.
6   Ibid, par. 27.
7   Ibid, par. 28.
8   Which are published for the first time in chapter nine of this book.

he had whispered to himself for years came back to him. They were not about nothing."[9]

Lewis was a great admirer of Milton's having taught him in the 30s[10] and written *A Preface to Paradise Lost*, in the early 40s.[11] In the *Preface*, Lewis writes of Satan's visit to the sun in Book III of Milton's great poem. He notes that Milton's description avoids the "bog of superlatives which is the destination of many bad poets,"[12] while making the description as utterly solar as possible. After summarizing Milton, Lewis says, "This is not, of course, the sun of modern science; but almost everything which the sun had meant to man up till Milton's day has been gathered together and the whole passage in his own phrase, 'runs with potable gold.'" The lines to which Lewis is referring, the lines which he summarizes in the *Preface*, include the following *brilliant* description:

> There lands the Fiend, a spot like which perhaps
> Astronomer in the sun's lucent orb
> Through his glazed optic tube yet never saw.
> The place he found beyond expression bright,
> Compared with aught on earth, metal or stone;
> Not all parts like, but all alike informed
> With radiant light, as glowing iron with fire;
> If metal, part seemed gold, part silver clear;
> If stone, carbuncle most or chrysolite,
> Ruby or topaz, to the twelve that shone
> In Aaron's breastplate, and a stone besides
> Imagined rather oft than elsewhere seen,
> That stone, or like to that which here below
> Philosophers in vain so long have sought,
> In vain, though by their powerful art they bind
> Volatile Hermes, and call up unbound
> In various shapes old Proteus from the sea,
> Drained through a limbec to his native form.
> What wonder then if fields and regions here
> Breathe forth elixir pure, and rivers run
> Potable gold, when with one virtuous touch
> Th' Arch-chemic sun so far from us remote
> Produces with terrestrial humor mixed

---

9   See chapter nine for revision three, paragraph two.
10 Hooper, *Companion & Guide*, 459.
11 Ibid, 461-62.
12 *A Preface to Paradise Lost*, 44.

> Here in the dark so many precious things
> Of color glorious and effect so rare?[13]

These (and more) are the lines Robin read which convinced him of the heavenly, otherworldly power and palpability of light and filled him with a mystical wonder for it.

The reference to "Potable gold" which Lewis quotes in the *Preface* is significant for its connection to the "Light" story and the concept of *drinkable light* or at least *liquid* light which appears several times in Lewis's works. In the third revision in the MBB notebook, Robin can't keep from picturing light as "something like flowing water. It wd. be flowing from somewhere you cd. not see—pure ethereal stream whose fountain who can tell.[14] He wd. slip down & bathe his eyes in it as one bathed one's hands in water."[15] And near the end of "Light" the painter makes clear what both Robin and he are after: "solid light—light you could drink in a cup or swim in!"[16] Robin thinks literally what the painter intends as a metaphor and so dives into *Light* once its existence has been confirmed by another. Unfortunately light lacks the thickness of water, at least in our earthly experience.[17] But what about other-earthly experiences?

Elwin Ransom, the hero of Lewis's first science fiction novel, *Out of the Silent Planet*, is surprised by his experiences of light while journeying in a ship through space. The light is "paler" than any he'd ever seen and "not pure white but the palest of all imaginable golds."[18] He had always thought that space would be "dark and cold." But he finds, instead an "irresistible attraction to the regions of light,"[19] and he spends a great deal of time on the light side of the space ship fulfilling one of Robin's desires: Ransom lies "immersed in a bath of pure ethereal colour and of unrelenting though unwounding brightness" where he feels "his body and mind daily rubbed and scoured and filled with new vitality."[20] He concludes that, far from being empty space, it is the heavens through which he and his shipmates are traveling, an "empyrean ocean of radiance in which they swam."

For Lewis, light is often a metaphor for higher, more concrete realities, especially when he describes light in such realms as a thing very much like

---

13 Milton, *Paradise Lost*, book III, lines 588-612.
14 Here is another connection between Milton and "Light": the last phrase of this sentence quotes, almost word-for-word, *Paradise Lost*, Book III, lines 7-8.
15 Revision three, paragraph one; "wd." and "cd." are ubiquitous Lewis abbreviations for "would" and "could."
16 "Light," par. 33.
17 We would doubtless think differently if we could fly close to the sun.
18 *Out of the Silent Planet*, 31. My thanks to Devin Brown for this reference.
19 Ibid, 33.
20 Ibid, 34.

water. One of the most powerful liquid light metaphors in Lewis's writings appears in *The Voyage of the Dawn Treader*. As the heroes near the eastern edge of the Narnian world, drawing as close as they can to the heavenly world of Aslan's country, they discover that the waters on which they sail have grown sweet. When King Caspian first tastes the water, he notes that he isn't sure that it won't kill him (any sailor would be naturally cautious when testing ocean water), but he adds that he would choose such a death by this water which he describes as "like light more than anything else." Reepicheep agrees: "That is what it is….Drinkable light."[21] Lucy finds the water to be the "loveliest thing I have ever tasted," but so strong that "We shan't need to *eat* anything now."[22] Life-sustaining water of light—Lewis is echoing his favorite gospel: "whoever drinks the water I give him will never thirst. Indeed, the water I give him will become in him a spring of water welling up to eternal life."[23] And for the clear connection between life, water, and light, pair this verse with John 8:12b: "Whoever follows me will never walk in darkness, but will have the light of life."

Christ uses water and light as images of life and water as an image of transformation. Lewis, then, makes water and light images of transformation to new life.[24] In *Dawn Treader*, such transformation occurs in the Narnian heroes as they drink the water from the world's end. First their tolerance of the incredible brightness around them increases.[25] Then they grow able to see things more clearly, even when looking directly at the sun.[26] Every day as they sail further east the light becomes brighter, and they are able to endure its power, neither eating nor sleeping.[27] Daily they draw buckets of the "dazzling water from the sea, stronger than wine and somehow wetter, more liquid, than ordinary water." When they reach the sea of lilies, their eyes have grown to the strength of an eagle's, and so they can bear the sunlight reflected from the white flowers floating on the water's surface.[28] The power of the water and the light is such that eventually Lucy and Caspian say to each other, "I feel that I can't stand much more of this, yet I don't want it to stop."

---

21   *Dawn Treader*, 248.
22   Ibid, 249.
23   John 4:13b-14, *New International Version*.
24   Regarding this theme of transformation, see Lewis's poem, "On a Theme from Nicolas of Cusa," where the human soul partaking of good and truth, the soul's most delightful food, is transformed by them by digesting their light and thus "turning luminous as they" (line 16, *Collected Poems*, 84). See also Lewis's poem, "A Pageant Played in Vain" (*Collected Poems*, 110) and Michael Ward's discussion of it in *Planet Narnia* (103-04).
25   *Dawn Treader*, 249.
26   Ibid, 250.
27   Ibid, 255.
28   Ibid, 258.

Water-like light also appears in *Out of the Silent Planet*, where angels, or eldila, are initially described as creatures which light passes through. Their appearance may sometimes be mistaken for a sunbeam or light passing among moving leaves.[29] Eldila have bodies, but they cannot be seen. This is because bodies have movement, and the manner in which they're perceived depends on the rate at which they're moving.[30] The wise sorn[31] Augray explains that

> The swiftest thing that touches our senses is light. We do not truly see light, we only see slower things lit by it, so that for us light is on the edge—the last thing we know before things become too swift for us. But the body of an *eldil* is a movement swift as light; you may say its body is made of light, but not of that which is light for the *eldil*. His "light" is a swifter movement which for us is nothing at all; and what we call light is for him a thing like water, a visible thing, a thing he can touch and bathe in—even a dark thing when not illumined by the swifter.[32]

Augray continues, saying that the things we consider to be solid—our bodies, the ground we walk on—are for an eldil very thin and hard to see, more like wisps of cloud.[33] While we see eldila as having a "thin, half-real body that can go through walls and rocks," an eldil sees himself as solid and walls and rocks like vapor. "And what is true light to him and fills the heaven, so that he will plunge into the rays of the sun to refresh himself from it, is to us the black nothing in the sky at night." Connections between the eldila and light continue in *Silent Planet*[34] and into its sequels *Perelandra*,[35] and *That Hideous Strength*,[36] but the image of thicknesses among disparate levels of reality carries us into the vision of heaven which Lewis offers in *The Great Divorce*.

Upon arriving in heaven, the narrator of *Divorce* finds to his surprise that the people from the city below, and he along with them, are transparent, in fact completely so when they stand between the narrator and the light of that heavenly world. He says they "were in fact ghosts: man-shaped stains on the brightness of that air."[37] Then the narrator reverses his point of view

---

29 *Silent Planet*, 77. Here we can return to our Milton discussion. In *The Four Loves*, Lewis writes that Milton envisioned "angelic creatures with bodies made of light who can achieve total interpenetration instead of our mere embraces."
30 *Silent Planet*, 94.
31 Sorns or Seroni: one of the three corporeal, sentient species on Mars.
32 *Silent Planet*, 94-95.
33 Ibid, 95.
34 See pages 117-18.
35 For example, pages 16-17.
36 For example, page 320.
37 *Divorce*, 20.

and realizes that the people are all the same as they'd always been, but that it was, instead, "the light, the grass, the trees that were different; made of some different substance, so much solider than things in our country that men were ghosts by comparison."[38] Lewis's Platonic envisioning of heaven is clear. Ours is a world of shadows, this a world of light, where the light, like everything else, is more solid than it is here. Lewis presents us a hierarchy of realities, each more real, more solid than the one below it. In *Silent Planet*, what is light to us is dark liquid to angels who then see a more real *Light* as light in their own perceptions.[39]

In *The Great Divorce*, heaven is so thick, so real, that the ghosts haven't even enough weight to bend the blades of grass beneath their feet. For this reason, to wander around in that place will hurt until a ghost's feet have been hardened, and so one ghost is told that "Reality is harsh to the feet of shadows."[40] The ghosts do not sink in the water of heaven,[41] nor can they lift even an apple from the ground without excruciating effort.[42] As noted previously, on earth, hell is smaller than a pebble for its lack of being and in heaven smaller than an atom. Even ideas in heaven are more solid things. What is known as mere abstraction on earth—the concept of truth, for example—is concrete reality in heaven,[43] representing Barfield's idea of concrete thought. Here we see Lewis offering his solution to the epistemological problem of not being able to experience concrete universals. In heaven we can.

Light is its most solid at the end of *The Great Divorce*: The narrator is turned away from the rising sun. Tree trunks grow bright. "Shadows deepened."[44] The narrator glances briefly over his shoulder at the sunrise and screams, "I am caught by the morning and I am a ghost." Then the light begins to hit him on the head. It is "like solid blocks, intolerable of edge and weight." From this the narrator wakes with a start to find he has fallen out of his bed and pulled some books from his shelf down on his head. Lewis also writes of this light of judgment in "The World's Last Night," admonishing us to ask ourselves how anything we say, do or fail to do

> will look when the irresistible light streams in upon it; that light which is so different from the light of this world—and yet, even now, we know just enough of it to take it into account. Women sometimes have the problem of trying to judge by artificial light how a dress will look by

---

38 Ibid, 21.
39 *Silent Planet*, 94-95.
40 *Divorce*, 39.
41 Ibid, 44.
42 Ibid, 48-49.
43 Ibid, 40.
44 Ibid, 145.

daylight. That is very like the problem of all of us: to dress our souls not for the electric lights of the present world but for the daylight of the next. The good dress is the one that will face that light. For that light will last longer.[45]

The Weight of Plato

There is a connection between the "Light" story and Lewis's use of light as a Platonic metaphor in what I have been calling the "third revision" in the MBB notebook. There Lewis writes, "Sometimes it seemed clear to him [Robin] that light had all along been only a name, an abstract noun wh. the un-blind used to mean nothing in particular." It is after this, as noted above, that Lewis writes of Robin's reaffirmation that what he'd read in Milton could not be about some non-existent thing. But focus on the phrase "abstract noun." It carries us to another Lewis text, one about Plato.

In *Studies in Words*, the chapter on "Life," Lewis writes that "Plato, as everyone remembers, talked as if Justice or Goodness were entities not only as real as particular just acts or good men but incomparably more so. Most emphatically of all, he talked thus about Beauty."[46] But modern man has rejected such concrete universals. "Indeed the whole Platonic position has been judged so hopelessly alien to our mode of thought as to be dismissed with the amusing formula 'Plato thought abstract nouns were proper names.'"[47] But as we have seen in this study, Lewis, following Plato, argues that abstract ideas can become concrete thought in the heavenly realm—that this is even an epistemological goal for human thinking. We've seen Lewis introduce us to the concrete universal of *Truth* in *The Great Divorce*. Here in *Studies in Words*, he continues his discussion on "Life," by using it as a means to rehabilitate modern thinking about Plato's vision. The way many modern writers use the word "life" indicates a continued belief in concrete universals.[48] In an outline for the "Life" chapter in *Studies*, Lewis specifically raises the issue of concrete universals, saying, "an interesting theory is to see whether we can at all recover the presence of mind in which it was possible to imagine say justice as something more than a concept purchased of abstraction for particular just acts: to recover in fact what has been called a Concrete Universal."[49] Lewis says doing so would give us a better understanding of the way ancient and medieval people thought.

Lewis's Platonic vision of nature and supernature, of shadowy lower realities giving way to light-filled higher heavens, is related to light in *Miracles*

---

45 "World's Last Night," 113.
46 *Studies in Words*, 294.
47 Ibid, 295.
48 See *Studies*, 296-300.
49 Bodleian Ms. Dep. d. 810, folio 85.

where Lewis speaks of our ascending with Christ: "When humanity, borne on His shoulders, passes with Him up from the cold dark water into the green warm water and out at last into the sunlight and the air, it also will be bright and coloured."[50] In his fourth Narnia book, *The Silver Chair*, Lewis attacks materialism, rejecting Freudian wish-fulfillment in the story of the Green Lady's attempt to convince the Narnian heroes that there is no other world above the space of her cavernous domain.[51] When she has almost convinced them of this truth, she is set back by Puddleglum's memory of the sun.[52] She retorts that the sun is merely an imagined expansion of a lamp—a product of dreamful wishes.[53] Lewis offers us something of a parable here: the witch is trying to convince the heroes that no world exists other than the one they currently see. We, of course, know better and so can see the ridiculousness of her position. When materialists try to convince us that this world is all there is and no heavenly world above it exists, we should not let the fact that we haven't seen that world deter us from seeing how equally ridiculous the materialist position is. There is a heaven. It's where the sun is, or, more specific to our non-Narnian-cave situation, it's where the *Light* behind the sun is which gives the sun its light. In a Platonic sense we *are* in a cavern (as per Plato's classic "Allegory of the Cave"[54]), but we can see our own sun and so the metaphor must shift a bit. It does so with Lewis in his description of God's glory as the "light from behind the sun" in *Letters to Malcolm*.[55] Here Lewis is quoting Charles Williams whom he had also quoted many years earlier in *Miracles*: "A light that shone from behind the sun; the sun was not so fierce as to pierce where that light could."[56]

We saw in the last chapter how Lewis connects heaven and Plato in *The Last Battle*: the old Narnia is just a shadow of the true Narnia. Digory explains that "It's all in Plato,"[57] and, in a very Platonic description, taking us back to the "Allegory of the Cave," Lewis calls our world "Shadowlands" at the novel's end.[58] All of life here on earth is just the "cover and the title page." The life to come is "Chapter One of the Great Story which no one on earth has read: which goes on forever: in which every chapter is better than the one before."

---

50 *Miracles*, 178.
51 *Silver Chair*, 181-91.
52 Ibid, 185.
53 Ibid, 186-87.
54 In Book Seven of *The Republic*.
55 *Malcolm*, 28.
56 *Miracles*, 143. The quote is from Williams's "The Calling of Taliessin," lines 308-09. Much thanks to several Lewis scholars who replied to my query to "hunt down" this quote: Bruce Edwards, Michael Ward, and Charles Beach.
57 *Last Battle*, 212.
58 Ibid, 228. See also Hebrews 8-9, especially 8:5.

Gems can sometimes be found in the most unlikely places. Lewis's clearest statements about the relationship among light, Plato, heaven, and God occur in some of his most esoteric literary criticism.[59] In *The Allegory of Love*, he specifically says, "the Sun is an image of Good for Plato."[60] He then adds that the sun is an image of God for Spenser, a writer Lewis loved and loved writing about.[61] As for his own opinion, Lewis writes that "God is, or is like, light" not just for any poetic purposes "but for every devotional, philosophical, and theological purpose imaginable within a Christian, or indeed a monotheistic, frame of reference."[62] The use of light to represent God is so perfect as to be "almost dictated…by the shape of the human mind."

It is also shaped by divine revelation: "I am the light of the world" says Christ in John 8:12,[63] and the apostle claims, "God is light; in him there is no darkness at all."[64] C. S. Lewis follows in kind: he describes the "light from behind the sun" in the context of the Incarnation: "The pure light walks the earth; the darkness received into the heart of Deity, is there swallowed up. Where, except in uncreated light, can the darkness be drowned?"[65] God in Christ is a "light from beyond the world."[66] Mythically, He is the true presence of which mythic gods and heroes of old were but shadowy representations.[67] Epistemologically, God is the "divine illumination" which makes it possible for us to know Him,[68] and He is the "Father of lights"[69] who illumined pagan Plato with an understanding of Creation.[70] Morally, God is unchanging Good; He is the "Light which has lightened every man from the beginning" which, though He "may shine more clearly…,cannot change."[71] God is *Light*, and Christians, therefore, can sympathize with Robin's longing for *Light*.

---

59 See Ward, *Planet Narnia*, 101.
60 Lewis, *The Allegory of Love*, 342. Lewis references Plato's *Republic* as the source.
61 See the entries by John Bremer, Anne Gardner, and Marjorie Lamp Mead in *The C. S. Lewis Readers' Encyclopedia*, 382-85. Among other places, Lewis wrote about Spenser in *The Allegory of Love, English Literature in the Sixteenth Century*, and in a lecture series which was edited into the book *Spenser's Images of Life*.
62 "Dante's Similes," 71.
63 *New International Version*.
64 Ibid, 1 John 1:5.
65 *Malcolm*, 71.
66 *Surprised*, 236.
67 "The Grand Miracle," 84.
68 *Four Loves*, 175.
69 Here Lewis is quoting James 1:17. He does so also in "The Language of Religion," (136), where he sees light as a proper metaphor for God.
70 *Reflections on the Psalms*, 69. See also 93 where God is involved in illuminating various pagan creation stories.
71 Ibid, 28.

C. S. Lewis's First and Final Short Story

Longing, Joy and Glory

The fact that throughout Lewis's writings light is a symbol of Platonic concrete universals, of higher realities, and of God invites us to consider its connection to one of Lewis's greatest themes. What has before been missing in a study of the "Light" story, besides the publication of the "Light" version itself, has been any transcription or publication of the three marginal revisions in the "Man Born Blind" notebook. What those revisions show us more clearly—which "Light" alludes to more subtly—is an emphasis on Robin's deep *longing* for *Light*. And while a careful analysis of those passages is reserved for chapters nine and ten, here we can survey Lewis's interrelated concepts of *longing*, *joy* and *glory* in his other works and touch on their relationship to "Light."

Ecclesiastes 3:11 tells us that God "has made everything beautiful in its time. He has also set eternity in the human heart."[72] This "setting" and its association with beauty find voice in Lewis's concept of *Sehnsucht* or *longing*.[73] In *Mere Christianity*, Lewis tells us that creatures do not have desires if such desires can't be satisfied. That babies are born hungry means that food exists somewhere in the world. That ducklings are born wanting to swim means water exists as well. So too, then, with sexual desire and various other pleasures. What then if we find a desire in ourselves which nothing in the world can satisfy? Lewis says, "the most probable explanation is that I was made for another world."[74] The desire within can be satisfied by no earthly pleasures, but not because we're being cheated. Instead it's because those pleasures are meant to wake us up to the thing we really want.

It is, as Lewis says, a thing we've never had:

> All the things that have ever deeply possessed your soul have been but hints of it—tantalising glimpses, promises never quite fulfilled, echoes that died away just as they caught your ear. But if it should really become manifest—if there ever came an echo that did not die away but swelled into the sound itself—you would know it. Beyond all possibility of doubt you would say "Here at last is the thing I was made for."[75]

Lewis admits that the idea is rather sentimental:

> In speaking of this desire for our own far-off country, which we find in ourselves even now, I feel a certain shyness. I am almost committing

---

72 New International Version.
73 Lewis most explores this idea in *The Pilgrim's Regress* (see especially his "Afterword to Third Edition") and *Surprised by Joy*.
74 *Mere Christianity*, 115.
75 *The Problem of Pain*, 146. And see *The Last Battle*, 213 where the unicorn Jewel exclaims, "I have come home at last!"

an indecency. I am trying to rip open the inconsolable secret in each one of you—the secret which hurts so much that you take revenge on it by calling it names like Nostalgia and Romanticism and Adolescence.[76]

We are in fact embarrassed to even speak of the longing because it's a "desire for something that has never actually appeared in our experience."[77] But neither can we hide the desire "because our experience is constantly suggesting it."[78] And so we call it being romantic or being nostalgic or we label it as an aesthetic experience—an experience of beauty—and think we've got a grasp on it. But the happy memories of nostalgia, the romantic feelings for a lover, or the experience of beauty are not the thing we really want; "they are only the scent of a flower we have not found, the echo of a tune we have not heard, news from a country we have never visited."

Lewis experienced this longing for a yet unnamed object throughout his life. He said it was "an unsatisfied desire which is itself more desirable than any other satisfaction. I call it Joy,"[79] and it is something to be distinguished from either "Happiness" or "Pleasure" in that it remains a desire unfulfilled, yet an experience we deeply long to have again.[80] Pleasures might be an indicator of it; they might lead to an experience of the longing called Joy, but in the end all such pleasures ever reveal is that they are not the thing truly being desired.[81]

Lewis calls the idea a romantic one "because inanimate nature and marvellous literature were among the things that evoked it"[82] throughout his early life. Lewis came to understand that the same things did not evoke this experience in other people, but he tries to describe it so that anyone can recognize it:

> The experience is one of intense longing. It is distinguished from other longings by two things. In the first place, though the sense of want is acute and even painful, yet the mere wanting is felt to be somehow a delight. Other desires are felt as pleasures only if satisfaction is expected in the near future; hunger is pleasant only while we know (or believe) that we are soon going to eat. But this desire, even when there is no hope of possible satisfaction, continues to be prized, and even to be preferred to anything else in the world, by those who have once felt it. This hunger is better than any other fullness.

---

76   "The Weight of Glory," 6.
77   Ibid, 6-7.
78   Ibid, 7.
79   *Surprised*, 17-18.
80   Ibid, 18.
81   Ibid, 169-70.
82   *Pilgrim's Regress*, 202.

Lewis even notes that, if the experience of desire disappears for a while, it can in itself become desired.

More peculiar than this experience of desire itself, however, is the mystery of its object. Few people ever understand what the object is. If a child has the experience while he is looking at hills in the distance, he thinks that what he wants is to be there. If it happens in a wonderful memory, he will desire to be back in those better times. Some years later, it may come when he's reading a great adventure story or when he sees a beautiful woman and longs for her, but none of these objects is the thing he truly desires.[83]

So what is it that he, that we, are all longing for? For Robin it is *Light*. It is the thing he would have more than anything else. He only wanted to have his sight so that he might see this thing called *Light* for himself. So that he could drink it, bathe in it, dive into it. The "visible world" becomes a "disappointment to him" because he cannot find his way to *Light*. The thing he most longs for is "nowhere to be found." Great poets like Milton may have spoken about it, but Robin cannot find it. He longs for a thing not of this world—an invisible something which may allow him to see everything else but which he cannot see directly.

Like Reepicheep, Robin is willing to die for *Light* (and he does). Reepicheep describes his longing for the utter East early in *Dawn Treader*, and though he doesn't reference *Light* specifically, his journey along with all the other Narnian heroes in this book is toward the light of the sun and Aslan's country, a journey whose progress is measured by ever increasing light.[84] Reepicheep tells of the song of a Dryad which she sang over him in his cradle: in that place where the water meets the sky and the water has grown sweet, Reep will find all he seeks. It is the "utter East."[85] Her song drives Reep's unflagging desire for the place. He later expresses his commitment to finding it:

> While I can, I sail east in the *Dawn Treader*. When she fails me, I paddle east in my coracle. When she sinks, I shall swim east with my four paws. And when I can swim no longer, if I have not reached Aslan's country, or shot over the edge of the world in some vast cataract, I shall sink with my nose to the sunrise.[86]

Of course Reepicheep doesn't die to get to the world of *Light*, as Robin does, but not for a lack of willingness on his part. How much does this difference matter? Caspian, after all, dies in the very next Narnia book to get to that world, but, having died, he is done with death. Aslan is completely nonchalant

---

83   Ibid, 203.
84   See *Dawn Treader*, chapters 15 and 16.
85   *Dawn Treader*, 22.
86   Ibid, 231.

about the matter of dying. When the children ask if Caspian has indeed died, Aslan says, "Yes," and adds, "Most people have, you know."[87]

As we've seen, Lewis associates the thing longed for with beauty. Amazingly, in his most famous sermon, "The Weight of Glory," he associates both the thing longed for and longed for beauty with *Light*. It should not surprise us that "The Weight of Glory," like "Meditation in a Toolshed," is contemporary with the "Light" manuscript, having been written just a few years before it and first preached in 1941.[88] As seen above, Lewis begins the sermon with longing, that deep desire we are so shy to admit. From there he considers how the promises of heaven might offer the fulfillment of that deepest longing. Of several promises he lists, he focuses most of his attention, indeed most of the sermon, on glory.

For Lewis, glory means two things. First, it means "good report with God, acceptance by God, response, acknowledgement, and welcome into the heart of things."[89] Paul says that those who love God "will be known by Him,"[90] but those who reject God will be rejected by Him: "I never knew you. Depart from me." They will be "both banished from the presence of Him who is present everywhere and erased from the knowledge of Him who knows all."[91] They will be "finally and unspeakably ignored." Lewis talks about being ignored in our own experiences of beauty. In those brief instances when we experience transcendent beauty on earth we find that our truest resulting heartache is not in beauty's subsequent fading away but in the fact that we "have been mere spectators. Beauty has smiled, but not to welcome us: her face was turned in our direction, but not to see us."[92] We have seen the dance but not been accepted into it. We have heard the message, but it doesn't seem meant for us. Beauty has ignored us, and the result is bitter pain.

But Lewis finds the solution to this heartbreaking exclusion in his second definition of glory. Glory means entering into God's beauty. It is imagined in "The Weight of Glory" as being most connected to light.[93] Glory is, at first, an unappealing idea for Lewis.[94] It conjures in his mind the idea of being famous (which leads him to the eternal recognition of God discussed above) and then the idea of "luminosity,"—light is in the very definition of glory—but then "who wishes to become a kind of living electric light bulb?" Quickly, though,

---

87   *Silver Chair*, 253.
88   Hooper, "Introduction," *The Weight of Glory*, xxi.
89   "Weight of Glory," 15.
90   Lewis is quoting I Cor. 8:3.
91   "Glory," 15.
92   Ibid, 14.
93   See also *Silent Planet*, 144 where the sun's intensity causes Ransom to reel back "almost blinded with the glory of that light."
94   "Glory," 11.

Lewis realizes that God's glory is connected to our aesthetic longings—our desire for beauty.[95] In *Miracles*, Lewis recalls from his reading of classical poetry that "brightness appealed to ancient and medieval man" more than it appeals to modern man.[96] He associates light with beauty in his own letters: writing to his friend Mary about a long spell of fog he notes that "One pines for lights and, scarcely less, *shadows*, which make up so much of the beauty of the world."[97] And a month later: "We are having beautiful winter weather at present: bright, pale sunshine (paler than you ever see—Joy [Lewis's wife] calls it the "arctic light"), still air, and just that sprinkling of hoar-frost which makes everything sparkle like sugar."[98] Lewis describes the pleasures of beauty in *Letters to Malcolm* as "shafts of the glory as it strikes our sensibility."[99] Such "pure and spontaneous pleasures are 'patches of Godlight' in the woods of our experience."[100] In his Postscript to *Out of the Silent Planet*, Lewis adds a beautiful description of light which the fictional Ransom had wanted in the book. It is night and the Milky Way rises from behind the mountains more clear than it can ever be seen on earth, "a dazzling necklace of lights brilliant as planets."[101] Then the native Martian hrossa cry out as this belt of beaded light gives way to the rising of Jupiter, forty million miles closer in appearance than ever seen by Terran eyes. The Martian landscape is "bathed in colourless light" as the king of planets rises in a "splendour" far greater than that of Earth's moon.[102]

Beauty has a power which can "build a bridge of light or sound or form"[103] to bring the human soul safely out of the pains of earthly life to encounter a greater light. So writes Lewis in his poem "Dungeon Grates." Then, when this miraculous moment fades, we hold onto our vision of it, and remember that we are not merely mortal and so can bear every trial which life hereafter brings.[104] We can do this because "we have seen the Glory—we have seen."[105]

The artist in *The Great Divorce* wants very much to capture the beauty of the heavenly landscape, a beauty which he first recognized existed in his love for light.[106] On earth he was a successful painter because he had been able to

---

95   Ibid, 16.
96   *Miracles*, 73.
97   25 December 1958; *Letters to an American Lady*, 80.
98   26 January 1959; *Letters to an American Lady*, 81.
99   *Malcolm*, 89.
100 Ibid, 91. My thanks to Peter Schakel for tracking this reference down.
101 *Silent Planet*, 157.
102 Ibid, 158.
103 Lewis, "Dungeon Grates," line 19, *Collected Poems*, 184.
104 Ibid, lines 27-37, *Collected Poems*, 184-5.
105 Ibid, line 40, *Collected Poems*, 185.
106 See *Divorce*, 83-87.

catch "glimpses of Heaven in the earthly landscape" and show it to others in his art.[107] But what started him on his aesthetic endeavors was a love for light: "Light itself was your first love" a heavenly friend reminds him.[108] For Lewis, light is a symbol of beauty,[109] beauty is a revelation of glory, and glory is made, in part, of *Light*.

But Lewis goes even further in "The Weight of Glory." We want so much more than just to "*see* beauty"[110] as wonderful as that is. "We want something else which can hardly be put into words—to be united with the beauty we see, to pass into it, to receive it into ourselves, to bathe in it to become part of it." Lovers of nature understand this desire. They don't want to just look at nature,[111] they "want to absorb it into themselves, to be coloured through and through by it."[112] We will bathe in glory just as Robin wants to bathe in it, just as the angels do in *Out of the Silent Planet*. God will one day "*give* us the Morning Star and cause us to *put on* the splendour of the sun."[113] To put on God's Glory is to put on His *Light*. Heaven is a place where the "Glory flows into everyone, and back from everyone like light and mirrors."[114] In *The Great Divorce*, when the only ghost in heaven who chooses to receive the fullness of Being begins his transformation into a wholly real soul—a person filled with the weight of God's Glory—that transformation is described in terms of light. He grows "brighter."[115] His face shines with what might be tears or what might only be the "liquid love and brightness…which flowed from him."[116] He leaps onto a horse and rides away "like a shooting star," himself "bright," on "into the rose-brightness of that everlasting morning." To be filled with God's Glory is to be filled with *Light*.

That Robin expects *Light* to be palpable, drinkable (like the "liquid light" water at the end of *Dawn Treader*), solid enough to buoy him when he leaps into it from the quarry's lip, is because God's Glory bears the weight—the thickness of Being. Lewis takes this idea of *weight* from Paul in 2 Corinthians 4:17: "For our light affliction, which is but for a moment, worketh for us a far more exceeding and eternal weight of glory."[117] Thus the title of Lewis's

---

107 *Divorce*, 83.
108 Ibid, 84.
109 As well as a beauty in and of itself.
110 "Glory," 16. Lewis's italics.
111 *Four Loves*, 34.
112 Ibid, 35. Lewis notes that, though nature did not teach him that God exists, it gave him a "meaning" for the word "*glory*" (Ibid, 37).
113 "Glory," 16-17.
114 *Divorce*, 86.
115 Ibid, 111.
116 Ibid, 112.
117 *King James Version*. We shouldn't confuse "light" as it is used here (something of little

most famous sermon, "The Weight of Glory" and thus the connections among weight, Being, Glory and *Light* in *The Great Divorce*. When we fill a balloon with air, what is its substance but a thin membrane filled, metaphorically, with nothing? But fill it with water instead (or liquid *Light* as Robin would have it), and it carries a far greater fullness, a literally heavier weight. The ghosts, upon first arriving in heaven, are stretched so thin they can't even bend the grass beneath their feet. They are unreal shadows, "stains on the brightness of that air."[118] But when transformed by being filled with the beautiful *Light* that is Glory, one of them finally becomes the real person he was meant to be.[119]

And so I offer this possible interpretation of the "Light" story, one with a very positive spin: Robin knows from the poets the fullness of being which *Light* really is. This is the palpable *Light* which Robin has been searching for; this is the *Light* we who are sighted cannot see, which Robin as a blind man knew was there. And so he leaps to his death for it, and, if his deepest longings are fulfilled (we do not know the state of his soul in the story), though he does not find it in this life (dying out of ignorance to the blindness that exists in all as part of the fall), he does soon find what he is looking for. Like the man in *The Great Divorce*, he is filled with the full *Light*, the full Being of God's Glory. It must have been the most beautiful thing he ever saw.

Unconclusion

So is this last interpretation of the "Light" story *my* interpretation of it? Would I argue that it's the *best* interpretation of the story? I'm going to go with a definite maybe though acknowledging a slightly but perhaps more equally definite maybe not. While I would *like* to put a positive spin on the story (I'm a sucker for happy endings), I have to acknowledge the reasons for hesitation.

First there is the epistemological emphasis on looking along rather than looking at suggested in such texts as "Meditation in a Toolshed" and "Myth Became Fact," which were written very near the time of "Light" and which therefore suggest the story had the same significance for Lewis in the 40s that it had at the time of the "Great War." Against this, however, I might point out that, just as "Myth" acknowledges the value of experiencing things directly, we might read Robin's dive into the quarry as his attempting a direct experience of *Light*—he doesn't want to look *at* light, he wants to step into it.

Or by contrary argument I might say that "Toolshed" *does* say there is value in looking *at* things. I can even point to two examples in Lewis's writings in which looking *at* something seems to provide a richer experience of it! One instance is in *The Voyage of the Dawn Treader*, which previously gave

---

weight) for the weighty *Light* we've been discussing.
118 *Divorce*, 20.
119 Ibid, 111-12.

us an example of how looking *along* was actually better. Before that encounter at the dark island, however, Lucy, on the island of the Dufflepuds, speaks a spell which makes invisible things visible. One of these things turns out to be Aslan who, though he was there all the time, was only made visible when Lucy spoke the spell. The result of this opportunity to look *at* Aslan is that Lucy's face lights up with radiant beauty.[120]

The second example where looking *at* is advantageous occurs in *Perelandra* when Ransom's conversations with the "Eve" of the planet Venus leads her to think by abstract reason for the first time. She describes the new phenomenon: "I have never done it before—stepping out of life into the Alongside and looking at oneself living as if one were not alive."[121] This is the first time the Queen of Perelandra has participated in abstract thinking separately from any act of learning or knowing she has experienced before. By doing so she has learned something new.[122]

But there is a far more difficult problem to surmount in attempting a positive reading of Robin's death, and it *is* the fact that he just dies—suddenly and to our dismay—and he doesn't merely die but leaps to his death. Lewis is not one to kill off the good guy and then just leave it at that. Aslan dies, but is resurrected in the same book—we see it happen.[123] If you'll pardon the pun, there is no cliff hanger in *The Lion, the Witch and the Wardrobe* as there is with the ending of our cliff leaper, Robin (if we're to take him as having resurrected). Reepicheep, whose longing is as powerful as Robin's (if not more so), reaches Aslan's country, successfully treading the light of dawn, if you will, but without dying.[124] Orual's story comes close to Robin's: each is in search of the beauty, the glory of *Light*. But in *Till We Have Faces*, we see a glimpse of that world of light, and, more importantly, we are given very strong evidence that Orual will reach that country of light in her final vision of herself as Psyche.[125] We could turn the argument somewhat and point out that Lewis does, in the persons of Aslan and Orual, offer characters whose deaths

---

120 *Dawn Treader*, 168-69.

121 *Perelandra*, 52.

122 Even as I offer this interpretation of the scene as a positive example of looking *at*, I see an alternative reading. Her reference to looking at oneself as if "not alive" is ominous, and just before she makes this statement, she finishes a conversation with Ransom on the nature of time by concluding, "I see that you come from a wise world…if this is wise." Is this last statement a questioning of what Ransom has just said about time or what she is about to say regarding abstract reason?

123 *Wardrobe*, 176-78. Aslan's resurrection happens in conjunction with the rising sun.

124 *Dawn Treader*, 266 and *Last Battle*, 220-21. We *do* get something of a cliff hanger in Reep's story since we do not know for certain that he has made it to Aslan's country till *The Last Battle*.

125 Lewis, *Till We Have Faces*, 306-08.

are positive, but the shock, suddenness and subsequent silence surrounding Robin's death pulls us away from such comparisons.

Still, two of Lewis's poems may push us back again. In the context of remembering friends lost through death, Lewis notes in his poem "Scazons" that God made us to be tied to particular things so that in such ties love might be transformed into a type of its universal source in us (recall from "Light" Robin's longing for "the light"[126]—a particular object, not a universal presence). Through such spiritual transformation we ourselves, though we are tiny and particular, come to burn with the same fire as does God, rather than only reflecting that fire. But then comes the poem's last line, stunning if considered in relation to Robin's death: "Gods are we, Thou hast said; and we pay dearly."[127] The poem builds to a vision of climactic transformation through its first nineteen lines—man burning with the flame of God. And then in an isolated final sentence, the poem ends (recalling the first stanza) with the price we dearly pay: the pain of particular death. The bluntness of the poem's finale mirrors that of "Light's."

Then there is the poem "Our Daily Bread" which Lewis wrote before he became a Christian. In this poem he glimpses a far off land and the face of a strange god and, longing to go there, knows that some day he will leave his home behind and go on a long journey as far as to the "last steep edges of the earth / Whence I may leap into that gulf of light"[128] to that place he truly belongs. The poem does not overtly mention death, but it absolutely allows for this reading of the leap into the gulf. It's a strong argument for a positive reading of Robin's leap.

And so is Ransom's attraction to death-by-light at the end of *Out of the Silent Planet*. Having come to believe that space is not a vast emptiness, an "abyss of death," Ransom sometimes feels that the light-filled heavens all around his "egg-shell" of a ship are the truest source of life. If it were to break through the shell, it would almost certainly kill the men riding inside, but "it would kill them by excess of its vitality."[129] He hopes to be killed rather by that than by suffocating within the ship, closed off from that life: "To be let out, to be free, to dissolve into the ocean of eternal noon, seemed to him at certain moments a consummation even more desirable than their return to Earth." Ransom's longing for light to break into the space ship and "unbody" him is not at all far from Robin's dive into light.

In addition, there is the idea of *Light* as a Platonic image—a Transcendent to be longed for. "Toolshed" seems closest to the content of "Light" on first

---

126 Par. 8.
127 "Scazons," line 20, *Collected Poems*, 132.
128 "Our Daily Bread," lines 17-18, *Collected Poems*, 213.
129 *Silent Planet*, 145. My thanks to Devin Brown for this reference.

review, but "Transposition" is much closer to "Light" in time of writing and, in using light as a metaphor for the appearance of supernature in the natural world, therefore makes light a metaphor for the heavenly, Platonic world of *Light*. To long for that world is to long to be released from prison, like the imprisoned artist in "Transposition" who wants her son to see the real world. Consider how the dwarfs in *The Last Battle* choose darkness rather than light. Where the heroes of Narnia tell them that there is light all around, the dwarfs choose to see only darkness.[130] In contrast to the woman in "Transposition," the dwarfs, by their own choice, create a dark prison of their own minds where they will forever remain.[131] Perhaps we should not, then, fault Robin for wanting to leap into *Light*. As we'll see in chapter nine, the endings of MBB and "Light" vary slightly. The former ends with "some rattling of loosened stones." But "Light" ends with "the momentary rattling of a dislodged stone." Might the difference be that Lewis intends in the revision an allusion to the stone rolled away at the moment of Christ's resurrection? Perhaps Robin leaps to his death to merely rise a moment later in new life and bathe in *Light*.

But even here I'm forced to consider the alternative, more negative, reading of "Light" because of Robin's attitude toward that great Platonic image, the sun. We've seen that the sun is an image for Plato of good, and that it is an image of God throughout history including for C. S. Lewis. But Robin seems to reject it. As the sun rises, Robin's "shadow lay before him, each moment blacker and more distinct. That violent yellow thing, the sun, which one could never see properly, stared at him on his left hand. He pulled the brim of his hat lower over his eyes, blinking. 'If only I could see any light!'"[132] Wanting to see "Light," Robin hides himself from the sun! And this suggests he is too much bent on looking *at* light rather than on experiencing it.

Let's consider again the ending of *The Great Divorce*, when the narrator is caught in the sunrise and light comes crashing down on him in blocks. The passage echoes "Light" in the description of shadows: "Shadows deepened"[133] in *Divorce* echoes the "blacker more distinct" shadows described above in "Light." Now does the narrator's terror arise because of his dread of "Light" or because he simply wasn't yet prepared for the full force of its power? If this is the only reason Robin shies away from the sun, it would not demand a negative interpretation of his story: searching for light, he naively does not know the dread intensity of the real *Light* for which he is searching. But I'm not convinced that this interpretation can stand. In looking away from the sun, Robin turns to a cheap substitute, and it costs him his life. Whether it is from

---

130 *Last Battle*, 180-83.
131 Ibid, 185-86.
132 "Light," par. 29.
133 *Divorce*, 145.

a demand to look *at* light, or mere naivety about its nature, Robin's choice, as evidenced by his turning from the sun, seems to be the wrong one. Can it be viewed otherwise?

Well consider this: Lewis says that, for medieval man, the sun "produces fortunate events."[134] For Robin it produces misfortune unless we read his death as a transition into new life. Or perhaps Robin turns from the sun because, following Lewis's other sun metaphor, he knows that what he really wants is the light that shines from behind the sun. Robin is looking for the higher Platonic *Light* which is ultimately found in God. You can see why I call this section "Unconclusion." Lewis gives me so many puzzle pieces with which to read his story.

All of these heavenly connections to light do at least open up a door (or roll away a stone) of possibility. I especially think this true considering the date of the "Light" manuscript. I don't doubt Owen Barfield's claim that the story was written by Lewis sometime around the "Great War," but two facts—that the story was recorded twice in the mid 1940s and that Lewis used light metaphors in connection to heaven and longing—give us enough reason to consider multiple interpretations. Barfield once said, "Somehow what Lewis thought about everything was secretly present in what he said about anything."[135] Maybe, then, there's more to "Light" than any single interpretation would allow, whether philosophical or theological, pre-conversion or post.

Lewis's artist in *The Great Divorce* has made the mistake of thinking he should paint to capture light (and for fame). He is like the artist in "Light" trying to "catch" light. But he is also reminded that his love for painting began with his love of light: "Light itself was your first love: you loved paint only as a means of telling about light."[136] There's nothing negative in this description. The artist's love for light is born of his desire for heaven—that's what made his painting so good: he was able to catch heavenly glimpses in his earthly paintings.[137] Again, the image is completely positive. Perhaps he represents two kinds of longing as seen in Robin and the painter in "Light," the first good, the latter bad. But my real point is that perhaps Lewis sees ambiguities in his "Light" story. Perhaps he sees an old meaning (the one intended by a younger Lewis in a story written for his friend in which Robin's death is a terrible thing) and a new meaning (one perceived by an older Christian Lewis who is looking at light both epistemologically and Platonically and so sees Robin's death as a transition into joy). Perhaps it's even a little of both. We do

---

134 In *The Discarded Image*, 106. Thanks again to Michael Ward for so many excellent solar references.
135 In his "Preface" to *The Taste of the Pineapple*, 2.
136 *Divorce*, 84.
137 Ibid., 83.

not know the state of Robin's soul when he dies. And so perhaps he does leap into the light for the wrong reason, but perhaps he awakens to *Light* on the other side of that leap just the same.

If I truly wanted to press the issue in favor of a positive reading of Robin's death—the choice to leap as well as the resulting rebirth—I might make an argument I don't intend to make. I offer it here because if I don't someone else will. In chapter four we looked at the mystery of Owen Barfield's claim about the date of the story versus the evidence that the extant versions were written in the 40s. I could likely eliminate the more negative interpretations of "Light" we covered in chapter five by simply arguing that Barfield was wrong. He did not first record his claim that the story was written in the late 20s until 1965, more than three decades after the fact, and no version of the story written either in the late 20s or early 30s exists. Perhaps Barfield simply remembered wrong. But if he did, he did so consistently for another three decades, plus! His testimony about when the story was written never wavered. And, as we saw in chapter four, Walter Hooper offers an effective explanation for the existence of later versions of the text in the form of a C. S. Lewis who loved to return to, and rewrite, material he'd worked on in the past.

I'm not convinced that Barfield's memory failed him. In fact, I rather like the mystery of the many interpretations of "Light" we've covered here, and so I do *not* conclude by siding with a single interpretation of the story. I hope I've laid a foundation so that other critics can come after me and offer more definitive answers to the interpretation of "Light." Otherwise, this is my only conclusion—the thesis if you will—of this book: "Light" is C. S. Lewis's most mysterious story and manuscript. In this I welcome others to try and prove me wrong.

One portion of this exploration yet remains—one more approach we can take which may tell us more about the mysterious meaning of "Light." Together, "The Man Born Blind," the revisions in the MBB notebook, and "Light" provide an interconnected history of the progress of a story—of Lewis's creative process as a writer. As we turn to a parallel examination of the manuscripts themselves, we will find that each individually and all together reveal even more about Lewis's first and final short story.

PART FOUR

Light by Letters and Lines

C. S. Lewis once described the importance of the Incarnation by comparing it to a lost manuscript: "Let us suppose we possess parts of a novel or a symphony. Someone now brings us a newly discovered piece of the manuscript and says, 'This is the missing part of the work. This is the chapter on which the whole plot of the novel really turned.'"[1] Here we have an opportunity to look at the new manuscript, the new piece of the puzzle which, especially when viewed side-by-side with its earlier version, shows us what the whole story of Robin, the man born blind, is really about.

The annotated manuscripts of MBB and "Light" follow with the marginal revisions appearing in their parallel positions midway through the story. Keep in mind that, though the revisions will appear on right facing pages next to MBB and "Light," they belong chronologically *between* MBB and "Light" as revisions written after MBB that led Lewis toward the final version of the story in "Light." Gaps between paragraphs and occasionally even sentences within paragraphs are not in the original manuscripts. I added them to maintain the parallel development among the various versions.

For a more formal and extended description of the MBB and "Light" manuscripts, see the Appendix. Here in Part Four, I have chosen less formal vocabulary for the sake of readability, and readers will want to be aware of a few points regarding pagination: The "Light" manuscript consists of four loose leaves which I refer to simply by number, thus "page one." The seven leaves of the MBB story are bound in a notebook. The story does not begin until folio (page) 22 of the notebook; however, I have chosen to reference these pages as if referring to a single manuscript. Rather than calling the story's first page "folio 22," I refer to it as "page one," and will do so through "page seven." The MBB story is written on the *recto*, or right hand, pages within the notebook. The *verso*, or left hand, pages are blank except for those opposite pages four (the *verso* side of page three), five (*verso* of four) and seven (*verso* of six). These contain the previously mentioned three revisions to a portion of the story. I refer to these revision pages in a manner like this: "the left hand page, opposite from page four."

---

1   *Miracles*, 145.

Chapter Nine

The Complete Parallel Light Stories

> Light
>
> From: C. S. Lewis,
> Magdalen College,
> Oxford
>
> 'Bless us!' said Anne, 'There's eleven o'clock. And you're nearly asleep, Robin.' She rose with a bustle of familiar noises, bundling her spools, and her little cardboard boxes into the work-basket. 'Come on, lazy-bones,' she added. 'You want to be nice and fresh for your first walk to-morrow.'
>
> 'That reminds me,' said Robin and then stopped. He had approached the subject three times already since his operation, once to the doctor, once to the nurse, and once before to Anne herself, and each time something seemed to have gone wrong. Now, he felt unreasonably nervous. 'I—I suppose,' he mumbled, 'there'll be lots of light out there— when we go for that walk?'
>
> 'You mean it will be lighter out of doors? Well, yes, of course. But I must say I always think this is a very light house. This room, now. We've had the sun on it all afternoon.'
>
> 'The sun makes it hot—?' said Robin tentatively.
>
> 'What are you talking about?' said Anne. That was what Robin couldn't understand; why they all sounded so angry or frightened whenever he got near the real question. It was as if they thought he was mad.
>
> 'I mean,' he said '— well, look here, dear. I've been wanting to ask you something ever since I got back from the nursing home. I expect it'll sound silly to you. But things must be different to a chap who's been blind all his life, mustn't they? It's all so new. As soon as I heard there was a chance of getting my sight— well, I looked forward. The last thing I thought of before the operation was light. Wondering what it would be like. Then all those days afterwards before they took the bandages off; wondering, waiting...'
>
> 'But of course, darling. That was only natural.'
>
> 'Then... then' (his voice shook a little) 'why don't I... I mean, where is the light?'

The First Page of the Light manuscript

C. S. Lewis's First and Final Short Story

[The Man Born Blind][1]

²'Bless us!,'³ said Mary, 'There's eleven o'clock. And you're nearly asleep, Robin.' She rose with a bustle of familiar noises, bundling her spools and her little cardboard boxes into the work basket. 'Come on, lazy-bones!,' she said. 'You want to be nice and fresh for your first walk to-morrow.'

'That reminds me,' said Robin and then stopped. His heart was beating so loudly that he was afraid it would make his voice sound odd. He had to wait before he went on.

<u>Light</u>

From C. S. Lewis, Magdalen College, Oxford.

'Bless us!' said Anne, 'There's eleven o'clock. And you're nearly asleep, Robin.' She rose with a bustle of familar noises, bundling[4] her spools and[5] her little cardboard boxes into the work basket. 'Come on, lazy-bones,' she added. 'You want to be nice and fresh for your first walk to-morrow.'

'That reminds me,' said Robin and then stopped. He had approached the subject three times already since his operation, once to the doctor, once to the nurse, and once before to Anne herself, and each time something seemed to have gone wrong. Now, he

---

1   This is the title given to the untitled notebook version of the story by Walter Hooper. It does not appear in the original text. "The Man Born Blind" was originally published in *Church Times*, No 5947 (4 February 1977), followed in the same year by *The Dark Tower and Other Stories*, ed. Walter Hooper. San Diego: Harcourt Brace, 1977, pages 99-103. Houghton Mifflin Harcourt graciously gave permission, *gratis*, for the publication of "The Man Born Blind" in this book: "The Man Born Blind" from THE DARK TOWER AND OTHER STORIES by C. S. Lewis. Copyright © 1977 by C. S. Lewis PTE Ltd. Used by permission of Houghton Mifflin Harcourt Publishing Company. All rights reserved.
2   While this transcription of MBB consulted Walter Hooper's published transcription of the text, it has been produced from the original MBB manuscript. Thus, it returns italics to their original underlines and restores any changes made out of editorial need. Even mistakes/omissions have been transcribed as per the original manuscript (ms).
3   Exclamation mark, comma, closed-single-quotation, (e.g. !,')—I've transcribed these and other seeming awkward punctuations exactly as they appear in the manuscripts.
4   The word "bundling" here is written in above a word which has been crossed out with a circular motion of the pen. Below the crossed out word are two arrows intended as editor's 'insert' marks. Most of Lewis's corrections in both manuscripts are made this way, though usually with a single editor's arrow. In this instance, the word crossed out is either a misspelling or an unclear (less legible) writing of "bundling" which Lewis wanted to correct or make legible (perhaps at the moment of the mistake). "Bundling" is the word which appears in "The Man Born Blind." Nowhere else in the "Light" manuscript (with one exception) does Lewis make a mistake or want to change a word and write the correction to the right of a crossed out word; it's always above, except for the last two words of the manuscript which are crossed out and rewritten, again, probably for legibility.
5   The word "and" is inserted above and between "spools" and "her" with an 'insert' arrow below the line, perhaps forgotten as Lewis was transcribing this paragraph from the MBB notebook.

Light

MBB	Light
'I suppose,'[6] he said[7] 'there[8]—[9]there'll be light[11] out there—when I go for that walk?'	'I felt unreasonably nervous. 'I—I suppose,' he mumbled, 'there'll[10] be lots of light out there—when we go for that walk.'[12]
'What do you mean, dear?', said Mary. 'You mean it will be lighter out of doors? Well, yes, I suppose it will.	'You mean it will be lighter out of doors? Well, yes, of course.

6   At the end of a line of dialog, Lewis generally follows punctuation marks with a closing single quotation mark throughout the ms (e.g.: .'). Every so often, however, the end quote is almost perfectly on top of the punctuation (as almost happens here) or even behind it (the punctuation being either a comma or a period). I take this as the random product of writing out a text by hand and, in the case of the "Light" ms, Lewis's being not too terribly worried about a typist's ability to transcribe his text according to an established form. I have therefore made the decision in this transcription to make end quotes appear after punctuation marks when they do so in the text or when they line up on top of each other, but to render the "mistake" of putting quote marks before a comma or period where Lewis did so in the manuscripts.
7   The comma needed here appears in Hooper's 1977 published "Man Born Blind." Lewis left it out.
8   Sometimes Lewis's 't's' when appearing with an 'h' appear to be capital 'T's.' In his teens and twenties, Lewis wrote lower case 't's' which look similar to these 'th' 't's.' Examples appear elsewhere in which context indicates a lower case 't.'
9   Lewis's dashes and ellipses present a challenge. Instances which appear from context to be dashes are written as two or three short lines (sometimes looking like periods) or one long line along the bottom of a line of text. If Lewis intends an ellipsis, however, he doesn't use anything different. Nor is he consistent between MBB and "Light" (for example, the sentence, "The sun makes it hot—?" in MBB uses three short lines [which could be periods] for its dash [or ellipsis] while "Light" uses two short lines which are clearly not periods). Rather than guessing from context, I've committed to dashes whenever I see two or three dots or dashes or a mix of them, as well as when Lewis draws a single long line, clearly indicating a dash. I am, therefore, excluding ellipses. In the current instance, there are two lines though one of them is barely more than a period.
10   Here another example of a 'th' in which Lewis's minuscule 't' looks like a capital.
11   Lewis underlined words which he wanted printed in italics (see for example, the sentence a few lines below in the text: 'What *are* you talking about?'—the original in both MBB and "Light" is underlined). Hooper italicized such underlined words in his transcription of MBB, and I follow his lead in chapter one of this book. While researching at the Wade Center, I noticed a few examples in comparing unpublished originals to published texts. In the typed manuscript of *The Screwtape Letters* (Wade Ms CSL/MS-107), the words "naïf" and "argument" (on page 13, the first paragraph of the first Screwtape letter), are underlined. I checked these against a second edition of the book which was released only a month after the first edition, and the words are italicized there as well. Additionally, the handwritten preface to *Screwtape* which Lewis sent to the publisher along with the typed manuscript contains a reference to Lewis's book *Out of the Silent Planet* (this reference was dropped from the published version). The title of Lewis's book is underlined as well. There's no doubt that he intended underlining to reference the need for italics. In this chapter, however, since the purpose of the presentation is to transcribe the manuscripts, I have left all words underlined.

C. S. Lewis's First and Final Short Story

MBB	Light
But I must say I always think this is a very light house. This room, now. We've had the sun on it all day'.	But I must say I always think this is a very light house. This room, now. We've had the sun on it all afternoon.'
'The sun makes it hot...?' said Robin tentatively.	'The sun makes it hot—?', said Robin tentatively.
'What <u>are</u> you talking about?', said Mary suddenly turning round. She spoke sharply, in what Robin called her governess voice.	'What <u>are</u> you talking about?' said Anne.[13] That was what Robin couldn't understand; why they all sounded so angry or frightened whenever he got near the real question. It was as if they thought he was mad.
'I mean,' said Robin—'Well, look here, Mary. There's a thing I've been meaning to ask you ever since I came back from the nursing home. I know it'll sound silly to you. But then it's different for me. As soon as I knew I had a chance of getting my sight, of course I looked forward. The last thing I thought before the operation was "Light".	'I mean', he said '—well, look here, dear. I've been wanting to ask you something[14] ever since I got back from the nursing home. I expect it'll sound silly to you. But things must be different to a chap who's been blind all his life, mustn't they? It's all so new. As soon as I heard there was a chance of getting my sight—well, I looked forward. The last thing I thought of before the operation[15] was <u>Light</u>.[16]

12   Instead of a question mark ending this sentence, it may be a period. If it's a question mark, Lewis forgot to close the quotation. The problem is that Lewis's question marks look like his single 'close-quotation' mark—a tiny, reversed and elevated "c" with a period beneath it. So, again, either Lewis forgot to close the quotation after the question mark or forgot to use a question mark, using a period with a closed quotation instead. Context leans toward a question mark, and the parallel sentence in MBB uses a question mark, but the high position of the "reverse c," especially when compared to other question marks in the ms, suggests a period and a closed quotation mark.

13   The word "Anne," here, is inserted above the crossed out word "Mary" which is Anne's name in the MBB ms. This is some of the clearest proof that "Light" is a revision from the earlier "Man Born Blind" ms.

14   Whenever Lewis splits a word between lines as he runs out of room at the end of a line on a page, he uses two hyphens to indicate the split, one at the end of the first part of the word, in this case, "some-" and the other at the beginning of the rest of the word on the next line, thus, "-thing."

15   The word "operation" is inserted above the line (with an 'insert' arrow) over what appears to be a crossed out attempt to begin to spell the word "chance." The letters "chan" are crossed out with two lines. Perhaps, as Lewis was copying this portion of "Light" from the MBB ms and looking back and forth between them, he turned his glance from "Light" and looked up and slightly to the left of the line he'd been on in the MBB ms and saw the word "chance" and started to write it, thinking that was where he had left off.

Light

MBB	Light
Then all those days afterwards, waiting till they took the bandages off—'	Wondering what it would be like. Then all those days afterwards before they took the bandages off; wondering, waiting—'
'Of[17] course, darling. That was only natural'[18]	'But of course, darling. That was only natural'
'Then, then, why don't I—I mean, where is the light?'	'Then—then' (his voice shook a little) 'why don't I—. I mean, where is the light?'
She laid her hand on his arm. Three[19] weeks of sight had not yet taught him to read the expression of a face, but he knew by her touch the great warm wave of stupid, frightened affection that had[21] welled up in her.	His three weeks of sight had not yet taught him to read the expression of her face, but he knew by her voice the warm wave of muddled,[20] frightened affection that had swelled up in her as she said 'Why not go to bed now, dearest? We can talk about all that in the morning. You know you're tired now'
'Why not come to bed, Robin dear?,' she said. 'If it's anything important,[22] can't we talk about it in the morning.[23] You know you're tired now'.	
'No. I've got to have this out. You've got to tell me about Light.	'No,' he said. 'I've got to have this out. You've got to tell me.

---

16   Lewis's cursive letter "L's" in the minuscule slant a bit to the right and curve at the bottom into the next letter. The "L" in "Light" here looks more like the capital "L" in the title: instead of curving at the bottom, the transition from vertical line to horizontal line is sharp and almost at a right angle. I found no other "L's" in the text like this except for the capital "L" in the title. In the parallel MBB passage, Lewis clearly capitalizes the word "Light" and puts double quotation marks around it. Here he underlines it for emphasis as well as capitalizing it. I'm convinced he intends to emphasize the word as something of a proper noun, probably along the level of a Platonic Ideal.
17   In size, Lewis's "o" appears to be lower case. This happens elsewhere. I take it as upper case.
18   The period at the end of this sentence is missing from the original. The first page of the MBB notebook ms ends here.
19   After the word "Three," Lewis wrote the word "weaks" and then crossed it out with a single line and wrote the correct "weeks."
20   The comma here is definitely a comma, but it looks more like a period. There is the barest hint of a hook (to the right rather than the normal left).
21   The word "had," here is written above the line between "that" and "welled" with an editor's insert arrow below the line and between the words to indicate the insertion.
22   This word is split at the end of a line with Lewis's typical hyphen system, thus "im-" on one line and "-portant" on the next.
23   There is a very faint period here where Lewis should have used a question mark.

C. S. Lewis's First and Final Short Story

MBB	Light
Great Scot—don't you <u>want</u> me to know?'	Great Scot, don't you <u>want</u> me to know?'[24]
She sat down suddenly with a formal calmness that alarmed him.	
'Very well,[25] Robin,' she said. 'Just ask me anything you like. There's nothing to be worried about—is there?'	'Know about what, Robin? Ask me anything you like. But there's nothing to worry about. Your sight is perfectly alright now. You're cured'
'Well then, first of all, there's light in this room at present?'	'Very well, then. Is there light in this room at present?'
'Of course there is'	'Of[26] course there is. Robin, do—'
'Then where is it?'	'Then where is it?'
'Why, all round us'	'Why, all round us.'
'Can you see it?'	'Can you see it?'
'Yes'	'Yes. But really, Robin dear—'
'Then why can't I?'	'Then why can't I?'
'But,[27] Robin, you can. Dear, do be sensible. You can see me, can't you, and the mantlepiece,[29] and the table and everything.'	'But, Robin, you can. You can see me, can't you?, and the mantlepiece,[28] and the table, and—'
	'That's what drives me mad. That's the sort of thing you all say. I want to see <u>light</u>. Are <u>you</u> light? Is the mantlepiece[32] light? Is light only another name for all the other things?'
'Are those light? Is that all it means? Are you light? Is the[30] mantlepiece[31] light? Is the table light?'	
'Oh! I see. No. Of course not. <u>That's</u> the light'—and she pointed to the bulb, roofed with its broad pink shade, that hung from the ceiling.	'Oh, I see what you mean. You're asking about <u>the</u> light. That's it there, hanging[33] from the ceiling with the pink shade.'

---

24   Page one of the "Light" manuscript ends here.
25   There's an elevated mark above and to the right of the comma here which is almost certainly a single quotation mark scribbled out.
26   As per previous insertions, "Of" appears above the crossed out phrase, "Why of" (as in "Why of course there is").
27   The comma here is only a little more than a dot on the page in MBB, but its counterpart in "Light" is definitely a comma.
28   *Sic.*
29   *Sic.*
30   Page two of the MBB ms ends here.
31   *Sic.*
32   *Sic.*
33   The word "hanging" is split between two lines.

Light

| MBB | Light |

'If that's light, why did you tell me the light was all round us?'

'I mean, that's what gives the light. The light comes from there.'

'Then where is the light itself? You see, you won't say. Nobody will say. You tell me the light is here and the light is there, and this is in the light and that is in the light, and yesterday you told me I was in your light, and now you say that light is a bit of yellow wire in a glass bulb hanging from the ceiling. Call that light? Is that what Milton was talking about? What are you crying about? If you don't know what light is, why can't you say so?

If the operation has been a failure and I can't see properly after all, tell me. If there's no such thing—if it was all a fairy tale from the beginning[34]—tell me. But for God's sake—

'Robin! Robin! Don't. Don't go on like that'

'Going[35] on like what?' Then he gave it up and apologised and comforted her and they went to bed.

A blind man has few friends;[36] a blind man who has recently received[37] his sight has, in a sense, none. He belongs neither to the world of the blind nor to that of the seeing and no one can share his[38] experiences. After

'Then why did you tell me the light was all round us?'

'Darling, I mean that's what gives the light. The light comes from there.'

'Then where is the light itself? You see, you won't say. Nobody will say. You tell me there's light here and light there, and this is in the light and that is in the light, and people get in one another's light. But you won't point me out the light itself.

If none of you know what light is, say so. If there's no such thing—if it was only a fairy tale all along—say so. If the operation was a failure and I still can't see what other people see, tell me. I can take that. It's this secrecy that I can't stand. You're all like conspirators. Why the devil—'

Anne began to cry and Robin apologised and comforted her. Then they went to bed.

This conversation made him more cautious. Clearly it was never going to be any use asking about light. Either there was no such thing or else he was all the time making some appalling mistake.

---

34   Lewis first wrote a comma in the manuscript here and then replaced it with a dash.
35   *Sic*.
36   This might be a colon, but looking at the original manuscript I noticed the slightest hook in the lower "dot," something I've seen in Lewis's commas before.
37   The word "received" is split between two lines in the same manner as described before, this split occurring between the "receiv-" and the "-ed."
38   After the word "his," Lewis writes the letters "diff" which are then crossed out with two lines. Lewis was probably going to write the word "difficulties" and decided on "experiences"

C. S. Lewis's First and Final Short Story

MBB

that night's conversation Robin never mentioned to[39] anyone his problem about light. He knew that he would only be suspected[41] of madness. When Mary[42] took him out next day for his first walk he replied to everything she said, 'It's lovely—all lovely. Just let me drink it in,' and she was satisfied. She interpreted his quick glances as glances of delight. In reality, of course, he was searching, searching with a hunger that had already something of desperation in it. Even had he dared, he knew it would be useless to ask her of any of the objects he saw 'Is that Light?' He could see for himself that she would only answer 'No. That's green—or blue—or yellow—or a field—or a tree —or a car.'[44] Nothing could be done until he had learned to go for walks by himself.

Light

If he was not careful he'd find himself[40] in the hands of doctors again—psychotherapists, as likely as not. When Anne took him out for his walk next day he was on his guard. He kept on saying 'It's lovely. All lovely. Just let me drink it in,' and that satisfied[43] her.

And he knew enough now to know that none of the things he saw could possibly be light. They were, as Anne volubly explained to him, only fields or cows or grass or the sun or trees or a quarry.

Nothing could be attempted until he was able to go for walks on his own.

---

instead. The latter suggests both the positives and the negatives of a blind man receiving sight (and so better fits the context of the passage) while the former emphasizes only the negatives.

39 Page three of the MBB ms ends here.
40 The word "himself" is split between two lines.
41 The word "suspected" is split between lines at the "s" and "p."
42 While Lewis changes the wife's name from Mary to Anne between MBB and "Light," here he apparently had another name in his head: the word "Jane" is crossed out with two lines and "Mary" written above it. An editor's insert arrow appears between the "a" and "n" of "Jane" with the point touching the cursive connecting line between them. Of course the character of "Jane" appears later in the MBB notebook (page 69) in a fragment that appears to be a first draft introduction of Jane Studdock in *That Hideous Strength*. I say first draft because in the MBB notebook she's called Jane Ruddock and her husband is named Peter rather than Mark. It's a bit of a stretch to say that this might be another proof that MBB was written in the 40s (when *Hideous* was written), but it's not a stretch I'm unwilling to make.
43 The word "satisfied" is split between pages two and three of "Light" with the same use of hyphens as is typical of Lewis.
44 Apart from the title, Walter Hooper made the most extensive editorial changes to this sentence in the published version of MBB, all having to do with punctuation, not content. Hooper's editorial work is faithful to the text while improving its readability and grammar.

Light

MBB	Light

45   This first revision is on the left hand page, opposite from page four of the MBB story, parallel to the paragraph that begins, "About five weeks later...."

46   This second revision begins at the top of the left hand page, opposite page five of the MBB story. It is a second attempt at revising the same material Lewis tried to rewrite in Revision One. This second revision follows naturally from the paragraph preceding the one being targeted for revision on page four. That preceding paragraph ends, "Nothing could be done until he had learned to go for walks by himself." The next paragraph in the original then begins, "About five weeks later...." In the first revision of that paragraph, the one opposite page four, Lewis wrote, "It was about six weeks later that he went out alone." But now take the ending of the previous paragraph with the beginning of the second revision, the one opposite page five: "Nothing could be done until he had learned to go for walks by himself. [par] It was about 6 weeks later that he did so." I argue that Lewis was not happy with the paragraph in the notebook (beginning on page four) which focuses on Robin's difficulty with transitioning from a life of blindness to a life of sight. He tried reworking it three times, but he was not satisfied for reasons I'll explain later and so almost completely deleted it from the "Light" version of the story.

47   The third revision is the last one in the notebook. Where the first two revisions are written opposite pages four and five in the MBB notebook, this one is *not* written on the opposite page from page six. Nevertheless, it appears to be Lewis's final attempt at rewriting the same paragraph he has tried to rewrite in the previous two revisions. This one is written opposite of page seven of MBB which is the last page of the story, but it does not fit the content of that final page in any way. The third revision consists of two paragraphs. The second paragraph begins, "About 6 weeks passed before he did so." This sentence alone places this paragraph in the same position in the story as the previous two attempts at revision. The paragraph above it however, parallels content in the "Light" ms which comes after the "six weeks" sentence. This acts as additional proof that each revision as it appears in the MBB notebook, was written after its predecessor, representing a progression of attempts by Lewis to rework a single section of the story. He tried it several ways, the end result—in "Light"—being the most abbreviated version of all.

C. S. Lewis's First and Final Short Story

MBB Revision One[45]	MBB Revision Two[46]	MBB Revision Three[47]
		He never doubted that if he did find light he would know it. He could not help picturing it as something like flowing water. It wd.[48] be flowing from somewhere you cd. not see—pure ethereal stream whose fountain who can tell.[49] He wd. slip down[50] & bathe his eyes in it as one[51] bathed ones hands in water. What tormented him was the

48   A favorite Lewis abbreviation is "wd." which stands for "would."
49   This word gave me a little trouble. Lewis's "t's" are often not so much crossed as merely marked with a dot to the right of the vertical line. Thus "tell" might look like "till" or "lift" (without the final "t" crossed) or even "life" in this instance. The phrase, "pure ethereal stream whose fountain who can tell" is an almost perfect rendering of *Paradise Lost*, Book III, lines 7-8, and a final proof that "tell" is the correct transcription here. Lewis did not end the sentence with a question mark.
50   One of the most difficult phrases to transcribe in this revision is "wd. slip down." I'm fairly comfortable with "wd." though it could be the word "and" with a stray dot appearing a bit further from it than where Lewis normally puts his periods. The word "down" looks like it could just as well be "door" or "clan" or "clear" with "down" being chosen as best fitting the context. But the hardest word is "slip." It looks far more like a five letter "sling" than a four letter "slip." I suppose Lewis might have meant to write "sling himself down" and left out the pronoun. "Slide down" would work well in the total sentence, but the final letter looks too much like a "p" or a "g." And then, once again, I'm faced with the problem of Lewis's dotted "t's." What if, instead of an "l" next to a dotted "i" in "sling," the dot actually indicates the crossing of a "t." In this case the options (such as "sting") make even less sense. The opening "s" might not even be an "s" but an "r," though probably not. If I grant myself the "s" and "l" at the beginning of the word, however, it looks like an "s-l-i-smudge-space-p." After the smudge there's a break in the cursive line and the "p" stands slightly disconnected from the rest of the word. In the end, "slip" is just my best guess.
51   The word "one" could be the word "we" but there's no first person narration anywhere else in the text and examining the original text as well as the digital copy of the text magnified makes me think "one" the correct word; what raises doubt is that the word "ones" (in the phrase "one bathed ones") which needs pronoun agreement with "one" looks much more like a three letter "our" (even magnified) than a four letter "ones" and there is no indication of a possessive apostrophe. The "u" could be an "n" and the last letter, which looks most like an "r" or "s," could indicate an "e's" if Lewis were indeed writing quickly to get his thoughts on paper and knew what he meant by the word. Thus the phrase looks most like, "one bathed our hands" and so is either a mistake of grammar or one of two phrases: "one bathed one's hands" or "we bathed our hands." The former seems less awkward.

Light

MBB	Light
About five weeks later Mary had a headache and took breakfast[58] in bed. As Robin came downstairs he was for a moment shocked to notice the sweet feeling of escape that came with her absence.	About six weeks went by[57] before he first did so. During that time he had passed through every fluctuation of hope and despair but the steady trend of his feelings was towards an increasing, and presently a tormenting, desire.[60] He no longer concealed from himself the fact that the visible world was a disappointment.

---

52   The similar sentence in the "Light" ms uses a clearly visible dash, while what first appears in this revision text is no more than a dot. But upon looking at the original text as well as magnifying it in digital copy, I noticed the faintest line beneath the dot suggesting the possibility that Lewis intended a colon. My choice to place a colon here is supported by a similar dot and faint line in revision two after the word "thing." There the context strongly indicates a colon.

53   This word is separated between two lines. A dot next to "some" indicates the intended hyphen. The "some" is barely recognizable apart from context and the "where" on the next line. "Some" looks like "car" more than "som" (no "e"); however, "some" best fits the context and, when magnified, there's enough of an "s" to make me confident in the transcription.

54   This is a problematic passage. After the word "mountains" ending the previous sentence, two clauses follow which are then crossed out. Those clauses read, "It was clear by now" and "But how if it did…." There is no period after "now," and the second clause begins with a capital "B" and has no question mark after "did." Above the second clause, the words in the transcription appear: "May[be] it all,…" The comma definitely seems to be present after the third word, but the "I" in "It" in the next sentence is clearly capitalized (which may indicate that "But how if it did" should've ended with a question mark and that Lewis wrote the next sentence, which does follow it contextually, before going back and trying a third option). In addition, "May[be]" looks more like "May" or "Mary," and "all" looks like it could be the word "can" (which would fit the context a little better). The phrase may not even be intended for the text given the capital "I" beginning the next sentence, in which case Lewis forgot to cross it out, and this is what I think most likely.

C. S. Lewis's First and Final Short Story

MBB Revision One	MBB Revision Two	MBB Revision Three
		fear that it might not exist:[52] or perhaps not in England. Perhaps somewhere[53] in the far East—perhaps rare deposits of it in deserts & high mountains. May[be] it all,[54] It must exist or why did they all talk about it? And yet that was no proof[55] for none of them cd. describe it[56]
It was about six weeks later that he went out alone. The novelty of the visible world had completely worn off and no longer concealed his disappointment with it.	It was about 6 weeks later that he did so. During that time the novelty of the visible world had worn off and there was nothing now to conceal his disappointment.	About 6 weeks passed before he did so. During that time he had passed thr.[59] every fluctuation of hope & despair.

---

55   The phrase, "that was no proof" is highly problematic: The word, "was" looks most like a "w" crammed into an "a" which finishes in the barest flick of an "s." The word "no" could be read as "are" or even "wd" or "cd" (though with no period to indicate abbreviation and with a very short "d"—very little *up-line* to speak of). And the word "proof" looks rather like two words which might read something like "pure of" or, with a few letters missing, "heard of." I'm nevertheless fairly confident about this transcription.
56   The first paragraph ends here with no punctuation.
57   The word "passed" is crossed out and replaced with the phrase "went by." This correction is significant because of its connection to the sentence, "About 6 weeks passed before he did so," in the third revision on the left hand page opposite page seven of the MBB notebook. That Lewis crossed out the word "passed" in the "Light" manuscript indicates that he was at that moment copying from the third revision in MBB.
58   The word "breakfast" is split between two lines at the "k" and the "f."
59   This word appears in the text as "thr." with the period definitely visible by magnification. A parallel sentence in the "Light" ms. indicates that Lewis intended the word "through."
60   The word "desire" appears in the light blue ink (in which the heading of "Light" is also written) above a word which is crossed out with the same color (circular marks—like a row of cursive "e's" with two editor's 'insert' arrows beneath the crossed out word). The original word in the text is "thirst."

MBB	Light

MBB

Then, with a long shameless sigh of comfort, he deliberately closed his eyes and groped across the dining room to his bookcase—for[64] this one morning he would give up the tedious business of guiding himself by his eyes and judging distances and would enjoy the old, easy methods of the blind. Without effort his fingers ran down the row of faithful Brayle[69] books and picked out the worn volume he wanted. He slipped his hand between the leaves and shuffled across to the table, reading as he went. Still with his eyes shut, he cut up his food, laid down the knife, took[70] the fork in his left[71] hand and began

---

61 The word "with" here appears above a crossed out "the" (with an 'insert' arrow below the "the").
62 This one's tricky: after the word "open" is a comma followed immediately by an 'insert' arrow. The word "carefully" is written above the two words "open," and "judging...." What makes the instance tricky is that the 'insert' arrow is right next to the comma and looks more like a letter "n" than an arrow—there's an extra line attached to the left side of the arrow. Sitting right next to the comma, the arrow and comma together look like the word "in." Thus we might read the sentence as, "He had learned how to walk about with eyes open in carefully judging distances by sight...." This reading seems awkward, and in the second revision of this paragraph, this phrase appears quite clearly as I have rendered it: "...open, carefully judging...." Additionally, there is an obvious 'insert' arrow in the third revision which looks similar to the one here, and I've seen Lewis add this little extra line to his insert arrows in many other instances.
63 This ampersand looks almost like a comma, but it is even with (not below) the line of writing, and comparing this ampersand to one in the third revision gives me confidence in this transcription.
64 The phrase "...bookcase—for..." is a bit unusual in the ms. The word "bookcase" ends one line and "for" begins another. The dash is a single line written in the margin of the page, suggesting it was inserted as an afterthought between the two words.
65 The phrase, "carefully judging distances by sight as he laboriously climbed the stairs..." is confusing. If I added the words, "for example," near the beginning it would make more sense, thus: "carefully judging distances by sight as he, for example, climbed the stairs...." But even then the phrasing is awkward. What helps a little bit here is that the phrase is revised twice. The phrase first appears as "carefully judging distance by sight even in the house where...." (and this is the end of the line in the text). The line that follows, "the stairs he cd. have run up..." clearly doesn't go with this original line. I think this next line was not written until the rewrites were done; in other words, the rewriting was done all at once before Lewis continued the sentence. The words "even in the house where" are crossed out and above them are penned "as in the home"

C. S. Lewis's First and Final Short Story

MBB Revision One	MBB Revision Two	MBB Revision Three
He had learned how to walk about with[61] eyes open, carefully[62] judging distances by sight as he laboriously climbed the stairs[65] he cd.[66] have run up so easily with his eyes shut. He had learned painfully to find with his eyes[68]	He learned to walk with his eyes open, carefully judging distances &[63] avoiding obstacles: but in doors where he cd. go everywhere so[67] much more easily with his eyes shut, it seemed a cumbersome and roundabout method.	

(possibly "as in the house") thus: "carefully judging distances by sight as in the home" (or "house")....But the options may be more complicated. As I look at the first crossed out phrase, "even in the house where," I see that "in the house" is crossed out with a single line and that "even in the house where" is crossed out with another line, slightly above the first line. Lewis may have only crossed out "in the house" and substituted "in the home," and only after that replaced the word "even" with the word "as" and deleted the word "where." At any rate, he also crossed out "in the home" and above it squeezed in the words "he laboriously." What we're left with, then, is a phrase that doesn't quite make sense: "carefully judging distances by sight as he laboriously climbed the stairs...." My explanation is pure speculation: Lewis was indeed revising, here. He was experimenting, playing, trying options. He was not looking at this revision as a final text which needed to be perfect (perhaps because he intended to rewrite the story on paper using the notebook as a guide). Lewis wrote a bad second sentence (after several tries) in this revision which he did not at first see as a bad sentence or which he intended to rewrite later. But then he pressed on, starting the next sentence, a sentence which he didn't finish, perhaps because he at that point realized that the sentence above it didn't make sense. What makes me think this most is that he did not continue this revision but, instead, on the left hand page opposite page five, Lewis started the paragraph revision over again.

66 One of Lewis's more famous abbreviations is "cd." for "could." The use of an abbreviation suggests that Lewis was working on revisions to the story intending to rewrite it on paper after the revisions were complete. Lewis would convert his "cd." to "could" at that time (which he never did, having abandoned this revision).

67 At least I think the squiggle in the manuscript here is the word "so."

68 The text of this first revision ends here with no punctuation.

69 *Sic*.

70 MBB page four ends here.

71 The word "right" is crossed out with two lines and an insert arrow both on and below the word. Above it appears the word "left."

MBB	Light
reading with his right. He realised[72] at once that this was the first meal he had really enjoyed since the recovery of his sight. It was also the first book he had enjoyed. He had been very quick, everyone told him, in learning to read by sight, but it would never be the real thing. W-A-T-E-R could be spelled out; but never, never would those black marks be wedded to their meaning as in Brayle where the very shape of the characters communicated an instantaneous sense of liquidity through his finger tips.	He realised that he had never really wanted it except for the sake of light and that unless somewhere amongst them he could find that pure stream and bathe his eyes in it and drink it in, all the clouds and colours and animals and what Anne called the 'views' were of no account.

72   The word "realised" is split between two lines at the "l" and the "i."
73   "Was" is inserted above and between "He" and "learning."
74   Lewis's spelling of "Brayle" instead of "Braille" both here and in the MBB manuscript is consistent, if wrong.
75   The word "had" is a tough read. In comparing this sentence to its almost identical original across the page, I noticed a real difference in the clarity of the script. The revision is "messier" than the original script (the writing in the "Light" manuscript is neater still). It suggests that Lewis was interested in his ideas, not his penmanship—that he was revising with the ultimate goal of rewriting the entire story.
76   This ampersand looks even more like a comma than the one referenced above, but, again, it is even with the other words in the line.
77   This is almost certainly the word "nothing," but there's a bit of a gap between "no" and "thing." This may be because Lewis used a dip pen to write: he begins a word just as his ink is running out, dips the pen, and continues the word without connecting the lines in cursive together and even placing some space between letters.
78   Read "which" for "wh."

C. S. Lewis's First and Final Short Story

MBB Revision One	MBB Revision Two	MBB Revision Three
	He was[73] learning to read too, but this eye reading wd. never be the same thing as Brayle.[74] One might spell out W-A-T-E-R: but never, never wd. those black marks be wedded to their meaning as in Brayle where the v. shape of the characters had[75] communicated an instantaneous sense of liquidity to his practiced fingers.	
	Meanwhile, of what he had longed &[76] hoped for—no thing[77]. All his life he had dreamed of light, whispering to himself the[79] words of Milton[80] or Shelley[81] or Ruskin[82] All the hopes that awoke in him	Sometimes it seemed clear to him that light had all along been only a name, an abstract noun wh.[78] the un-blind used to mean nothing in particular. Then again it seemed equally obvious that there was something

---

79   This "the" looks like the word "an" as well, or even a "Cn" or a "tn." Within context, and compared to another "the" on this page, my reading of "the" seems the best.

80   John Milton, 1608-1674. English poet most famous for writing *Paradise Lost*. The passage to which Robin is referring in the revision is most likely *Paradise Lost*, Book III, lines 572-621 which Lewis talks about on page 44 of *A Preface to Paradise Lost*, and/or lines 1-55 of Book III (see note 49).

81   Probably the English poet Percy Bysshe Shelley, 1792-1822 (though I suppose Mary Shelley, author of *Frankenstein* might not be out of the question). Shelley is categorized among the "Romantic" poets and is most famous for such poems as "Ozymandias," "Ode to the West Wind," and "Prometheus Unbound."

82   John Ruskin, 1819-1900. Culture and art critic. Lewis writes of reading volume three of his book *Modern Painters* in a letter of February 1937 (*Collected Letters* 2, 210). There is no visible period after the word "Ruskin" and the "A" in "All" might be a minuscule. But the sentence immediately preceding this one also begins with the word "All" (the period before being clearly visible), where the "A" is meant to be a capital letter. The "All" there and the "All" here look almost exactly alike. This plus context and grammar give sufficient reason to end one sentence and begin another.

Light

MBB	Light
He took a long time over breakfast. Then he went out.	
There was a mist that morning, but he had encountered mists before	On the morning when he first went out alone there was a mist, but he

---

83   The letters "w" and "h" are visible in "when"; the rest is a very slight scrawl. In context, no other word but "when" seems to work.
84   The phrase, "there was something wrong" is inserted between "that" and "his" with an 'insert' arrow. The word "with" which would complete the sentence is missing.
85   Or possibly "specialist."
86   Between "had" and "promised," five words are written and then crossed out with a single line: "said 'Yes. The nerve was" (though the words "nerve" and "was" are hard to make out). Throughout these revisions, I get the sense of Lewis wanting to turn attention away from the theme of blindness, even in rejecting the medical terminology here, and wanting to focus instead on the concept of light.
87   Lewis started to write another word, probably "But," and then wrote "And" over it.

C. S. Lewis's First and Final Short Story

MBB Revision One	MBB Revision Two	MBB Revision Three
	that awoke in him when[83] the specialists[85] had[86] promised to give him sight had been turned to that one thing: it was indeed the thing that all the un-blind boasted of. And[87] now[88] it was nowhere to be found. Every thing[90] you 'saw', as they called it, turned out to be not light but something else—the sun, or the moon,[91] or water, or a mirror, or a window. Yet maddeningly they continued to jabber about Light. If he could get away from them all, and on his own, perhaps there was still hope. Everyone agreed that there was more light out of doors[92]	wrong[84] his own eyes— or, more still, his own mind—which prevented him perceiving what was all about him. But that mood did not last long. Great lines from Milton that he had whispered to himself for years came back to him. They were not about no thing[89]

---

88   This word looks more like a series of zig-zags than anything else. "Now" seems best to fit the context.
89   The text of this third revision ends here with no punctuation.
90   "Every" and "thing" appear on separate lines with no visible hyphen between them.
91   "Moon" looks to be spelled with one "o," i.e. "mon."
92   The text of this second revision ends here with no punctuation. Most of the page opposite page five is filled with this text, but there is still an inch or so left on the bottom and Lewis ended on the word "doors" in the middle of a line. He had room to finish the paragraph so as to transition into the next one which, if this revision were meant to go where I have suggested, begins "There was a mist that morning…." The end of the second revision doesn't quite fit with the next paragraph. Perhaps this is because Lewis didn't like this version either. The other evidence for this possibility is that the final revision, the one opposite page seven, also seems to include an attempt to revise the same 'about 6 weeks later' paragraph.

MBB

and this did not trouble him. He walked through it, out of the little town and up the steep hill and then along the field path that ran round the lip of the quarry. Mary had taken him there a few days ago to show him what she called the 'view.' And while they had sat looking at it she had said 'What a lovely light that is on the hills over there.' It was a wretched clue, for he was now convinced that she knew no more about light than he did, that she used the word but meant nothing by it. He was even beginning to suspect that most of the un-blind were in the same position. What one heard among them was merely the parrot-like repetition of a[93] rumour—the rumour of something which perhaps (it was his last hope) great poets and prophets of[94] old had really known and seen. It was on their testimony alone that he still hoped. It was still just possible that somewhere in the world, not everywhere as fools had tried to make him believe, guarded in deep woods or divided by distant seas, the thing Light might actually exist, springing up like a fountain or growing like a flower.

The mist was thinning when he came to the lip of the quarry. To left and right more and more trees were

Light

had met mists before and this did not trouble him. He walked out over the railway bridge and up the steep hill and then along the field-path that skirted the lip of the quarry. Anne had taken him there a few days before to show him 'the view.'

She had said 'What a lovely light there is on the hills over there.' That clue he was now following, though with very faint hope. He was almost certain by now that she knew no more about light than he did. He was beginning to suspect that most of the un-blind were in the same position. What one heard among them was probably mere parrot-like repetition of a rumour—a rumour concerning something which the very few, the great poets and prophets, had really seen and known.[95] Somewhere[96] it must exist. Perhaps not in England—perhaps only rare deposits of it existed, far away to the East in deserts or high mountains. In that case, he would never see it. But if he did—ah yes, if—he would dive into its very heart,[97] give all himself away to it, drink, drink, drink it till he died drinking.

The mist thinned rapidly. Trees brightened out of it, birds began singing. He found he was hot. His

---

93   The word "a" appears above, and its accompanying insert arrow below, the crossed out word "some."
94   MBB page five ends here.
95   The section of "Light" which follows has its parallel in part of the first paragraph of revision three which, though it appears previously in terms of order (and so is printed earlier), is printed again here in italics for the reader's convenience.

C. S. Lewis's First and Final Short Story

MBB Revision One	MBB Revision Two	MBB Revision Three
		What tormented him was the fear that it might not exist: or perhaps not in England. Perhaps somewhere in the far East—perhaps rare deposits of it in deserts & high mountains. May[be] it all, It must exist or why did they all talk about it? And yet that was no proof for none of them cd. describe it[98]

96 The word "somewhere" is split between two lines.
97 While Lewis's hand written commas are sometimes 'stubby,' the comma which clearly belongs here is so short that it looks like a period, even when magnified. Only context says otherwise.
98 See note 95.

MBB	Light
visible and their colours grew brighter every moment. His own shadow lay before him; he noticed that it became blacker and firmer-edged while he looked at it. The birds were singing too and he was quite hot. 'But still no Light',[101] he muttered. The sun was visible behind him but the pit of the quarry was still full of mist—a shapeless whiteness, now almost blindingly white.	shadow lay before him, each moment blacker and more distinct. That violent yellow thing, the sun, which one[99] could never see properly, stared at him on his left hand. He pulled the[100] brim of his hat lower over his eyes, blinking.[102] 'If only I could see any light!' he muttered.
Suddenly he heard a man singing. Someone whom he had not noticed before was standing near the cliff-edge with his legs wide apart dabbing at an object which Robin could not recognise.	At that moment he caught sight of a young man who was standing with his legs wide apart on the edge of the cliff, singing and making jabs with some slender instrument at a complicated two-legged object about the same height as himself. If Robin had had more experience he would have recognised[103] this as a canvas on an easel. As it was, his eyes and those of the wild looking stranger met so unexpectedly that Robin blurted out 'What are you doing?' before he had time to be self-conscious
If he had been more experienced he would have recognised it as a canvas on an easel. As it was, his eyes met the eyes of this wild-looking stranger so unexpectedly that he had blurted out 'What are you doing?' before he[104] realised it.	
'Doing?', said the stranger with a certain savagery. 'Doing? I'm trying to catch Light, if you want to know. Damn it.'	'Doing?' said the stranger with a certain light-hearted savagery. 'Doing? I'm trying to catch light, if you want to know. Damn it'

---

99   The word "one" appears above the crossed out word "would" (Lewis then makes the very next word in the sentence "could").
100   Page three of the "Light" manuscript ends here.
101   The punctuation is obviously a comma, but in the manuscript it's no more than a dot on the page.
102   At the end of "eyes," a period has been covered by an 'insert' arrow above which (roughly between the word "eyes" and the "If" of the next sentence) are a comma, followed by the word "blinking" and a period (thus: ", blinking."). The 'insert' arrow, punctuation, and word are in the blue ink mentioned above, making it clear that the word was a later addition to the manuscript.
103   The word "recognised" is split between two lines at the 'g-' and the '-n.'
104   An illegible letter (perhaps two) is scribbled out here.

C. S. Lewis's First and Final Short Story

MBB	Light
A smile came over Robin's face. 'So am I,' he said, and came[105] a step nearer.	'Good God![106] So am I', said Robin.
'Oh—you know too, do you?' said the other. Then, almost vindictively, 'They're all fools. How many of them come out to paint on a day like this, eh? How many of them will recognize it if you show 'em? And yet if they could open their eyes, it's the only sort of day in the whole year when you can really see light, solid light, that you could drink in a cup or bathe in! Look at it.'	'Oh—you know too, do you?', said the man. Then, almost vindictively, 'They're[107] all fools. How many come out to paint on a day like this? How many will see it even if you show it 'em? And yet this is the only sort of day[108] when you can see light—solid light—light you could drink in a cup or swim in! Look at it!'
He caught Robin roughly by the arm and pointed into the depths at their feet. The fog was at death-grips with the sun, but not a stone on the quarry floor was yet visible. The bath of vapour shone like[110] white metal and unfolded itself continually in ever widening spirals towards them.	He pointed into the quarry. The fog was[109] at death grips with the sun but not a stone on the quarry floor was yet visible. The bath of[111] vapour shone like white metal and unfolded itself in ever widening spirals towards them.

---

105   Page six of the MBB ms ends here.
106   Lewis's capital "G's" look very much like his minuscule "g's." They are written a little bit bigger; otherwise, context, indentations and punctuation provide the clues needed to know when to capitalize a Lewisian letter "G."
107   The word, "They're" is split between two lines, but the typical hyphens are missing. "They" appears at the end of one line, and the apostrophe and "re" ('re) begin the next.
108   An 'insert' arrow appears, as usual, below a twice crossed out word. The word written above the crossed out word is the word "day." But the crossed out word is also the word "day." The ink is fairly heavy—perhaps Lewis was concerned that the "y" looked too much like a "g" and wanted to rewrite the word for clarity. But it's not really all that unclear, which makes me think Lewis wrote "day," crossed it out, thinking or trying to think of another word, and then thought better of his choice and wrote "day" again.
109   There is a faint dot after "was" which I do not include. It's too faint to be an intended period. It's a stray mark.
110   Before the word "white" is also written (and then crossed out with two lines) the word "white." Perhaps Lewis was going to change his mind and choose another word and then decided to stick with "white."
111   Between the words "of" and "vapour," the word "white" is marked out, doubtless because the "vapour" is described as looking "like white metal" in the very next phrase.

Light

MBB	Light
'Do you see that', shouted the violent stranger. 'There's light for you if you like it!.'[112]	'Do you see that?', shouted the violent stranger. 'There's light for you if you like it'
A second later the expression on the painter's face changed. 'Here,'[113] he cried, 'Are you mad?.' He made a grab at Robin. But he was too late. Already he was alone on the path. From beneath a new-made and rapidly vanishing rift in the fog there came up no cry but only a sound so sharp and definite that you would hardly expect it to have been made by the fall of anything so soft as a human body; that, and some rattling of loosened stones.	A second later the expression on the painter's face changed. 'Here!', he cried, 'Are you mad?' The grab he made at Robin was too late. Already he was alone on the path.[114] From a new-made and rapidly vanishing rift in the fog beneath him there came up no cry but only a sound so sharp and definite[115] that you would hardly expect it to have been made by the fall of anything so soft as a human body: that, and the momentary rattling of a dislodged stone.[116]

---

112   The extra period here is Lewis's as is the one in the second sentence of the next paragraph.
113   The comma here looks like a period. Magnified, a small tail is visible.
114   The period here is jammed against the "h" in "path." It is barely visible, but visible nevertheless. Also, the next word is clearly capitalized.
115   The word "definite" is split (at the "e" and the "f") between two lines.
116   After the word "a," the phrase "dislodged stone" is crossed out (with circular lines) and then rewritten to the side where the blank line on the page continues. The "ed" in the crossed out "dislodged" looks to be inked with such thickness as to have run close enough together (and the "s" in "stone" a bit illegible as well) that Lewis perhaps thought the words too messy for a typist or publisher to read, so he crossed them out and rewrote them more neatly. Or, again, perhaps Lewis was trying to think of another option, failed to do so, and went with his original.

Chapter Ten

Shedding Light on the Blind

Lewis the Reviser

The first thing we learn from a parallel analysis of the texts is that Lewis was a writer who revised. It has been generally held that Lewis wrote his books quickly and in single drafts with little revision.[1] A new, book length study by Diana Glyer, however, questions this conclusion. In her book, *The Company They Keep*, Glyer finds Lewis to be a frequent reviser,[2] noting that Lewis revised *Out of the Silent Planet* based on a critique by Tolkien,[3] that Lewis produced abridged versions of *Perelandra* and *That Hideous Strength*, that he revised his various broadcast talks for publication in *Mere Christianity*, and that he rewrote chapter three of *Miracles*.[4] Lewis abandoned his first attempt at what would become *The Magician's Nephew* and wrote several other Narnia books before returning to that one.[5] Glyer further notes that *The Inklings*, of which Lewis and Tolkien were members, existed foremost for the reading and critique of writings in progress,[6] and she reminds us that there is ample evidence of Lewis's revising activity in the often multiple versions of many

---

1 Walter Hooper made this claim in an interview with Justin Phillips. *The Screwtape Letters*, for example was written in only one draft as was *Letters to Malcolm* (Phillips 113). At the same time Hooper has noted that Lewis was a constant reviser when it came to his poetry (see King 298). However, in his interview with me, Hooper pointed out Lewis's love for rewriting texts and that these rewrites often became revisions. He acknowledged Lewis's rewriting of poetry especially and said he could easily believe that Lewis rewrote the "Light" story several times.
2 I saw Lewis's revision work myself at the Wade Center in such manuscripts as the hand written original of "Donne and Love Poetry in the Seventeenth Century" (Wade Ms. CSL/MS-39). Revisions occur throughout the manuscript, including a page 15A between pages 15 and 16 which has five lines and then a note in large pencil: "Type straight on (with new para.) on next page."
3 Glyer, *Company*, 2.
4 Ibid, 120. Lewis rewrote chapter three of *Miracles*, after its publication, in response to Elizabeth Anscombe's critique of the original chapter (Hooper, *Companion & Guide*, 619).
5 See the "Lefay Fragment" and its introduction in Walter Hooper's *Past Watchful Dragons*, 48-68.
6 Glyer, *Company*, 17, 76.

of his poems.[7] That there is not *more* evidence of Lewis as a reviser Glyer attributes to "the oft-made distinction in composition circles between external processors (like Tolkien and Bach) and internal processors (like Lewis and Mozart)."[8] Glyer explained to me that "internal processors do a great deal of revision.…They just don't tend to leave an extensive paper trail." But in the case of "Light" there are two manuscripts for comparison plus three revisions (of the same part of the story) in the left hand pages of the MBB notebook. Lewis was a reviser. What do these revisions tell us?

Style

In part they tell us that Lewis revised for style. The simple addition of the word "added" in place of the word "said" in the opening paragraph of "Light," for example, better unifies Anne's dialog within the paragraph. The second paragraph of "Light" pulls back from the sudden panic of the "loud heart beat" and "fear" in its counterpart in MBB so as to draw the reader more gently into the story. Even the two-word revision in the final sentence of this paragraph—"there'll be lots of light out there"—is superior to MBB's "there'll be light out there" because its more standard phraseology does not too early awaken the reader's sense that something strange having to do with *light* is going on. The original makes the reader wonder at the phrasing. Isn't there light indoors as well as out? But "lots of light" makes sense to us—more light outdoors than in. Lewis carries us a little further into the story before revealing Robin's strange obsession. Additionally, removing the unnecessary first line of paragraph three in MBB ("What do you mean, dear?") improves the pace of the story.

A recurring revision from MBB to "Light" has to do with the tone Lewis uses in describing Robin's wife ("Mary" in MBB, "Anne" in "Light"). In MBB paragraph five, Lewis refers to Mary speaking "sharply, in…her governess voice." He abandons this description in "Light" to focus instead on building the suspense he more subtly initiates in "Light" paragraph two. He mentions Anne's sounding "angry or frightened" in this paragraph but only in building the issue toward the question of light. Anne's attitude is no longer the primary issue. Overall, Lewis's treatment of Anne in "Light" tends to be more sympathetic than his treatment of her in MBB.

Paragraph six of "Light" emphasizes the issue of light over Robin's blindness and is a bit smoother in its language. Diving further down into the dialog between Robin and his wife we find these two sentences:

---

7   Ibid, 121.
8   Glyer, 3 March 2011; Email to Starr. Glyer pointed me to an example in her book of Lewis as internal reviser in the form of his relationship with Clifford Morris (see pages 121-22). I wonder if we might not consider, however, that evidence for Lewis as an external processor might have burned up in the "bon fire" after his death.

C. S. Lewis's First and Final Short Story

MBB: "Well then, first of all, there's light in this room at present?"[9]

"Light": "Very well, then. Is there light in this room at present?"[10]

The latter removes unnecessary language and eliminates the awkwardness of asking a question in the form of a statement. The longer paragraphs at the end of the husband-wife dialog and following are tighter, and several individual sentences after that show stylistic improvement: MBB's "He took a long time over breakfast. Then he went out. There was a mist that morning"[11] is nicely tightened in "Light": "On the morning when he first went out alone there was a mist"[12]; and, there's better word choice over MBB's "ran round the lip of the quarry" in "Light's" "skirted the lip of the quarry" as well as in "Light's" "a few days before" over MBB's "a few days ago."

We also see in this same paragraph the difference in tone regarding Robin's wife. There's a tone of fault finding in Mary in MBB—an air of something conspiratorial even in the description of her ignorance: "It was a wretched clue, for he was now convinced that she knew no more about light than he did, that she used the word but meant nothing by it." The version in "Light" is far more neutral toward Anne: "That clue he was now following, though with very faint hope. He was almost certain by now that she knew no more about light than he did." The remainder of the paragraph is tighter in "Light," including the deletion of a repetitive "It was on their testimony alone that he still hoped" from MBB.

In the final ten or so paragraphs, Lewis's revisions show real writing craft. The improvements may be minor, but the cumulative effect is for a much stronger, better written story. In the paragraph which begins "The mist was thinning" in MBB[13] and "The mist thinned rapidly" in "Light,"[14] the latter version consists of short, staccato sentences which increase the story's pace and heighten the sense of urgency in Robin's desperate search. The last sentence in the MBB version, referencing the "shapeless whiteness, now almost blindingly white" of the mist, is deleted in the "Light" version so that Robin's (and the reader's) experience of the solid light he hopes to find occurs at the last moment of the story. Robin's reaction, upon *seeing* the thing he has most desired to see is more immediate in "Light" and the audience more stunned by his actions.

The description of the painter and his easel is smoother, more sophisticated in "Light."[15] The word "recognise(d)" appears in back-to-back sentences in the

---

9   Par. 14.
10 Par. 15.
11 Par. 30.
12 Par. 28.
13 Par. 32.
14 Par. 29.
15 Par. 30.

MBB description[16]; the reader screams for a thesaurus when reading them. Lewis qualifies the artist's "savagery" in MBB[17] as "light-hearted savagery" in "Light"[18] lest the reader mistake the painter's creative intensity for mere anger. Robin's response to the painter's "I'm trying to catch light"[19] is almost sheepish in MBB[20] when compared to the "Good God! So am I" of "Light."[21] The latter far more anticipates the leap into the quarry which follows. The "Oh—you know too, do you?"[22] paragraph is tightened up in "Light"—needless repetition is removed. The line "He caught Robin roughly by the arm..." in MBB[23] is removed in "Light," to again avoid any sense that the artist is angry and also because there's no indication in the story that Robin had yet moved close enough to the painter to be grabbed by him. Instead, "Light" picks up saying, "He pointed into the quarry,"[24] which sentence gives the reader a reason for Robin's moving closer to the painter as he then shouts "Do you see that?"

Here's a subtle but effective change in the last paragraph:

> MBB: "He made a grab at Robin. But he was too late."[25]

> "Light": "The grab he made at Robin was too late."[26]

I also prefer the final clause of "Light" to that of MBB:

> MBB: "that, and some rattling of loosened stones."

> "Light": "that, and the momentary rattling of a dislodged stone."

In part, the rhythm of the words within the phrase makes me prefer the latter to the former, and, as I've said before, there may be an image of resurrection in the idea of the "dislodged stone."

Order and Emphasis

There is one more revision worth discussing which is easy to miss but which completely changes the meaning of the story's end. In MBB, especially with its emphasis on the experiences of blindness and not just a focus on light, Robin has only one reason to jump into the quarry. Of course he has a strong desire for light which he refers to as possibly existing in some "guarded...deep

---

16 Par. 33.
17 Par. 35.
18 Par. 31.
19 MBB, par. 35, "Light," par. 31.
20 Par. 36.
21 Par. 32.
22 MBB, par. 37, "Light," par. 33.
23 Par. 38.
24 Par. 33.
25 Par. 39.
26 Par. 34.

woods…springing up like a fountain or growing like a flower,"[27] but his only reason to jump into the quarry after the light is his inexperience as a sighted person. This leads him to take literally the painter's metaphor of "solid light, that you could drink in a cup or bathe in"[28] and so jump into the quarry by almost dumb mistake.

But in "Light," it is not the painter's description alone that sends Robin to his death, nor merely his inexperience with sight. It is *Light* itself which Robin most wants. It was the only reason he really wanted sight. And in his own thoughts he had determined that Light must be a concrete thing. Twice in "Light" he thinks about this solidity, first wanting to "find that pure stream and bathe his eyes in it and drink it in,"[29] then wanting to find those hidden deposits of the substance and "dive into its very heart" and "give all himself away to it, drink, drink, drink it till he died drinking."[30] In "Light" he gets his wish. Thus in MBB, Robin naively jumps to his death. In the revised version of "Light," he dives into it with purpose.

What I have alluded to here is Lewis's major revision or rather re-vision of the story which we will consider as we also look at the various proofs that Lewis wrote "Light" after MBB and intended it for publication. There is first of all the fact that the "Light" manuscript has a heading—Lewis's name and address. Then there is the fact that it is written on individual sheets of paper rather than in a notebook as is the MBB version of the story. Even more important is the fact that "Light" has a title where MBB does not.

Perhaps an even stronger piece of evidence is in the first sentence of the fifth paragraph of the "Light" manuscript: "'What are you talking about?' said Anne." In the "Light" manuscript, the word "Anne" is inserted above the crossed out word "Mary." The sentence in MBB is the same as the one here, save for an extra comma and the name. Clearly Lewis was copying word-for-word from MBB to "Light," and he accidentally wrote the name "Mary" when he intended to write Anne. He caught his mistake and made the appropriate change. There is no way to explain how this mistake might work in reverse, that is, if "Light" were the earlier version. The first time I read "Light," I was immediately struck by the name change (since it occurs in the first sentence) and wondered why Lewis had made it. It's pure speculation, but I think Lewis might have wanted to avoid any Robin Hood allusions readers might derive from the names Robin and Mary (i.e. Robin and Marion). While this copying mistake is among the strongest proofs that "Light" is the later version of the story, there are several others.

---

27 Par. 31.
28 Par. 37.
29 Par. 27.
30 Par. 28.

In the ninth paragraph of "Light," Lewis substitutes the word "muddled" for the word "stupid" in MBB.[31] In either version Lewis meant something like "confused," and, as mentioned above, Lewis makes several revisions which lighten an otherwise negative view of Mary (Anne). A bit stronger than this argument is that Lewis removes the single sentence paragraph twelve from MBB: "She sat down suddenly with a formal calmness that alarmed him." Lewis removed this sentence because he saw an obvious flaw in the logic of the story. Only a few paragraphs above (in both versions), Lewis had noted that "three weeks of sight"[32] were not enough for Robin to read his wife's facial expressions. How then would he be alarmed by her sitting down "suddenly with a formal calmness"? He wouldn't have been able to read that expression either. So Lewis removed the sentence.

In the one line conversation which follows, Lewis is more careful with his end punctuation in "Light" than in MBB where he placed only question marks and forgot periods. Furthermore, there are no major grammatical *gaffes* in "Light" where in MBB, at the end of the couple's conversation, Lewis writes, "Robin! Robin! Don't. Don't go on like that"[33] to which Robin replies, "Going on like what?"[34] Hooper rightly corrected this sentence to "Go on like what?" in the published version.

The very next paragraph of MBB begins with two sentences which are deleted in "Light": "A blind man has few friends; a blind man who has recently received his sight has, in a sense, none. He belongs neither to the world of the blind nor to that of the seeing and no one can share his experiences."[35] By themselves, the removal of these two sentences indicates little. But this removal is the first hint of a process of rewriting which I have already alluded to, one which runs through the three revisions and culminates in "Light," as Lewis here begins the process of deleting references to Robin's experiences as a blind man.

The first sentence of revisions one and two and first sentence of revision three, paragraph two, along with the parallel sentences in MBB and "Light," again provide strong evidence that "Light" is the later version of the story. Compare the texts:

> MBB: "About five weeks later Mary had a headache and took breakfast in bed."[36]

---

31 Par. 9.
32 MBB, par. 9, "Light," par. 9.
33 Par. 27.
34 Par. 28.
35 Par. 29.
36 Par. 30.

> Rev. 1: "It was about six weeks later that he went out alone."
>
> Rev. 2: "It was about 6 weeks later that he did so."
>
> Rev. 3: "About 6 weeks passed before he did so."
>
> "Light": "About six weeks went by before he did so."[37]

Most significantly, the words "went by" in the "Light" manuscript are written above the word "passed" which has been scratched out. Lewis was clearly copying from the third revision onto page three of "Light."

A similar progression occurs in sentence two of each version[38] after MBB:

> Rev. 1: "The novelty of the visible world had completely worn off and no longer concealed his disappointment with it."
>
> Rev. 2: "During that time the novelty of the visible world had worn off and there was nothing now to conceal his disappointment."
>
> Rev. 3: "During that time he passed thr. every fluctuation of hope and despair."
>
> "Light": During that time he had passed through every fluctuation of hope and despair...." [and the next sentence:] "He no longer concealed from himself the fact that the visible world was a disappointment."[39]

Notice how the "Light" version incorporates the very different third revision as well as elements from revisions one and two.

The longest portion cut from MBB is about the life of a blind man (beginning with the third sentence of paragraph 30). Such references are completely missing from the "Light" version, a deletion which Owen Barfield regretted: "I suppose the later ["Light"] revision is on the whole an improvement, but I am sorry Lewis cut out the touching episode of Robin going back to Braille, and his other habits when blind, for the comfort of them."[40] Why did Lewis make this change? Rather than giving insight on the life of the blind, "Light" moves straight from the visible world being a disappointment to Robin realizing he only wanted sight for the sake of seeing light. More telling are the revisions which reveal Lewis's struggle with the issue of blindness and light. The remainder of revision one is entirely about Robin's difficulties with "judging distances" visually. Revision two takes up the same content adding the need for "avoiding obstacles" and then turning to parallel the Braille content of MBB—the difficulties of spelling out words like "W-A-T-E-R" by sight. But then revision two adds a lengthy section—about

---

37 Par. 27.
38 Sentence two of paragraph two in the third revision.
39 Par. 27.
40 Barfield, 17 November 1986; Letter to Brown.

half its content—on light and its significance to Robin. When Lewis gets to revision three, he abandons the references to blindness completely. The Braille references are completely missing and the only thing that survives of "W-A-T-E-R" in "Light" is a reference to its liquidity (see below). The third and longest of the revisions is entirely about the nature, whereabouts, and Robin's longing for light. It is this emphasis and this revision which echoes most in the "Light" version of the story.

In the last parallel between revisions two and three, the focus is on lines from poets who wrote of "light"—these Robin clings to in hope, but his hope is fading. Revision two blames the ignorance of the unblind while revision three (which is more succinct than revision two) focuses on that ignorance *and* Robin's fear that something might be wrong with his eyes. These emphases disappear or are greatly reduced in the "Light" version, primarily because of repetition, but also—in the case of the more philosophical material—because Lewis, perhaps, wanted to move away from any hints of didacticism or needless exposition—he didn't want to overtly state his meanings regarding the significance of light. But what we clearly see happening in examining all five versions of the story's center is that Lewis is shifting attention.

An additional proof of this shift in emphasis is in the paragraph order of revision three. The first paragraph of revision three both stands alone in my parallel transcription of the texts (because it precedes the "six weeks" paragraph), and is also placed, italicized, in parallel position to "Light." This paragraph focuses specifically on the issue of light: its substance, origin, solidity, location. Lewis stops the action of the story in order to describe light as a Platonic essence. He thinks better of this in "Light" and retains only some of the elements, repositioned as part of a paragraph which continues to carry the plot forward (again, I think he wanted to avoid didacticism and allow the story to carry the meaning more subtly). When Lewis discusses light in paragraph two of revision three, it is through a character focus on Robin. Even then he reduces both paragraphs by the time he gets to "Light." The indicated progression is of completely removing references to blindness[41] and of streamlining ideas about light into abbreviated hints,[42] thus allowing the action of the story to carry its meaning without needless exposition. And so the first four sentences of revision three, paragraph one on light-as-water are reduced to the phrase, "that pure stream and bathe his eyes in it and drink it in" in "Light." Additionally, the three poets in revision two are reduced to "Milton" in revision three and "great poets and prophets" in "Light" (which is actually a phrase in the MBB version). But, overall, the various ideas in revisions two and three which treat of *Light* itself are distilled into the "Light"

---

41   Between revisions two and three.
42   Between revision three and "Light."

C. S. Lewis's First and Final Short Story

version of the story, for the most part, in paragraph 28.

It makes perfect sense that Walter Hooper called this short story as he first knew of it, "The Man Born Blind." That is certainly what it's about. The insight into a former blind man's experiences with sight in regard to his walking, eating and reading are brilliant. But Lewis shifted his attention to focus on a single purpose. This is not a story about blindness; it is a story about sight—about perception and its problems (both physical and spiritual) and about spirituality as perceived in the metaphor of light. "The Man Born Blind," is about a man born blind. Lewis revised that story into one about *Light*. He gave it a good title.

Appendix

Describing the Manuscripts

Since this book is about the "Light" *manuscript*, as well as the "Light" story, physical descriptions of the MBB and "Light" documents themselves are here included.

The Man Born Blind

The manuscript published under the title, "The Man Born Blind" is part of a notebook which contains additional material, all in Lewis's hand. The notebook stands a little under nine inches tall. When closed it is a shade under seven inches wide.[1] The cover is dark blue with a maroonish-brown binding at the spine and blue cloth covering the boards. The front and back of the cover are beat up, scratched, worn at the edges and water-stained. There's a prominent Roman numeral V on the front cover in silver or grey about three inches from the top and off center to the left inside (though not centered in) what appears to be a double-circled tea or coffee mug stain. There's another less prominent V an inch from the top and a little more right of center than the first V is left. This one is in blue or black ink and visible only at a second glance. The leaves of the notebook are lightly ruled and yellowed with age.[2]

---

1   Thus, when opened it's about 14 inches wide.
2   A description of the notebook is provided by Judith Priestman, Curator, Modern Literary Manuscript Collections, Bodleian Library: "Notebook containing miscellaneous literary and theological notes and drafts, including <u>a</u> (fols. 2-8) a fair copy of an Arthurian poem beginning: 'When the year dies in preparation for the birth'; <u>b</u> (fols. 22-8) a draft of 'The Man Born Blind'; <u>c</u> (fols. 37ᵛ-61) notes on medieval and Renaissance literature; <u>d</u> (fols. 64-5ᵛ) <u>rev</u>. a poem beginning: "We're proud of Finchley Avenue", and <u>e</u> (fol. 68ᵛ) a fragment of <u>That Hideous Strength</u>. The entries are undated, with the exception of a mathematical calculation on the front pastedown which is dated 'Sept. 1946'. The figure 'V' is inscribed on the top board and the words 'Lewis MS No. 31', in the hand of W. Hooper are written on fol. i. Lewis's signature appears at fol. 70ᵛ. 71 leaves; blue cloth boards, maroon linen spine. Deposited by W. Hooper, January 1989. **Dep. d. 809**" (Priestman 9). The letters and numbers in bold are the manuscript's reference number at the Bodleian.

C. S. Lewis's First and Final Short Story

Lewis wrote from both ends of the notebook in toward the middle. Most of the writing is written from one end only, what we would for that reason call the "front" of the book. But at various times he occasionally flipped the book over and upside down to write from the "reverse" end. The content is truly a flotsam and jetsam of Lewis writing: poems, essays, outlines, pictures, book fragments and research notes.[3]

The MBB story occupies folios 22-28 (*rectos* only) in the library penciled foliation, seven pages total. All the pages are full save for the very last where the story ends a few lines from the bottom. All but the first of these are numbered separately, 2 through 7[4] (with some errors that had to be corrected[5]) presumably by Walter Hooper before he placed the book in the Bodleian, so that the library's folio numbers for these leaves had to be placed a little lower. The story is written in Lewis's hand with his traditional steel nibbed, dip pen,[6] in a light blue ink. Three of the *versos* also contain writing, in a blue-black ink: fol. 3ᵛ only six lines; 4ᵛ and 6ᵛ almost full. These entries are three attempts by Lewis at revising a single paragraph that begins on folio 4.[7]

Light

The "Light" manuscript consists of four loose leaves[8] of "'foolscap' (a lined sheet of paper, 8"x13", in standard use in Britain"[9] in Lewis's time) which are yellowish in color and ruled with faint purple lines. Two thin oval stains (the lines of the ovals being incomplete in several places), side-by-side and less than an inch long are visible at the top left of the first page and one such mark at the bottom left. These are marks from rusted paper clips which must have held the

---

3   Especially for Lewis's *English Literature in the Sixteenth Century*.
4   The numbers are lightly circled.
5   The last four pages of the story are misnumbered, and so there is a "4" written over a "5" on the fourth page, followed by a "5" written over a "4," a "6" over a "5," and a "7" next to a crossed out "6."
6   Confirmed by Walter Hooper: Lewis used a fountain pen for a while in the 20s but "then went back to his dip pen," because, as Lewis explained it, that pause between writing and dipping allows one to think. Words become darker and lighter in MBB and "Light," indicating the use of a dip pen (Hooper, Interview).
7   My thanks to Charles Huttar for his assistance with the wording of this description.
8   In his book, Brown says it's five pages (82), a mistake which occurred during the writing of his book as Ed explained to me in an email of 24 January, 2011. Upon my asking about the discrepancy, Brown replied, "I went through my files to see everything I have relative to the manuscript—and found my original draft for page 82 of my Lewis book, which notes that the manuscript is <u>four</u> pages. Somewhere along the line in writing several redrafts that number erroneously became five."
9   Brown, 82.

manuscript together for quite some time.[10] The paper clip mark on the bottom of the first page appears to be from the same paper clip which made one of the marks at the top. The back side of page one, both sides of pages two and three, and the front side of page four of the manuscript show indentations from two paper clips side-by-side. Additionally, the back side of page four shows two oval (paper clip shaped) indentations as well as rust marks along the indentations (though, again, these marks do not fill up the ovals completely). The back side, bottom of page four does not have a paper clip mark. The paper clip mark on the bottom of the first page is not at the very edge, indicating that the page was folded not exactly in half; the top of the page was folded onto the bottom with about half an inch of the bottom still showing. In short, then, the manuscript was double paper clipped at the top and then folded over.[11] Creases on all four pages indicate that they were folded in half, probably multiple times as there appear to be multiple crease marks. They may even have been folded in both directions at different times. The creases in the middle of each page are angled slightly downward from left to right (more prominently on the first page and running a little more parallel to the lines on the paper on each successive page. In addition to these center creases, there are creases at the tops and bottoms of each page about two inches from the horizontal edges. At some point in its history, the manuscript was quadri-folded. The "outside" folds[12] are not at all near an exact quarter point of the page (they are only a couple of inches from the top or bottom but then almost twice as many inches from the middle fold). The impression I get from these folds taken together is that the middle fold was present before the end folds and that these were added later, perhaps so the manuscript could be fit into a coat pocket or an envelope for mailing.[13]

---

10   Other original Lewis manuscripts contain similar paper clip rust marks including, for example, Wade Ms. CSL/MS-39, a handwritten essay entitled "Donne and Love Poetry in the Seventeenth Century."

11   There are additional stains on the top right of page one around and in the heading. These look like rust stains but the possibility of a paper clip is less defined, and there are no creases on any other page and no marks on the back of page four. Additionally, there is a partial paper clip "rust oval" on the back of page four, about two inches from the bottom and half an inch in. The oval is not complete, but curved stains at the top and bottom end of it indicate the paper clip was not attached to the page. The oval is at a diagonal to the page and seems haphazardly present. My best guess is that the manuscript was sitting on top of some other manuscript at some point—long enough to have picked up a rust stain from the paper clip holding the other manuscript together.

12   The horizontal folds closer to the upper and lower edges of the page as opposed to the fold in the center.

13   Ed Brown told me the manuscript was mailed to him in the States from England by Peter Jolliffe, I asked Brown if it was folded when he received it in the mail. He replied, "I'm sure it was folded" (Brown, Interview).

C. S. Lewis's First and Final Short Story

Various other dots, smudges or stains appear throughout the manuscript, but one more set of marks is worth noting. On the bottom of page one there are impressions of words and possibly numbers scattered across several inches of the page. In the very bottom right corner is a tiny impression of two lines. The second is illegible, even with some digital technology applied to enhance it.[14] The first line is backwards on the page and reads something like, "17 to s?smer Mr. Y" (with some question about the "Y"). The first "s" in the long word in the line is suspect. It's followed by an unreadable smudge. The "smer" is pretty clear. To the right of center are the clearest impressions. There appear to be three groups of letters or numbers backwards on the page, angling up left to right from near the center of the page. These marks, are definitely transferred from type, not hand writing. When read in reverse they say, "Hours 50 Minutes." There may be a number before the word "Hours"—there's a smudge in the right place for one—but it is illegible. I think the "Light" manuscript probably spent some time folded but also some time open and in a pile. It either sat upside down on something or something sat upside down on it in the middle of a stack of books, magazines, or papers, and this led to the transference of the above impressions which may have even come from multiple sources.[15] The "Hours 50 Minutes" phrase makes me wonder if "Light" shared some compressed space with a train schedule. There are a few other stray recognizable marks, none of them whole words or of any other significance as far as I can tell.

The entire manuscript is in Lewis's own hand. Pages two, three and four are numbered, and a heading and title appear on the first page. The heading begins at the very top of the page, the first line ending about an inch from the page's right side, the second line about three quarters of an inch, and the final line almost the same distance as the first. The title of the manuscript is underlined, written in letters a little larger than the rest of the text, and placed just off center, slightly below the first line of the heading and slightly above the second line. The heading and title are written in a light blue, almost violet, ink (which may be the same color of ink in which the entire MBB story is written) while the rest of the manuscript is written in black or perhaps blue-black ink.

---

14 The fun of doing a project which works with an original manuscript is getting to plumb its mysteries as something of an archaeological artifact. My wife Becky and I, along with my tech-savvy friend John Harvey, had fun working with a digital photocopy of "Light" in *Photoshop* where we were able to flip the page in several directions, reverse it, zoom in and out, and use various adjustment tools to make some of the vague impressions on page one readable (or almost so). None of the discoveries were earth shattering, but the search, as I say, was fun.

15 There's no telling whether it was Lewis who kept the story in a stack as I've described or the later possessor of the story who did so. According to Douglas Gresham, most of Lewis's writing that "was 'pending' i.e. not finished with but not rejected, lived in the drawers of his central desk in his upstairs office" (16 April 2011; Email to Starr).

Light

The same shade of light blue ink in the heading and title appears in two other places in the manuscript, one each on pages three and four where Lewis has crossed out and replaced (page three) or inserted (page four) a word in the text. This leads me to conjecture that Lewis wrote out the manuscript, starting from the first ruled line on the first page and later read through the manuscript to proof it, during which time he added the title and heading to the top of page one and made the corrections on pages two and three, all in the same color of ink.

C.S. Lewis's First and Final Short Story

Light

BIBLIOGRAPHY

Adey, Lionel. "The Barfield-Lewis 'Great War." *CSL: The Bulletin of the New York C. S. Lewis Society* 6.10 (August 1975): 10-14.

—. *C. S. Lewis' 'Great War' with Owen Barfield*. Rosley, UK: Ink Books, 1978.

Alexander, Samuel. *Space, Time, and Deity: the Gifford Lectures at Glasgow 1916-1918*. 1920. New York: Dover Publications, 1966.

Barfield, Owen. "C. S. L. Biographia Theologia." First published in Glyer, *The Company They Keep*, 177.

—. "Great War Letter to C. S. Lewis." Bodleian, Ms. Facs. c. 54, folio 17, par. 4.

—. "Introduction." *Light on Lewis*. Ed. Jocelyn Gibb. New York: Harcourt Brace, 1965. ix-xxi.

—. "Letter to Ed Brown." 17 November 1986. MS.

—. *Owen Barfield on C. S. Lewis*. Middletown, CT: Wesleyan UP, 1989.

—. "Owen Barfield's Response to John Fitzpatrick's Essay on 'The Man Born Blind.'" *CSL: The Bulletin of the New York C. S. Lewis Society* 14.8 (June 1983): 5.

—. *Poetic Diction: A Study in Meaning*. 1928. Middletown, CT: Wesleyan UP, 1973.

—. "Preface." *The Taste of the Pineapple: Essays on C. S. Lewis as a Reader, Critic, and Imaginative Writer*. Ed. Bruce Edwards. Bowling Green: Bowling Green State UP, 1988.

—. *Saving the Appearances: A Study in Idolatry*. 1965. 2nd ed. Middletown: Wesleyan UP, 1988.

Barker, Nicolas. "C. S. Lewis, Darkly." *Essays in Criticism* 40.4 (1990): 358-67.

Bramlett, Perry C. "The Great War." *The C. S. Lewis Readers' Encyclopedia*. Eds. Jeffrey D. Schultz and John G. West Jr. Grand Rapids: Zondervan, 1998. 188-89.

—. "Transposition." *The C. S. Lewis Readers' Encyclopedia*. Eds. Jeffrey D. Schultz and John G. West Jr. Grand Rapids: Zondervan, 1998. 408-09.

Bremer, John. "Edmund Spenser (c.1551-1559)." *The C. S. Lewis Readers' Encyclopedia*. Eds. Jeffrey D. Schultz and John G. West Jr. Grand Rapids: Zondervan, 1998. 382-83.

—. "*Spenser's Images of Life.*" *The C. S. Lewis Readers' Encyclopedia.* Eds. Jeffrey D. Schultz and John G. West Jr. Grand Rapids: Zondervan, 1998. 383-85.
Brown, Edwin W., M.D. with Dan Hamilton. *In Pursuit of C. S. Lewis: Adventures in Collecting His Works.* Bloomington, IN: Author House, 2006.
—. Email to Charlie W. Starr. 24 January, 2011. TS.
—. Email to Charlie W. Starr. 6 February, 2011. TS.
—. Email to Charlie W. Starr. 23 March 2011. TS.
—. Email to Charlie W. Starr. 18 April 2011. TS.
—. Personal Interview. 13 March 2011. Author. Indianapolis, Indiana.
Camery-Hoggatt, Jerry. "God in the Plot: Storytelling and the Many-Sided Truth of the Christian Faith." *Christian Scholars Review* 35 (2006): 451-470.
Carnell, Corbin Scott. "Imagination." *The C. S. Lewis Readers' Encyclopedia.* Eds. Jeffrey D. Schultz and John G. West Jr. Grand Rapids: Zondervan, 1998: 214-15.
Damen, Mark. Online Course: *Ancient Literature and Language.* Chapter 11: "Vergil and *The Aeneid*," Part II, "Vergil's *Aeneid*: Books 1-2," Subsection B, "An Introduction to *The Aeneid*," par. 5. Utah State University, 2004. Web. 1 September 2011. http://www.usu.edu/markdamen/1320AncLit/chapters/11verg.htm.
"Edwin W. Brown Collection." *Taylor University.* Web. 1 March 2011. http://library.taylor.edu/cslewis/collection/.
Feinendegen, Norbert. "Contemplating C. S. Lewis's Epistemology: Reflections on C. S. Lewis's Argument with Owen Barfield about the Distinction Between Enjoyment and Contemplation During the 'Great War.'" *Seven: An Anglo-American Literary Review* 24 (2007): 29-52.
—. "A Reply to Stephen Thorson." *Seven: An Anglo-American Literary Review* 25 (2008): 69-79.
Fischier, Tony. Email to Charlie W. Starr. 16 April 2011. TS.
—. *Parkercollector.com.* Web. 10 April 2011. http://parkercollector.com.
Fitzpatrick, John. "The Short Stories: A Critical Introduction." *CSL: The Bulletin of the New York C. S. Lewis Society* 14.6 (April 1983): 1-5.
Gardner, Anne. "'Spenser's Cruel Cupid.'" *The C. S. Lewis Readers' Encyclopedia.* Eds. Jeffrey D. Schultz and John G. West Jr. Grand Rapids: Zondervan, 1998. 383.

Glyer, Diana Pavlac. *The Company They Keep: C. S. Lewis and J. R. R. Tolkien as Writers in Community*. Kent, OH: Kent State UP, 2007.
—. Email to Charlie W. Starr. 3 March 2011. TS.
Green, Roger Lancelyn, and Walter Hooper. *C. S. Lewis: A Biography*. San Diego: Harvest/HBJ, 1974.
Gresham, Douglas H. *Lenten Lands: My Childhood with Joy Davidman and C. S. Lewis*. San Francisco: Harper, 1988.
—. Email to Charlie W. Starr. 7 January 1997. TS.
—. Email to Charlie W. Starr. 22 February 2011. TS.
—. Email to Charlie W. Starr. 23 February 2011. TS.
—. Email to Charlie W. Starr. 24 February 2011. TS.
—. Email to Charlie W. Starr. 25 February 2011. TS.
—. Email to Charlie W. Starr. 16 April 2011. TS.
—. Email to Charlie W. Starr. 26 April 2011 4:47 a.m. EDT. TS.
—. Email to Charlie W. Starr: 26 April 2011. 10:50 a.m. EDT. TS.
Holy Bible. King James Version.
Holy Bible. New American Standard Version.
Holy Bible. New International Version.
Honda, Mineko. *The Imaginative World of C. S. Lewis: A Way to Participate in Reality*. New York: University Press of America, 2000.
Hooper, Walter. *C. S. Lewis: Companion & Guide*. San Francisco: Harper San Francisco, 1996.
—. Email to Charlie W. Starr. 31 August 2011. TS.
—. Email to Robert Trexler. 30 January 2012. TS.
—. "Introduction." C. S. Lewis. *They Stand Together: The Letters of C. S. Lewis to Arthur Greeves (1914-1963)*. Ed. Walter Hooper. New York: Macmillan, 1979. 9-45.
—. "Introduction." C. S. Lewis. *The Weight of Glory and Other Addresses*. Ed. Walter Hooper. New York: Macmillan, 1980. ix-xxvi.
—. *Past Watchful Dragons: The Narnia Chronicles of C. S. Lewis*. New York: Collier, 1979.
—. Personal Interview. 18 July 2011. Author. Oxford, UK.
—. "Oxford's Bonny Fighter." *C. S. Lewis at the Breakfast Table: and Other Reminiscences*. Ed. James T. Como. New York: Macmillan, 1979. 137-185.
—. "Preface." C. S. Lewis. *Collected Letters, Vol. I: Family Letters, 1905-1931*. Ed. Walter Hooper. London: Harper Collins, 2000. vii-xii.

—. "Preface." C. S. Lewis. *The Dark Tower and Other Stories*. Ed. Walter Hooper. San Diego: Harcourt Brace, 1977. 7-14.

—. "Preface." C. S. Lewis. *Narrative Poems*. Ed. Walter Hooper. San Diego: Harcourt Brace, 1969. vii-xiv.

Kilby, Clyde S. *Tolkien & the* Silmarillion. Wheaton: Harold Shaw, 1976.

King, Don W. *C. S. Lewis, Poet: The Legacy of His Poetic Impulse*. Kent, OH: Kent State UP, 2001.

Lewis, C. S. *The Allegory of Love: A Study in Medieval Tradition*. 1936. Oxford: Oxford UP, 1958.

—. "—And Became Fact." Wade MS. CSL/MS-4. Wheaton: Marion E. Wade Center, Wheaton College.

—. "The Birth of Language." Bodleian MS. Eng. lett. c. 220/3. 21. Oxford: Bodleian Library.

—. "Bluspels and Flalansferes." *Selected Literary Essays*. Ed. Walter Hooper. Cambridge: Cambridge UP, 1969. 251-65.

—. "Caught." *The Collected Poems of C. S. Lewis*. Ed. Walter Hooper. London: Fount, 1994. 129-30.

—. *Clivi Hamiltonis Summae Metaphysices Contra Anthroposophos Libri II* (The *Summa*). Original MS. Upland: The Edwin W. Brown Collection, Taylor University. Transcription by Norbert Feinendegen, Bonn Germany.

—. *Collected Letters, Vol. I: Family Letters, 1905-1931*. Ed. Walter Hooper. London: Harper Collins, 2000.

—. *Collected Letters, Vol. II: Books, Broadcasts, and the War, 1931-1949*. Ed. Walter Hooper. San Francisco: Harper Collins, 2004.

—. *Collected Letters, Vol. III: Narnia, Cambridge and Joy, 1950-1963*. Ed. Walter Hooper. London: Harper Collins, 2006.

—. "The Country of the Blind." *The Collected Poems of C. S. Lewis*. Ed. Walter Hooper. London: Fount, 1994. 47-48.

—. "Dante's Similes." *Studies in Medieval & Renaissance Literature*. Ed. Walter Hooper. Cambridge: Cambridge UP, 1966. 64-77.

—. "De Audiendis Poetis." *Studies in Medieval & Renaissance Literature*. Ed. Walter Hooper. Cambridge: Cambridge UP, 1966. 1-17.

—. *The Discarded Image: An Introduction to Medieval and Renaissance Literature*. Cambridge: Cambridge UP, 1964.

—. "Donne and Love Poetry in the Seventeenth Century." Wade MS. CSL/MS-39. Wheaton: Marion E. Wade Center, Wheaton College.

—. "Dungeon Grates." *The Collected Poems of C. S. Lewis*. Ed. Walter

Hooper. London: Fount, 1994. 184-85.
—. *Dymer*. 1926. *Narrative Poem.* Ed. Walter Hooper. San Diego: Harcourt Brace, 1969. 3-91.
—. "The Empty Universe." *Present Concerns: Essays by C. S. Lewis.* Ed. Walter Hooper. San Diego: HBJ, 1986. 81-86.
—. *English Literature in the Sixteenth Century Excluding Drama. The Oxford History of English Literature* 3. Oxford: Clarendon, 1954.
—. *An Experiment in Criticism.* "Canto" ed, 1992. Cambridge: Cambridge UP, 1961.
—. *The Four Loves.* San Diego. Harvest/HBJ, 1960.
—. "The Grand Miracle." *God in the Dock: Essays on Theology and Ethics.* Ed. Walter Hooper. Grand Rapids: Eerdmans, 1970. 80-88.
—. *The Great Divorce.* New York: Collier, 1946.
—. *The Great Divorce* (Partial). Bodleian MS. Dep. d. 241. Oxford: Bodleian Library.
—. "'Great War' Letters to Owen Barfield." Bodleian MS. Facs. c. 54. Oxford: Bodleian Library.
—. *A Grief Observed.* 1961. San Francisco: HarperCollins, 1989.
—. "Horrid Red Things." *God in the Dock: Essays on Theology and Ethics.* Ed. Walter Hooper. Grand Rapids: Eerdmans, 1970. 68-71.
—. "The Humanitarian Theory of Punishment." *God in the Dock: Essays on Theology and Ethics.* Ed. Walter Hooper. Grand Rapids: Eerdmans, 1970. 287-300.
—. "Is Theology Poetry?" *The Weight of Glory and Other Addresses.* Ed. Walter Hooper. New York: Macmillan, 1980. 74-92.
—. "Launcelot." *Narrative Poems.* Ed. Walter Hooper. San Diego: Harcourt Brace, 1969. 93-103.
—. "Language and Human Nature." *Seven: An Anglo-American Literary Review* 27 (2010): 25-28.
—. "The Language of Religion." *Christian Reflections.* Ed. Walter Hooper. Grand Rapids: Eerdmans, 1967. 129-41.
—. *The Last Battle.* 1956. New York: HarperCollins, 1984.
—. "The Lefay Fragment." Bodleian MS. Dep. d. 811. Oxford: Bodleian Library. Published in Hooper, *Past Watchful Dragons*, 48-65.
—. *The Letters of C. S. Lewis.* Ed. W. H. Lewis. Rev. ed. Ed. Walter Hooper. San Diego: Harvest/HBJ, 1993.
—. *Letters to an American Lady.* Ed. Clyde S. Kilby. Grand Rapids: Eerdmans, 1967.

—. *Letters to Malcolm: Chiefly on Prayer.* San Diego: Harvest/HBJ, 1964.
—. "Letter." 10 June 1930. Wade MS. CSL/MS 140. Wheaton: Marion E. Wade Center, Wheaton College.
—. "Letter." 11 May 1942. Bodleian MS. Eng. lett. c. 220/1. Oxford: Bodleian Library.
—. "Letter to Arthur Greeves." 25 July 1922. Wade MS. Letters to Arthur Greeves, vol. 5, 1920-27. Wheaton: Marion E. Wade Center, Wheaton College.
—. "Letter to Arthur Greeves." 6 March 1926. Bodleian MS. Facs b 50. Oxford: Bodleian Library.
—. "Letter to Arthur Greeves." 26 June 1927. Wade MS. Letters to Arthur Greeves, vol. 5, 1920-27. Wheaton: Marion E. Wade Center, Wheaton College.
—. "Letter to Arthur Greeves." 24 December 1930. Bodleian MS. Facs. b. 51. Oxford: Bodleian Library.
—. "Letter to Arthur Greeves." 18 October 1931. Bodleian MS. Facs. b. 51. Oxford: Bodleian Library.
—. "Letter to Arthur Greeves." 8 November 1931. Bodleian MS. Facs. b. 51. Oxford: Bodleian Library.
—. "Letter to Arthur Greeves." 1 October 1934. Bodleian MS. Facs. b. 51. Oxford: Bodleian Library.
—. "Letter to Arthur Greeves." 23 December 1941. Bodleian MS. Facs. b. 51. Oxford: Bodleian Library.
—. "Letter to Cecil Harwood." 28 October 1926. Bodleian MS. Eng. lett. c. 861. Oxford: Bodleian Library.
—. "Letter to Cecil Harwood." 11 September 1945. Bodleian MS. Eng. lett. c. 861. Oxford: Bodleian Library.
—. "Letter to Cecil Harwood." Boxing Day [26 December] 1945. Bodleian MS. Eng. let. c. 861. Folio 43. Oxford: Bodleian Library.
—. "Letter to Jill Flewett (Freud)." 7 January 1948. MS. Upland: The Edwin W. Brown Collection, Taylor University.
—. "Letter to Mary Neylan." 17 April 1942. MS. Upland: The Edwin W. Brown Collection, Taylor University.
—. "Letter to Mr. Irwin." 28 August 1947. Bodleian MS. Dep. d. 415. Oxford: Bodleian Library.
—. "Letter to Mr. Neylan." 29 October 1941. Wade MS. CSL/MS-107. Wheaton: Marion E. Wade Center, Wheaton College.
—. "Letter to Owen Barfield. 19 December 1945. Wade MS. CSL/MS-8. Wheaton: Marion E. Wade Center, Wheaton College.

—. "Letter with Poem, 'Caught.'" Wade MS. CSL/MS-135. Wheaton: Marion E. Wade Center, Wheaton College.

—. "Letters to Arthur Greeves." Wade MS. Letters to Arthur Greeves, vol. 2, 1916-17. Wheaton: Marion E. Wade Center, Wheaton College.

—. "Light." MS. Upland: The Edwin W. Brown Collection, Taylor University.

—. *The Lion, the Witch and the Wardrobe*. 1950. New York: HarperCollins, 1978.

—. *The Magician's Nephew*. 1955. New York: HarperCollins, 1983.

—. "The Man Born Blind." Ed. Walter Hooper. *Church Times*, No 5947 (4 February 1977). Rpt. in *The Dark Tower and Other Stories*. Ed. Walter Hooper. San Diego: Harcourt Brace, 1977. 99-103.

—. "The Man Born Blind" (Untitled Original MS). Notebook entitled, *Lewis Ms No. 31*. Bodleian Manuscript Dep. d. 809. Oxford: Bodleian Library. 22-28.

—. "Meditation in a Toolshed." *God in the Dock: Essays on Theology and Ethics*. Ed. Walter Hooper. Grand Rapids: Eerdmans, 1970. 212-15.

—. *Mere Christianity*. "Christian Library" ed. Westwood, NJ: Barbour and Company, 1952.

—. *Miracles: A Preliminary Study*. 1947. New York: Touchstone, 1975.

—. *The Moral Good: It's Place Among the Values*. Wade MS. CSL/MS-76X. Wheaton: Marion E. Wade Center, Wheaton College.

—. "Myth Became Fact." *The Grand Miracle and Other Selected Essays on Theology and Ethics from God in the Dock*. Ed. Walter Hooper. New York: Ballentine Books, 1970. 38-42.

—. "Noon's Intensity." *The Collected Poems of C. S. Lewis*. Ed. Walter Hooper. London: Fount, 1994. 128.

—. *Notes on Henry More*. Wade MS. CSL/MS-170. Wheaton: Marion E. Wade Center, Wheaton College.

—. "On Forgiveness." Bodleian MS. d. 415. Oxford: Bodleian Library.

—. "On a Theme from Nicolas of Cusa." *The Collected Poems of C. S. Lewis*. Ed. Walter Hooper. London: Fount, 1994. 84.

—. "On Three Ways of Writing for Children." *Of Other Worlds: Essays and Stories*. Ed. Walter Hooper. New York: Harcourt Brace Jovanovich, 1966. 22-34.

—. "Our Daily Bread." *Spirits in Bondage: A Cycle of Lyrics*. 1919. Ed. Walter Hooper. San Diego: Harcourt Brace Jovanovich, 1984. 60.

—. *Out of the Silent Planet.* 1938. New York: Scribner, 2003.

—. "A Pageant Played in Vain." *The Collected Poems of C. S. Lewis.* Ed. Walter Hooper. London: Fount, 1994. 110.

—. *Perelandra.* 1944. New York: Scribner, 1972.

—. *The Pilgrim's Regress: An Allegorical Apology for Christianity, Reason, and Romanticism.* 1933. Grand Rapids: Eerdmans, 1981.

—. "The Planets." *The Collected Poems of C. S. Lewis.* Ed. Walter Hooper. London: Fount, 1994. 26-29.

—. "The Poison of Subjectivism." *Christian Reflections.* Ed. Walter Hooper. Grand Rapids: Eerdmans, 1967. 72-81.

—. *A Preface to Paradise Lost.* 1942. London: Oxford UP, 1961.

—. *The Problem of Pain.* New York: Macmillan, 1940.

—. "Psycho-Analysis and Literary Criticism." *Selected Literary Essays.* Ed. Walter Hooper. Cambridge: Cambridge UP, 1969. 286-300.

—. "Reason." *Poems.* Ed. Walter Hooper. San Diego: Harvest/HBJ, 1992. 81.

—. *Reflections on the Psalms.* London: Fontana, 1958.

—. "Relapse." *Poems.* Ed. Walter Hooper. San Diego: Harvest/HBJ, 1992. 103.

—. "Religion: Reality or Substitute." *Essay Collection & Other Short Pieces.* Ed. Lesley Walmsley. London: HarperCollins, 2000. 131-137.

—. "Scazons." *The Collected Poems of C. S. Lewis.* Ed. Walter Hooper. London: Fount, 1994. 132.

—. *The Screwtape Letters.* Wade MS. CSL/MS-107. Wheaton: Marion E. Wade Center, Wheaton College.

—. *The Screwtape Letters with Screwtape Proposes a Toast.* 1942. 1961. San Francisco: HarperCollins, 1996.

—. *The Silver Chair.* 1953. New York: HarperCollins, 1981.

—. *Spenser's Images of Life.* Ed. Alistair Fowler. Cambridge: Cambridge UP, 1967.

—. *Studies in Words.* 2nd ed. "Canto" ed, 1996. Cambridge: Cambridge UP, 1960.

—. *Surprised by Joy: The Shape of My Early Life.* San Diego: Harvest/HBJ, 1955.

—. *That Hideous Strength: A Modern Fairy-Tale for Grown-Ups.* 1945. New York: Scribner, 1974.

—. *They Stand Together: The Letters of C. S. Lewis to Arthur Greeves (1914-1963).* Ed. Walter Hooper. New York: Macmillan, 1979.

—. *Till We Have Faces: A Myth Retold.* 1956. San Diego: Harcourt Brace, 1985.

—. *Transposition and Other Addresses*. London: Geoffrey Bles, 1949.

—. "Transposition." *C. S. Lewis: Essay Collection and Other Short Pieces*. Ed. Lesley Walmsley. London: HarperCollins, 2000. 267-278.

—. "Unpublished Outline for 'Life' Chapter in *Studies in Words*." Notebook entitled, *Lewis Ms No. 27*. Bodleian MS. Dep. d. 810. Oxford: Bodleian Library.

—. "Unpublished Paragraph about Community Going Blind." Bodleian MS. Dep. d. 811. Oxford: Bodleian Library.

—. *The Voyage of the Dawn Treader*. 1952. New York: HarperCollins, 1980.

—. "The Weight of Glory." *The Weight of Glory and Other Addresses*. 1949. Ed. Walter Hooper. New York: Macmillan, 1980.

—. "The World's Last Night." *The World's Last Night and Other Essays*. San Diego: Harcourt, Brace, 1987. 93-113.

Mead, Marjorie L. "Spenser's Irish Experiences and *The Faerie Queene* (Letter)." *The C. S. Lewis Readers' Encyclopedia*. Eds. Jeffrey D. Schultz and John G. West Jr. Grand Rapids: Zondervan, 1998. 385.

Milton, John. *Paradise Lost. Norton Critical Edition*. Ed. Scott Elledge. New York: Norton, 1975.

"Nicolas Barker." *Fathom: The Source for Online Learning*. 2002. Web. 5 December 2011. http://www.fathom.com/contributors/4276.html.

Neuhouser, David. "Higher Dimensions: C. S. Lewis and Mathematics." *Seven: An Anglo-American Literary Review* 13 (1996): 45-64.

"Parker Pen Company." *Wikipedia*. Web. 26 August 2011. http://en.wikipedia.org/wiki/Parker_Pen_Company.

"The Parker Pen History." *Parkerpen.com*. Web. 26 August 2011. http://www.parkerpen.com/en/discovery/making_of/timeline.

Phillips, Justin. *C. S. Lewis at the BBC: Messages of Hope in the Darkness of War*. London: HarperCollins, 2002.

Plato. *The Republic*. Trans. Allan Bloom. New York: Basic Books, 1968.

Priestman, Judith. *A Selective Catalogue of the Papers of C. S. Lewis (1898-1963)*. Oxford: Bodleian Library. Compiled 1989.

"Quink." *Wikipedia*. Web. 30 March 2011. http://en.wikipedia.org/wiki/Quink.

"Quink Advertisement." *Boys Life* (March 1935): 35. *Google Books*. Web. 31 May 2011. http://books.google.com/books?id=uNvVyIetZwC&pg=pg=PA34&lpg=PA34&dq=When+did+Parker+release+Royal+Blue+Quink?&source=bl&ots=3CoD9rZam&sig=6

g308Pt 60y1IdxfHrXNZk_kN90&hl=en&ei=UuvTTdKXDu bb0QGmsYzeCw&sa=X&oi=book_result&ct=result&resnum =5&ved=0CCQQ6AEwBDgK#v=onepage &q&f=false.

Sammons, Martha. *"A Far Off Country": A Guide to C. S. Lewis's Fantasy Fiction.* New York: University Press of America, 2000.

—. "'The Man Born Blind': Light in C. S. Lewis." *CSL: The Bulletin of the New York C. S. Lewis Society* 9.2 (December 1977): 1-7.

Sayer, George. *Jack: A Life of C. S. Lewis.* 1988. Wheaton: Crossway, 1994.

Schakel, Peter J. *Reason and Imagination in C. S. Lewis: A Study of Till We Have Faces.* Grand Rapids: Eerdmans, 1984.

—. "Seeing and Knowing: The Epistemology of C. S. Lewis's *Till We Have Faces.*" *Seven: An Anglo-American Literary Review* 4 (1983): 84-97.

—. Smith-Theobald, Sharon and Edwin Posey. *Appraisal of the Brown Collection.* Appraisal Associates International. West Lafayette Indiana. 10 December 1996.

Starr, Charlie W. "Contemplating Norbert Feinendegen's Epistemological Contemplation: Greater Understanding of and Next Steps Toward Grasping C. S. Lewis's Theory of Knowledge." *Seven: An Anglo-American Literary Review* 25 (2008): 81-86.

Thorson, Stephen. "Enjoying the Spirit, Enjoying the Soul: A Response to Norbert Feinendegen." *Seven: An Anglo-American Literary Review* 25 (2008): 61-69.

—. "Knowing and Being in C. S. Lewis's 'Great War' with Owen Barfield." *CSL: The Bulletin of the New York C. S. Lewis Society* 15.1 (November 1983): 1-9.

—. "Two Clarifying Points." *Seven: An Anglo-American Literary Review* 25 (2008): 79-80.

—. and Norbert Feinendegen. "A Dialogue Concluded: 'Enjoyment' and 'Contemplation' as Used in Owen Barfield and C. S. Lewis's 'Great War.'" *Seven An Anglo-American Literary Review.* On-Line. Web. http://www2.wheaton.edu/wadecenter/seven/Feinendegen-Thorson-Dialogue_web.pdf.

Walmsley, Lesley, ed. *C. S. Lewis: Essay Collection and Other Short Pieces.* London: HarperCollins, 2000.

Ward, Michael. *Planet Narnia: The Seven Heavens in the Imagination of C. S. Lewis.* Oxford: Oxford UP, 2008.

Warner, Francis and R. E. Alton. "C. S. Lewis Manuscripts: A Report." 24 July 1989. Oxford.

Wells, H. G. "The Country of the Blind." *The Country of the Blind and Other Short Stories: Electronic Classics Series*. Ed. Jim Manis. Hazelton PA: Penn State UP, 376-399. Web. 7 March 2012. http://www2.hn.psu.edu/faculty/jmanis/hgwells/Country-Blind.pdf.

Williams, Charles. "The Calling of Taliessin." *The Region of Summer Stars*. London: Oxford UP, 1944. 5-20.

—. *He Came Down from Heaven*. 1938. Grand Rapids: Eerdmans, 1984.

Light

INDEX

A

Anthroposophy, 46, 47, n47, 52, 54, 76
Alexander, Samuel, 50, 51, n51, n74, n75, 84, 87
Aesthetic(s), 47, 87, 104, 107, 108 (see also Beauty and Glory)

B

Barfield, Owen, 1, 2, 16, 18, 21, n21, 22, n22, 23, 24, 25, 26, 28, n28, 29, n31, 32, 33, n33, n34, 37, 38, 39, 42, 43, 46-48, n46, n48, 49, n49, 51, 52-56, n52-55, 57, 58, 72, n73, 76, n76, 77, 86, 99, 113, 114, 145, n145
Beauty (see also Aesthetics and Glory), 64, 80, n82, 87, 100, 103-04, 106-108, n108, 110
Blindness (Blind), 21, 49, 63-69, 85, n86, 87, 94, 100, n106, 109, 140, 142, 145, 146, 147 (see also Epistemology)
Brown Collection, iii, 34, 35, n36, n53
Brown, Edwin, iii, 1, 2, n5, n14, n15, 16-19, n16-19, 20, n20, n21, 22-23, n22-23, 24-25, n24, 26, n28, 29, n29, n34, 38, n145, n149, n150

E

Enjoyment/Contemplation, 2, 50-51, n51, 52, 53, 54, 55, 58, 59, 63, 66, 67, 69, 71, 72, 73, 74, 75, 76, 78, 81, 87
Epistemology (Epistemological, Knowing), 48, n48 49, n49, 50, 51, n51, 55, 56, 57-59, 62, 64, 66, 69, 71, n71, 72, n72, 73-78, 86, 87, 99, 100, 102, 109, 113 (see also Blindness, Looking and Seeing)
Abstract/Concrete Thinking, 51, 53, n73, 74-76, 77, 78, 79, n79, 81-83, 99, 100, 103, 110, n110, 131
Experience, 2, 50-54, n50-51, 59-67, n62, 69, 70-79, 81-83, 85, 86, 87, 91, 92, 93, 96, 99, 104-105, 106, 107, 109, 110, 112, 143, 144
Imagination, x, 2, 52, 55, 56, 69, 71-79, n71-73, 80, 82-83, 86, 91, 92, 100
Myth, 2, 52, 64, 68, 73-79, 80-81, n81, 83, 102, 109
Reality (the Real, Fact), x, 2, 21, 41, 47, 48, n48, 51, 52-54, 63, 66-68, 72-79, n73, n79, 80-83, n80, n82, 85, 86-92,

94, 96, 98-99, 100, 103, 108, 109, 112,
Reason (Thinking, Thought), 2, 41-42, 47, 49, 52, 53, 55, 57, 61, 65, 66, 67, 71-73, n71-73, 75-77, 79, 81-83, 86, 110, n110
Truth (true), 47, 52, 56, 57-59, 61, 64-65, 71-73, n72, 77-79, 80, 81-83, 85, n97, 99, 100, 101, 102
Experience (see Epistemology)

F

Fact (see Epistemology: Reality)

G

God (Christ), 29, 33, 41, n47, n48, 49, n49, 51, 55, 58, 59, 68, 71, n72, n74, 78, 89, n80, n82, 83, 85, 86, 87, 90, 91, 97, 101, 102, n102, 103, 106, 107, 108, n108, 109, 112, 113
The "Great War," 21, 31, n31, n32, 33, n33, 43, 46-47, n47, n48, 49, n49, 51-56, n52-53, 57, 71, 109, 113
Glory (see also Aesthetics and Beauty), 48, 90, 101, 103, 106-109, n106, n108, 110
Gresham, Douglas, 1, 12, n12, 13, n13-14, 16, n16, 24-26, n25-26 27,
28-29, n28-29, 32, 39, 57, n151

H

Hooper, Walter, ix, 1, 5, n5, 11-15, n11-15, 16, 19, 21, n21, 22, n22, 24, n24, 25, n25, 26, 28, 30, n30, 36, n36, 37-40, n37, n38, n40, n41, 43, n43, n46, n47, n48, n59, 71, n71, n73, n95, n106, 114, n117, n118, n123, n139, 144, 147, n148, 149, n149

I

Idealism v. Realism, 47-49, n49, n53
Imagination (see Epistemology)
Incarnation, 55, 58, n58, 68, 79, 90, n91, 102, 115

J

Joy (see Longing)

K

Knowing (see Epistemology)

L

Lewis, C. S.,
Biographical, ix-xi, 11-14, 22, 23, 24, 25, 28, 30, 38-39, 41, 46-47, 69, 107, 139
Books and Essays, "Bluspels and Flalansferes," 82, n82

Clivi Hamiltonis Summae Metaphysices Contra Anthroposophos Libri II (the *Summa*), n31, 32, 33, n33, 53, n53, 54, n54, 55
"Dante's Similes," 62, n62
The Dark Tower and Other Stories, n5, n14, 15, n21, 24, 34, n46, n48, n59, n11
"De Audiendis Poetis," n80
The Discarded Image, n24, 58, n58, 113, n113
"Donne and Love Poetry in the Seventeenth Century," n139, n150
"The Empty Universe," n64
English Literature in the Sixteenth Century, 40, n40, 77, n77, n102, n149
An Experiment in Criticism, n24, 72, n72
The Four Loves, 58, n58, 65, n65, 90, n90, n98, n102, n108
"The Grand Miracle," n58, n102
The Great Divorce, n36, 81, n81, 98-99, n98-99, 100, 107-08, n107-108, 109, n109, 112, n112, 113, n113
A Grief Observed, 69, n69, n91
"Horrid Red Things," n83
"The Humanitarian Theory of Punishment," n64
"Is Theology Poetry?", n49, n58
"Language and Human Nature," n20
"The Language of Religion," n64, n102
The Last Battle, nx, 68, n69, 81, n81, 101, n101, n103, n110, 112, n112
"The Lefay Fragment," n40, n139
Letters to Malcolm, x, xi, n90-91, 101, n101, n102, 107, n107, n139
"Light," 1, 2, 5, 6-9, 16, 17, n17, 18, n18, 20, 22, n22, 23, 24, n24, 25, n25, 26, 28-39, n36, n38, 42-49, 51, n53, 54-57, n54, 59, 63, 70-73, 78, 85-89, n89, 93, 94, 96, n96, 100, 103, 106, n108, 109, 111-116, 117-138, n117-121, n123, n124, n126, n127, n130, n134, n136, n139, 140-147, 148, 149, 151, n151

The Lion, the Witch and the Wardrobe, x, 39, n85, 110, n110
The Magician's Nephew, n40, 139
"The Man Born Blind" (MBB), 5, 19-22, n19, n22, 24-29, n30, 31-44, n31, n36, n38, n40, n41, 48, n48, 57, n59, 71, 73, 86, 94, 96, 100, 112, 114, 115, 117-138, n117-121, n123, n124, n127, n129, n130, n134, n137, 140-146, n142, n144, 148, 149, n149, 151
"Meditation in a Toolshed," 50, 59-63, n59-61, n63, 69, 78, 84, 87, 106, 109, 111
Mere Christianity, n67, 68, n68, n80, n82, n86, 103, n103, 139
Miracles, 57, n57, n58, 65-67, n65, n66, n68, 77, n77, n80, 82, n82, 83, n83, n90, 100, 101, n101, 107, n107, n115, 139, n139
The Moral Good: It's Place Among the Values, 30
"Myth Became Fact," 23, n23, 60, 66, 73-75, n74-75, 78-79, n78- 79, 87, 109

Notes on Henry More, 30
"On Forgiveness," n24
"On Three Ways of Writing for Children," n80
Out of the Silent Planet, 96, n96, 98, n98, 99, n99, n106, 107, n107, 108, 111, n111, n118, 139
Perelandra, 66, n66, 73, 73, 77, n77, n80, 98, n98, 110, n110, 139
The Pilgrim's Regress, n103, 104, n104
"The Poison of Subjectivism," 63, n82
A Preface to Paradise Lost, 41, n74, 95, n95, 96, n131
The Problem of Pain, n80-81, n103
"Psycho-Analysis and Literary Criticism," n80
Reflections on the Psalms, n58, n59, n102
"Religion: Reality or Substitute," n82
The Screwtape Letters, 1, n23, 26, n82, n118, n139
The Silver Chair, 101, n101, 105-106, n106
Spenser's Images of Life, n102
Studies in Words, 100, n100
Surprised by Joy, 21, n46, n47, 50, n50, n51,

n55, n68, n73, n83, n102, n103, n104
That Hideous Strength, x, xi, 38, n62, n63-64, 77, n77, 98, n98, n123, 139, n148
Till We Have Faces, n71, 110, n110,
"Transposition" (and Transposition), 41, 42, 86-92, n86-89, n91, 93, 112
The Voyage of the Drawn *Treader*, n63, 83, 84, n84, 97, n97, 105, n105, 108, 109, n110
"The Weight of Glory," 103-104, n104, 106, n106, n108, 109
"The World's Last Night," n72, 99, n100
Poems (Narrative Poems), 30, n31, n36, 40, n40, 58, n58, 64, n64, 73, n73, 82, n82, n89, n97, 107, n107, 111, n111, n148, 149
Light, 2, 6-9, 21, 29, 48, n58, 61, 62, n62, n63, 65, 68, 70, 84, 85, 87, 90, 94, 107, 110-114, 117-138, n132, 140-143, 145-147
  as Divine Symbol, n48, n49, 55, 58, 59, n61, 68, 78, n82, 90-92, 102, n102, 107-109
  as Epistemological Symbol, 48, n48, 49, 54, 55, 57-59, n58, 60, 61, 65-66, 67, 68, 69, 70, 85, 86, 89, 90, 92, 113
  as Platonic Reality, n48, 62, 68, 70, 78, 88, 89, n89, 90, 92, 93-101, n97, n98, 102-109 n106, n109, 110-114, 141, 143, 146, 147
  as Reflection, 61, 62, 68, 78, 86, n86, 88-90, n90, 92, 106, n106, 107-109, 112, 113
Logical Positivism, 63-65
Longing (Sehnsucht, Joy), 2, 51, 87, 93, 102, 103-107, 109, 110, 111, 113, 146
Looking At/Along, n50, 51, 55, 59-63, n62, 65-69, 73, 75, 78-79, 83-85, 87, 92, 109-110, n110, 112 (see also Epistemology and Seeing)

M

Modern Thought, 52, 60, 63, 64, 100
Morality (Morals), 30, 47, 52, 57, n58, 63, 67, 72, 83, 86, 102
Milton, John (see *Paradise Lost*)
Myth (see Epistemology)

N

Narnia, x, xi, 1, n16, 37, 40, n46, 48, n48, n58, n63, 68, 69, 81, 84, n84, n85, n89, 97, n97,

101, n102, 105, 112, 139
Naturalism (Materialism), 49, 65-68, 77, 101

P

Paradise Lost (Milton), 41, n74, 94-96, n96, n98, 100, 105, 122, 125, n131, 133, 146
Philosophy (Philosopher, Philosophical), 41, 46, 47, 49, n51, 54, 56, n58, 62, n63, 67, 68, 74, 76, 95, 102, 113, 146
Plato (Platonic, Platonism), 48, 64, 68, 77, 79, 81, n89, 99, 100-102, n101-102, 103, 111, 112, 113, n120, 146,

Q

Quink Ink, 26-28, n27-28, 32, 36

R

Reality (see Epistemology)
Reason (see Epistemology)

S

Seeing (Sight), 6-9, 21, 48, 49-51, n53, 54, 55, 58-62, n61, 63-69, 70, n70, n71, 78, 83, 88-92, n90, 93-94, 96-99, 101, 105-109, 112, 119-122, n123, n124, 125, n128, 129, n129, 130, 133, 134, 136-138, 141, 143-145, 147

(see also Epistemology and Looking)
Sehnsucht (See Longing)

T

Tolkien, J. R. R., xi, 21, n21, 24, 139, 140
Transposition (see "Transposition")
Truth (see Epistemology)

W

Wells, H. G., 64
Williams, Charles, 18, n90, 101, n101

C. S. Lewis's First and Final Short Story

C. S. LEWIS & FRIENDS BOOK SERIES

With the cooperation of Winged Lion Press, the Center for the Study of C. S. Lewis and Friends at Taylor University plans to publish one volume of distinguished scholarship every two years. *Light: C. S. Lewis's First and Final Short Story* is the second book in this series. Our interest centers on work concerning C. S. Lewis, George MacDonald, Dorothy L. Sayers, Owen Barfield, and Charles Williams. Authors with book-length manuscripts who would like their work considered for future volumes may send a cover letter and proposal to Pam Jordan-Long / Program Director / Center for the Study of C. S. Lewis and Friends / Taylor University / Upland, IN 46989. http://library.taylor.edu/cslewis/index.shtml

The Center for the Study of C. S. Lewis & Friends is housed at Taylor University in Upland, Indiana, located in the Midwest of the U.S.A. With a mission to promote the kingdom of God through the study of exemplary Christian authors, the Center serves the Taylor University campus, the local community, and a worldwide academic and lay audience. We offer several programs to reach these various groups. For our students, we hold classes on the works of C. S. Lewis and several related authors—primarily, but not exclusively, George MacDonald, Dorothy L. Sayers, Charles Williams, and Owen Barfield. For our local community, we present regular C. S. Lewis Society Meetings, featuring lectures and discussions on the works of Lewis and related authors. And for our more distant friends, we organize the biennial Frances White Ewbank Colloquium on C. S. Lewis & Friends, which gathers scholars and readers from across the United States and around the world. For all of these groups, we maintain one of the finest rare book and manuscript collections, which we have named after its collector, Edwin W. Brown.

The Edwin W. Brown Collection includes first English and American editions of books authored, edited, or with prefaces by C. S. Lewis, published essays and lectures of Lewis, several Lewis letters, and two Lewis manuscripts ("Light" and *Clivi Hamiltonis Summae Metaphysics Contra Anthroposophos Libri II*). The collection also contains books about C. S. Lewis, as well as first and reprint editions of Charles Williams, Dorothy L. Sayers, George MacDonald, and Owen Barfield. Individuals or groups interested in visiting the collection are welcome during the academic year, when we hold regular hours; special arrangements can also be made for other times. We are always eager to share our collection with new friends.

Pam Jordan-Long, Program Director

ABOUT THE AUTHOR

Dr. Charlie W. Starr teaches English, Humanities, and Film at Kentucky Christian University in Eastern Kentucky where he also makes movies with his students and family. He writes a monthly column on Christians and the Arts and Media for *Lookout* magazine and has published four books: two biblical studies, a science-fiction novel, and, most recently, a children's book entitled *King Lesserlight's Crown*. Charlie has published several scholarly and popular articles on C. S. Lewis, especially on Lewis and film. His essay, "The Silver Chair and the Silver Screen" is the lead chapter in the book *Revisiting Narnia*. Besides writing for print, Charlie has acted as a consultant, writer, actor and/or producer on over a dozen short film projects. His most recent film (as producer), a music video entitled "Recollection," was accepted into three national film festivals and featured internationally on the U. S. Military's Pentagon Channel.

Charlie enjoys caving, writing, reading, watching bad television, and movies of every kind. His areas of expertise as a teacher include literature, film, and all things C. S. Lewis. Charlie and his wife Becky have two mostly grown-up children, Bryan and Alathia, and a four pound family dog named Phydeaux.

OTHER BOOKS OF INTEREST

C. S. Lewis

C. S. Lewis: Views From Wake Forest - Essays on C. S. Lewis
Michael Travers, editor

Contains sixteen scholarly presentations from the international C. S. Lewis convention in Wake Forest, NC. Walter Hooper shares his important essay "Editing C. S. Lewis," a chronicle of publishing decisions after Lewis' death in 1963.

"Scholars from a variety of disciplines address a wide range of issues. The happy result is a fresh and expansive view of an author who well deserves this kind of thoughtful attention."
Diana Pavlac Glyer, author of *The Company They Keep*

The Hidden Story of Narnia:
A Book-By-Book Guide to Lewis' Spiritual Themes
Will Vaus

A book of insightful commentary equally suited for teens or adults – Will Vaus points out connections between the *Narnia* books and spiritual/biblical themes, as well as between ideas in the *Narnia* books and C. S. Lewis' other books. Learn what Lewis himself said about the overarching and unifying thematic structure of the Narnia books. That is what this book explores; what C. S. Lewis called "the hidden story" of Narnia. Each chapter includes questions for individual use or small group discussion.

Why I Believe in Narnia:
33 Reviews and Essays on the Life and Work of C. S. Lewis
James Como

Chapters range from reviews of critical books, documentaries and movies to evaluations of Lewis' books to biographical analysis.

"A valuable, wide-ranging collection of essays by one of the best informed and most accute commentators on Lewis' work and ideas."
Peter Schakel, author of *Imagination & the Arts in C. S. Lewis*

C. S. Lewis Goes to Heaven: A Reader's Guide to The Great Divorce
David G. Clark

This is the first book devoted solely to this often neglected book and the first to reveal several important secrets Lewis concealed within the story. Lewis felt his imaginary trip to Hell and Heaven was far better than his book *The Screwtape Letters*, which has become a classic. Clark is an ordained minister who has taught courses on Lewis for more than 30 years and is a New Testament and Greek scholar with a Doctor of Philosophy degree in Biblical Studies from the University of Notre Dame. Readers will discover the many literary and biblical influences Lewis utilized in writing his brilliant novel.

C. S. Lewis & Philosophy as a Way of Life
Adam Barkman

C. S. Lewis is rarely thought of as a "philosopher" per se despite having both studied and taught philosophy for several years at Oxford. Lewis's long journey to Christianity was essentially philosophical – passing through seven different stages. This 624 page book is an invaluable reference for C. S. Lewis scholars and fans alike

C. S. Lewis: His Literary Achievement
Colin Manlove

"This is a positively brilliant book, written with splendor, elegance, profundity and evidencing an enormous amount of learning. This is probably not a book to give a first-time reader of Lewis. But for those who are more broadly read in the Lewis corpus this book is an absolute gold mine of information. The author gives us a magnificent overview of Lewis' many writings, tracing for us thoughts and ideas which recur throughout, and at the same time telling us how each book differs from the others. I think it is not extravagant to call C. S. Lewis: His Literary Achievement a tour de force."
     Robert Merchant, *St. Austin Review*, Book Review Editor

Mythopoeic Narnia:
Memory, Metaphor, and Metamorphoses in The Chronicles of Narnia
Salwa Khoddam

Dr. Khoddam, the founder of the C. S. Lewis and Inklings Society (2004), has been teaching university courses using Lewis' books for over 25 years. Her book offers a fresh approach to the *Narnia* books based on an inquiry into Lewis' readings and use of classical and Christian symbols. She explores the literary and intellectual contexts of these stories, the traditional myths and motifs, and places them in the company of the greatest Christian mythopoeic works of Western literature. In Lewis' imagination, memory and metaphor interact to advance his purpose – a Christian metamorphosis. *Mythopoeic Narnia* helps to open the door for readers into the magical world of the Western imagination.

Speaking of Jack: A C. S. Lewis Discussion Guide
Will Vaus

C. S. Lewis societies have been forming around the world since the first one started in New York City in 1969. Will Vaus has started and led three groups himself. *Speaking of Jack* is the result of Vaus' experience in leading those Lewis societies. Included here are introductions to most of Lewis' books as well as questions designed to stimulate discussion about Lewis' life and work. These materials have been "road-tested" with real groups made up of young and old, some very familiar with Lewis and some newcomers. *Speaking of Jack* may be used in an existing book discussion group, to start a C. S. Lewis society, or to guide your own exploration of Lewis' books.

George MacDonald

Diary of an Old Soul & The White Page Poems
George MacDonald and Betty Aberlin

The first edition of George MacDonald's book of daily poems included a blank page opposite each page of poems. Readers were invited to write their own reflections on the "white page." MacDonald wrote: "Let your white page be ground, my print be seed, growing to golden ears, that faith and hope may feed." Betty Aberlin responded to MacDonald's invitation with daily poems of her own.

"Betty Aberlin's close readings of George MacDonald's verses and her thoughtful responses to them speak clearly of her poetic gifts and spiritual intelligence."
    Luci Shaw, poet

George MacDonald: Literary Heritage and Heirs
Roderick McGillis, editor

This latest collection of 14 essays sets a new standard that will influence MacDonald studies for many more years. George MacDonald experts are increasingly evaluating his entire corpus within the nineteenth century context.

"This comprehensive collection represents the best of contemporary scholarship on George MacDonald."
    Rolland Hein, author of *George MacDonald: Victorian Mythmaker*

In the Near Loss of Everything: George MacDonald's Son in America
Dale Wayne Slusser

In the summer of 1887, George MacDonald's son Ronald, newly engaged to artist Louise Blandy, sailed from England to America to teach school. The next summer he returned to England to marry Louise and bring her back to America. On August 27, 1890, Louise died, leaving him with an infant daughter. Ronald once described losing a beloved spouse as "the near loss of everything". Dale Wayne Slusser unfolds this poignant story with unpublished letters and photos that give readers a glimpse into the close-knit MacDonald family.

A Novel Pulpit: Sermons From George MacDonald's Fiction
David L. Neuhouser

"In MacDonald's novels, the Christian teaching emerges out of the characters and story line, the narrator's comments, and inclusion of sermons given by the fictional preachers. The sermons in the novels are shorter than the ones in collections of MacDonald's sermons and so are perhaps more accessible for some. In any case, they are both stimulating and thought-provoking. This collection of sermons from ten novels serve to bring out the 'freshness and brilliance' of MacDonald's message."
    From the author's introduction

Through the Year with George MacDonald: 366 Daily Readings
Rolland Hein, editor

These page-length excerpts from sermons, novels and letters are given an appropriate theme/heading and a complementary Scripture passage for daily reading. An inspiring introduction to the artistic soul and Christian vision of George MacDonald.

Behind the Back of the North Wind:
Critical Essays on George MacDonald's Classic Children's Book
John Pennington and Roderick McGillis, editors

The unique blend of fairy tale atmosphere and social realism in this novel laid the groundwork for modern fantasy literature. Sixteen essays by various authors are accompanied by an instructive introduction, extensive index, and beautiful illustrations.

Shadows and Chivalry:
C. S. Lewis and George MacDonald on Suffering, Evil, and Death
Jeff McInnis

Shadows and Chivalry studies the influence of George MacDonald, a nineteenth-century Scottish novelist and fantasy writer, upon one of the most influential writers of modern times, C. S. Lewis – the creator of Narnia, literary critic, and best-selling apologist. This study attempts to trace the overall affect of MacDonald's work on Lewis's thought and imagination. Without ever ceasing to be a story of one man's influence upon another, the study also serves as an exploration of each writer's thought on, and literary visions of, good and evil.

Christian Living

The Living Word of the Living God:
A Beginner's Guide to Reading and Understanding the Bible
Rev. Tom Furrer

This book is based on over 20 years experience of teaching the Bible to confirmation classes at Episcopal churches in Connecticut. Chapters from Genesis to Revelation.

Keys to Growth: Meditations on the Acts of the Apostles
Will Vaus

Every living things or person requires certain ingredients in order to grow, and if a thing or person is not growing, it is dying. *The Acts of the Apostles* is a book that is all about growth. Will Vaus has been meditating and preaching on *Acts* for the past 30 years. In this volume, he offers the reader forty-one keys from the entire book of Acts to unlock spiritual growth in everyday life.

Called to Serve: Life as a Firefighter-Deacon
Deacon Anthony R. Surozenski

Called to Serve is the story of one man's dream to be a firefighter. But dreams have a way of taking detours – so Tony Surozenski became a teacher and eventually a volunteer firefighter. And when God enters the picture, Tony is faced with a choice. Will he give up firefighting to follow another call? After many years, Tony's two callings are finally united – in service as a fire chaplain at Ground Zero after the 9-11 attacks and in other ways he could not have imagined. Tony is Chief Chaplain's aid for the Massachusetts Corp of Fire Chaplains and Director for the Office of the Diaconate of the Diocese of Worchester, Massachusetts.

Harry Potter

The Order of Harry Potter: The Literary Skill of the Hogwarts Epic
Colin Manlove

Colin Manlove, a popular conference speaker and author of over a dozen books, has earned an international reputation as an expert on fantasy and children's literature. His book, *From Alice to Harry Potter*, is a survey of 400 English fantasy books. In *The Order of Harry Potter*, he compares and contrasts *Harry Potter* with works by "Inklings" writers J.R.R. Tolkien, C.S. Lewis and Charles Williams; he also examines Rowling's treatment of the topic of imagination; her skill in organization and the use of language; and the book's underlying motifs and themes.

Harry Potter & Imagination: The Way Between Two Worlds
Travis Prinzi

Imaginative literature places a reader between two worlds: the story world and the world of daily life, and challenges the reader to imagine and to act for a better world. Starting with discussion of Harry Potter's more important themes, *Harry Potter & Imagination* takes readers on a journey through the transformative power of those themes for both the individual and for culture by placing Rowling's series in its literary, historical, and cultural contexts.

Repotting Harry Potter: A Professor's Guide for the Serious Re-Reader
Rowling Revisited: Return Trips to Harry, Fantastic Beasts, Quidditch, & Beedle the Bard
James W. Thomas

In *Repotting Harry Potter* and his sequel book *Rowling Revisited*, Dr. James W. Thomas points out the humor, puns, foreshadowing and literary parallels in the Potter books. In *Rowling Revisited*, readers will especially find useful three extensive appendixes – "Fantastic Beasts and the Pages Where You'll Find Them," "Quidditch Through the Pages," and "The Books in the Potter Books." Dr. Thomas makes re-reading the Potter books even more rewarding and enjoyable.

The Deathly Hallows Lectures:
The Hogwarts Professor Explains Harry's Final Adventure
John Granger

In *The Deathly Hallows Lectures,* John Granger reveals the finale's brilliant details, themes, and meanings. *Harry Potter* fans will be surprised by and delighted with Granger's explanations of the three dimensions of meaning in *Deathly Hallows*. Ms. Rowling has said that alchemy sets the "parameters of magic" in the series; after reading the chapter-length explanation of *Deathly Hallows* as the final stage of the alchemical Great Work, the serious reader will understand how important literary alchemy is in understanding Rowling's artistry and accomplishment.

Sociology and Harry Potter: 22 Enchanting Essays on the Wizarding World
Jenn Simms, editor

Modeled on an Introduction to Sociology textbook. this books is not simply about the series, but also used the series to facilitate reader's understanding of the discipline of sociology and a development of a sociological approach to viewing social reality. It is a case of high quality academic scholarship written in a form and on a topic accessible to non-academics. As such, it is written to appeal to Harry Potter fans and the general reading public. Contributors include professional sociologists from eight countries.

Harry Potter, Still Recruiting:
Essays on Harry Potter and Pop Culture
Valerie Frankel, editor

Chapters include a wide variety of topics such as social networking, Pottermore, college quidditch, fan art, fan fiction, conferences, exhibitions, Wizard Rock, websites, and fan locations such as the Wizarding World of Harry Potter. Includes interviews with prominent Harry Potter community members such as Muggle Net, Harry and the Potters, and Whimsic Alley. Frankel emphasizes the recent effects on society ranging from the Simpsons to Facebook.

Hog's Head Conversations: Essays on Harry Potter
Travis Prinzi, editor

Ten fascinating essays on Harry Potter are divided into five sections: Conversations on 1) Literary Value, 2) Eternal Truth, 3) Imagination, 4) Literary Criticiam, and 5) Characters. Contributors include the following popular Potter writers and speakers: John Granger, James W. Thomas, Colin Manlove, and Travis Prinzi.

Fiction

The Iona Conspiracy (from The Remnant Chronicles book series)
Gary Gregg

Readers find themselves on a modern adventure through ancient Celtic myth and legend as thirteen year old Jacob uncovers his destiny within "the remnant" of the Sporrai Order. As the Iona Academy comes under the control of educational reformers and ideological scientists, Jacob finds himself on a dangerous mission to the sacred Scottish island of Iona and discovers how his life is wrapped up with the fate of the long lost cover of *The Book of Kells*. From its connections to Arthurian legend to references to real-life people, places, and historical mysteries, *Iona* is an adventure that speaks to eternal truths as well as the challenges of the modern world. A young adult novel, *Iona* can be enjoyed by the entire family.

Poets and Poetry

Remembering Roy Campbell: The Memoirs of his Daughters, Anna and Tess
Introduction by Judith Lütge Coullie, editor
Preface by Joseph Pearce

Anna and Teresa Campbell were the daughters of the handsome young South African poet and writer, Roy Campbell (1901-1957), and his beautiful English wife, Mary Garman. In their frank and moving memoirs, Anna and Tess recall the extraordinary, and often very difficult, lives they shared with their exceptional parents. The book includes over 50 photos, 344 footnotes, a timeline of Campbell's life, and a complete index.

In the Eye of the Beholder: How to See the World Like a Romantic Poet
Louis Markos

Born out of the French Revolution and its radical faith that a nation could be shaped and altered by the dreams and visions of its people, British Romantic Poetry was founded on a belief that the objects and realities of our world, whether natural or human, are not fixed in stone but can be molded and transformed by the visionary eye of the poet. Unlike many of the books written on Romanticism, which devote many pages to the poets and few pages to their poetry, the focus here is firmly on the poems themselves. The author thereby draws the reader intimately into the life of these poems. A separate bibliographical essay is provided for readers listing accessible biographies of each poet and critical studies of their work.

The Cat on the Catamaran: A Christmas Tale
John Martin

Here is a modern-day parable of a modern-day cat with modern-day attitudes. Riverboat Dan is a "cool" cat on a perpetual vacation from responsibility. He's *The Cat on the Catamaran* – sailing down the river of life. Dan keeps his guilty conscience from interfering with his fun until he runs into trouble. But will he have the courage to believe that it's never too late to change course? (For ages 10 to adult)

"Cat lovers and poetry lovers alike will enjoy this whimsical story about Riverboat Dan, a philosophical cat in search of meaning."
    Regina Doman, author of *Angel in the Water*

The Half Blood Poems
Inspired by the Stories of J.K. Rowling
Christine Lowther

Like Harry Potter, Christine's poetry can soar above the tragic to discover the heroic and beautiful in such poems as "Neville, Unlikely Rebel", "For Our Wide-Armed Mothers," and "A Boy's Hands." There are 71 poems divided into seven chapters that correspond to the seven books. Fans of Harry Potter will experience once again many of the emotions they felt reading the books – emotions presented most effectively through a poet's words.

Pop Culture

To Love Another Person: A Spiritual Journey Through Les Miserables
John Morrison

The powerful story of Jean Valjean's redemption is beloved by readers and theatergoers everywhere. In this companion and guide to Victor Hugo's masterpiece, author John Morrison unfolds the spiritual depth and breadth of this classic novel and broadway musical.

Through Common Things: Philosophical Reflections on Popular Culture
Adam Barkman

"*Barkman presents us with an amazingly wide-ranging collection of philosophical reflections grounded in the everyday things of popular culture – past and present, eastern and western, factual and fictional. Throughout his encounters with often surprising subject-matter (the value of darkness?), he writes clearly and concisely, moving seamlessly between Aristotle and anime, Lord Buddha and Lord Voldemort.... This is an informative and entertaining book to read!*"
Doug Bloomberg, Professor of Philosophy, Institute for Christian Studies

Above All Things: Essays on Christian Ethics and Popular Culture
Adam Barkman

"*Whether discussing Winnie the Pooh or The Walking Dead, this book digs up buried philosophical treasure. Those who don't normally think of themselves as philosophically inclined will be surprised and delighted as Barkman rescues philosophy from dry classroom abstractions and reveals how it fills the glorious messiness of everyday life.*"
Dr. Kevin Flatt, Assistant Professor of History, Redeemer University College

Spotlight:
A Close-up Look at the Artistry and Meaning of Stephenie Meyer's Twilight Novels
John Granger

Stephenie Meyer's *Twilight* saga has taken the world by storm. But is there more to *Twilight* than a love story for teen girls crossed with a cheesy vampire-werewolf drama? *Spotlight* reveals the literary backdrop, themes, artistry, and meaning of the four Bella Swan adventures. *Spotlight* is the perfect gift for serious *Twilight* readers.

Virtuous Worlds: The Video Gamer's Guide to Spiritual Truth
John Stanifer

Popular titles like *Halo 3* and *The Legend of Zelda: Twilight Princess* fly off shelves at a mind-blowing rate. John Stanifer, an avid gamer, shows readers specific parallels between Christian faith and the content of their favorite games. Written with wry humor (including a heckler who frequently pokes fun at the author) this book will appeal to gamers and non-gamers alike. Those unfamiliar with video games may be pleasantly surprised to find that many elements in those "virtual worlds" also qualify them as "virtuous worlds."